ALSO BY MARY MORRIS

FICTION

*Revenge*

*Acts of God*

*The Lifeguard: Stories*

*House Arrest*

*The Night Sky*

*The Waiting Room*

*The Bus of Dreams*

*Vanishing Animals & Other Stories*

NONFICTION

*Angels & Aliens: A Journey West*

*Maiden Voyages: Writings of Women Travelers*

*Wall to Wall: From Beijing to Berlin by Rail*

*Nothing to Declare: Memoirs of a Woman Traveling Alone*

# THE
# RIVER QUEEN

# THE
# RIVER QUEEN

A Memoir

## Mary Morris

Henry Holt and Company
New York

Henry Holt and Company, LLC
*Publishers since 1866*
175 Fifth Avenue
New York, New York 10010
www.henryholt.com

Distributed in Canada by H. B. Fenn and Company Ltd.

Library of Congress Cataloging-in-Publication Data

Morris, Mary, date.
  The River Queen : a memoir / Mary Morris.—1st ed.
    p.   cm.
  ISBN-13: 978-0-8050-7827-5
  ISBN-10: 0-8050-7827-4
  1. Morris, Mary, 1947—Travel—Mississippi River.   2. Novelists, American—
20th century—Biography.   3. Mississippi River—Description and travel.   I. Title.
  PS3563.087445Z46 2007
  813'.54—dc22                                                      2006050681

Henry Holt books are available for special promotions and premiums.
For details contact: Director, Special Markets.

First Edition 2007

Designed by Meryl Sussman Levavi
Printed in the United States of America

1   3   5   7   9   10   8   6   4   2

To S.H.M.

1902–2005

The face of the river, in time, became a wonderful book which told me ... its most cherished secrets ... not a book to be read once and thrown aside for it had a new story to tell every day.

—MARK TWAIN

# CONTENTS

# THE
# RIVER QUEEN

# DOWNSTREAM

~ 1 ~

IT'S FOUR in the morning and I'm sitting upright in bed. I've been awakened by a fork of lightning that illumines the sky; thunder rattles the boat. I'm lying on top of my sleeping bag in a nook near the engines and next to the head. The bed is on wheels and, as water strikes the hull, it rolls into the wall, then bangs back into the nook. I was hoping that by September I'd feel a hint of fall. But it's pouring out and hot and muggy on board. My clothes, the sleeping bag, everything is damp.

My river pilot, Jerry, who has gone to his other houseboat for the night, says I'm safe unless there's an electric storm—which there is. I've got my river planner open to the page that reads: "Lightning: Not the Type of Electricity to Mess With." I read a brief description of something called a dielectric breakdown and a tale of an exploding boat. The advice under these circumstances is quite specific: Get off the river. But I've got nowhere to go.

I am in a place called Richmond Bay at a marina located on the Black River. Four miles downstream the Black merges with the Mississippi. There is an Ojibwa saying: At the place where the three rivers meet, there will be no wind. That place is La Crosse, Wisconsin, where this marina is located. According to the Ojibwa, there will never be a tornado in La Crosse and there never has been.

But there is a great deal of lightning and thunder. And there's also a deluge. In the heaviness of the air mosquitos buzz. In the morning we are supposed to sail down the Mississippi on this houseboat. But when I arrived last night from New York, where I live, it was obvious that a good deal remained to be done. We have no running water. No electricity. The refrigerator isn't hooked up. Neither is the stove.

There are no screens on the windows above my bed. If I crack one, the cabin fills with bugs. Our marine toilet lies in pieces on the bathroom floor, along with the instructions for assembly, which I have briefly perused. I'm not sure what else we don't have, but I believe there is an issue with the starboard engine.

The drugs I've been taking these past few months for sleep and anxiety have worn off. Since my father's death last May, I've awakened in the night, short of breath. Now it is the storm that frightens me. I hear strange noises—footsteps, and, I think, voices. Maybe it's a radio. Someone or something runs along the pier.

In the shower stall, which is being used for storage, there's an axe and a baseball bat, which Jerry showed me before he and Tom, our mechanic, left for the night. For now I'm alone as bolts shoot from the sky and waves slap the hull. My bed rolls as other houseboats clang into the dock.

In the flashes of light I see a mist rising, blending with the fog and rain into a gray soup. An electric palm tree, which marks this harbor, glows green in the night. There's a gun on board, but Jerry didn't say where.

><

When I look at the Mississippi and all its tributaries, I see the left hand of a musician with a twelve-note reach. A big hand that stretches clear across the country with its palm covering the Midwest. The thumb comes down somewhere in upstate New York, not far from Lake Ontario, first knuckle in Pittsburgh. The little finger keeps the beat in Helena, Montana, while the middle fingers play the blues up north in Bismarck, Minneapolis, Chicago. The wrist narrows at New Orleans.

My father played jazz piano years before I was born. He played house parties, bar mitzvahs, and for his friends. He never played on the South Side of Chicago, though he went to the "black and tans" on a Saturday night. He used to tell me he wasn't very good, but that's not how I remember it.

He still did what he called "fiddling" when I was a girl. He accompanied himself to corny tunes like "Smile" or "Smoke Gets in Your Eyes" or lively ones like "I'm Looking Over a Four-Leaf Clover" with a little Art Tatum or Eddie Duchin swing. My mother claims, for reasons of her own, that I never heard my father play. He was a businessman, she'll tell me, not a musician. But I recall the wide reach of his fingers. His foot tapping and head shaking as he kept the beat.

In the 1920s my father lived on the banks of the Mississippi and I was raised on his river tales. He sold ladies' garments at Klein's Department Store in Hannibal, Missouri, and my childhood was peppered with stories of the bucolic life. He had friends who kept a farm in the middle of the river on an island between Hannibal and Quincy, Illinois, and he spent his weekends there. For a time he told me he lived next door to Mark Twain's boyhood home and that Twain's house wasn't any bigger "than a shoe box." He said you could throw a stone into the river from his front porch.

The Mississippi, if you include its major branch, the Missouri, is over four thousand miles long, making it the longest river in the world. Only the Amazon and the Congo have as large a drainage basin—over 1,250,000 square miles. On a normal day the Mississippi carries one hundred thousand cubic feet downstream per second. At the peak of the great floods of 1993, which I witnessed from the vantage point of a hotel room in Kansas City, it carried one million cubic feet per second.

All my life I've thought about the river. I grew up in Illinois, and the Mississippi was its western border. I imagined that cowboys, Indians, and pioneers fought bloody battles on the other side. The first time I crossed the river was on a train going to Idaho. I was no more than five or six, but I had the run of that train, which had a dome car where I spent hours up high, watching the prairie zip by. That evening we sat in the dining car as the orange sun was disappearing behind the grassy plains. I'd never had dinner on a train before and I remember the white linen tablecloth, a red carnation in a vase, the Illinois towns speeding past.

We were going for a summer vacation, but my father wasn't with us. He had stayed in Chicago for work and would join us in a week or two. My mother sat primly, riding backward, across from my brother, John, and me. In her blue dress with patent leather purse and white gloves resting in her lap, my mother puffed on a Pall Mall, wishing she was heading to Paris or Rome instead of to Idaho with her two rowdy children. Trains and dust and horses weren't her idea of a dream holiday, but they were certainly, for a time at least, mine.

My brother and I were amazed that we could eat a hamburger on a moving train. We kept our eyes glued to the miles and miles of fields as they sped by. We pointed, shouting, "Cows, a barn!" Suddenly we clanged onto a bridge and there it was—wide and blue and churning. The river seemed to go on forever, and we were silent as we crossed it. As soon as we were on the other side, my mother turned to us and said, "Well, that's it. We're in the West now." Then she glanced at the menu and ordered Dover sole and a Rob Roy.

After that I traveled back and forth across the Mississippi many times—going to Idaho in the summers, to camp in Colorado, driving with a rather wild cousin to her college in St. Louis—but the river never lost its allure. It became part of my landscape, my natural terrain. My father's stories of living in Hannibal and his friend's farm on the river took hold of my imagination. It became a piece of what I called home.

Unlike my mother who hungered for the big cities of Europe, and a man who'd take her there, my father always wanted a farm, and he spoke longingly of this one. Cattle grazed on these islands and the scent of apples filled the air. The house was white and clean and there wasn't a sound except for rushing water and laundry flapping on a line. In the winter the water froze and you could put on your skates and glide across. He'd put his hands behind his back and slide along the carpet of our suburban home to show me.

At my house in Brooklyn I have a picture of him, taken in the 1920s. He is wearing a linen suit, a fedora, leaning against a Model T. The car is stopped on what looks like a dirt road and my father has a woman in a flapper dress on each arm and a cigarette dangling from his lips. He looks dashing with a slightly gangster air.

I hardly recognize him. I like to think he's on his way to a speakeasy or a private club on the Indiana Dunes. He'll stay until the wee hours, listening to the great cornet player Bix Beiderbecke and the Wolverines. I'll never know who those women were hanging on his arms.

~ 2 ~

IN THE morning I wake to the sound of hammer on metal and someone shuffling on deck. Peering out from behind my green curtain, I see Jerry, who looks a bit like an aging Jimmy Buffett in his khakis, Hawaiian shirt, and baseball cap, carting provisions on board. He must hear me rummaging about. "Aloha," he says. I gaze at my watch and it is just past six.

"Good morning," I mutter back, still half asleep. The banging gets louder and seems nearby. Pulling the curtain on the aft door, I find myself staring at Tom's burly back in a sleeveless, red Harley-Davidson T-shirt, muscles bulging, bent over the engine, not two feet from my sleeping nook. Grunting to himself, Tom stands inside the engine pit. At any moment I expect his girlfriend, Kim, will show up as well.

Tom's big hands dip into the bowels of the engine, as he shakes his head. Around him are assorted wrenches, bolts, screws, things that look like fan belts. He's got a can of diet Dew and about a dozen Chips Ahoy sitting on a rag. I hear a loud bang. "Hey, Tom," Jerry shouts, "what's happening?"

"Hole in the exhaust manifold, Sir," Tom shouts back across the nook as I pretend to sleep.

"Hmm," I hear Jerry mutter. "Can you fix her?"

"Gonna try."

There is a yanking noise, like the guts of something being ripped out. "Violation!" Jerry shouts.

"Only way to do it, Sir."

I am not a mechanic, but I know this does not look good. My head is reeling from the drugs I finally took to get back to sleep. Ativan, half an Ambien. Whatever the doctor would allow. I never used to do this. Pop pills. But after my father died, I found myself with my heart pounding in my chest. When my doctor asked how I was doing, I told him, "I don't know how to explain it, but it's as if something keeps jumping out from behind a door and shouting 'boo!'"

He sent me to a therapist who sent me to a psychopharmacologist. A very nice man. The first time I met him I cried for two straight hours. "It hasn't been a good summer," I said. I told him that my father had just died and I wasn't speaking to my mother, who refused to mourn his passing. My daughter, Kate, was leaving for college, and my last book hadn't done very well. I told him I was heading down the Mississippi River in a houseboat with two strangers, and my husband was planning on spending his weekends doing road trips with our dog and some Creedence Clearwater Revival tapes.

When he asked how I was dealing with my anxiety, I replied, "With vodka." He made a special note of this.

Since then I have been on an assortment of medications. Zoloft to make me happy, Ativan to calm me down. Ambien to make me sleep. I'm trying to wake up, but the cocktail is taking its toll. I'm groggy. I'm also desperate to pee into something that is not a jelly jar and have a cup of coffee, none of which seem imminent.

I ease my way out of my nook into a pair of flip-flops and my Uncle Sidney's hospital robe from thirty years ago, which for some reason I have brought along, and pull aside the lime green curtain that separates me from the galley and the helm. Jerry greets me with a double shot of mocha from a machine in town and a copy of *USA Today*.

"Thanks," I say.

He mentions that Tom's girlfriend, Kim, has "aborted the mission." The night before I had dinner with Kim as she made her case for going down the river with us. She ambushed me over sauteed trout, telling me she'd worked hard on the boat and wanted to come with us. When I said no, there wasn't really room, she asked if she could just sail with us for a day or two. I couldn't say no to that.

"I got a note from her," he explains. "She's not coming with."

"Really?" I could still see Kim, a blue-eyed woman with a mane of auburn hair, talking nonstop about her five children and the farm they all live on. Kim told me, "I've got pigs, cows, and lambs. I raise them by hand. I cuddle and give them names. They come when I call. When it's time to harvest, I take out my .44 and shoot them right between the eyes."

"Maybe it's for the best," I reply.

Jerry shrugs. "Kim's a good woman. She worked hard to get this boat into the water." He pauses, "But, as they say in Norwegian, less to worry about."

I glance at the headlines of *USA Today*. It is September 12, 2005, just two weeks after Hurricane Katrina struck the Gulf Coast. "Some Say Congress Is Going Too Far on Aid; Officials: Rush May Encourage Waste, Fraud." And "Disaster Stays on New Yorkers' Minds." An image of people sleeping on cots in the Astrodome catches my eye. This journey was to take me to New Orleans. But nothing is certain now.

Clutching my towel and cosmetic bag, I clasp my robe around me. "I think I'll get a shower."

"Oh, take your time," Jerry says, and I have a feeling he means it.

❦

The boathouse up the hill is a kind of warehouse filled with machines, pumps, a message board, assorted boating manuals, sporting-life magazines, a refrigerator, showers, and a toilet. In the shower I put the water on full blast. I slip out of my Uncle

Sidney's robe, though I am careful to keep my flip-flops on (athlete's foot, my daughter swears, loves communal showers). Hot water spills over my body.

As I walk out, towel-drying my hair, I find Tom with a large metal object that resembles a horse's stomach in a vise. He's poking a finger through a rusty hole. "I've gotta fix this manifold before we can sail," he says.

"Yes." I'm standing on the concrete floor in my bathrobe, looking at his grease-stained finger. "I can see the problem."

"Well, you know, Mary, you sleep right next to the engines." He looks at me with his dark, serious eyes. "I don't want you to die of exhaustion."

It takes me a moment. "Right, thanks. I wouldn't want to either." Tom turns back to the manifold with his soldering iron. Carly Simon is singing the words "Don't go away" on his boom box. On the wall there's a poster of half a dozen golden retriever puppies and a sign that reads IF THIS IS THE FIRST DAY OF THE REST OF MY LIFE, THEN I'M IN REAL TROUBLE.

In the parking lot I walk by a pickup truck. A little black dog with beady eyes and wiry hair sits in the driver's seat. It looks just like Toto. When I go up to say hello, the dog goes nuts, barking, flipping in the seat, baring its teeth, ready to rip my throat out. "Jesus," I say, backing away.

"Hey!" Tom shouts as he comes out of the boathouse. "Samantha Jean, cut that out!"

"That's Samantha Jean?" I recognize the name of Tom's houseboat, and I know it's named after the dog who will be traveling with us.

"Yeah," Tom says. "She's a little territorial about the car." He goes over and bends his face toward the rat terrier. "Aw, she'll get used to you after a while. Just don't go near her or try and pet her or anything like that until she comes to you. Sammy, you be a good girl now. That's right. Gimme five."

And the dog slaps his hand with her paw.

As I head back down to the boat, I ponder why I am doing this. I have a nice house, a loving husband, a dog that doesn't want to kill me. Surely I could have stayed home. But for whatever reason, this river has gotten under my skin. Shuffling through a shaded picnic area, I pass two old guys, one pudgy, one thin, pouring their morning coffee from a thermos. I smell the rich, dark liquid steaming in their plastic mugs.

I'm sniffing the air and trying to sneak by when one of the men—moon-faced with glasses—says, "So you going downriver with those fellows?"

"Yes, I am," I say. He takes a big sip of coffee. If he offered me some, I wouldn't say no. But he doesn't.

"And that dog?"

"That's right."

He raises his mug at me. "Well, I wish you luck." He goes back to looking out at the river. "I used to keep a boat and a slip here."

I sit down at a table a few feet from theirs. "You don't take her out anymore?"

He shakes his head. "My wife's got Alzheimer's. She'll tell you the day of the week when our daughter was born, but she can't remember if she left the gas on. Can't leave her alone anymore." His eyes gaze down the bank and settle on our boat. A pair of swans with their cygnets swim by. "I'm gonna sell mine soon."

"You ever been downstream?" I ask them.

"Oh, yeah," the thin man says. "But I like it up here between Wabasha and Dubuque."

"Naw, I like it further south," his friend chimes in. "From Davenport to Alton. There's more to see."

"It's God's Country where we are," the other replies. "Hey, that big guy, Tom, he used to work on boats before, didn't he?"

"Before what?" I ask.

"I don't know. I think something happened. . . ."

"What happened?" I ask.

He waves it off with his hand. "Oh, if he's going downriver with Jerry, I'm sure he's a good guy."

"Yeah," the thin man nods as if he's trying to convince himself. Suddenly Tom emerges from the boathouse, holding up the manifold in a clenched fist like a barbarian with his spoils. He shouts down to the boat to Jerry, "I think she'll hold for now!"

"For now?" I ask, "What does that mean?"

Tom looks at me through disgruntled eyes. "For as long as she holds."

This seems to satisfy Jerry, who begins transporting the food he's been keeping in the marina workshop fridge onto the boat and into the cooler on the deck. Eggs, orange juice, the largest loaf of Wonder Bread I've ever seen. Milk, a two-pound slab of Wisconsin cheddar. A family-size package of Chips Ahoy, which Tom stows above the fridge and devours by the fistful. There's also two loaves of chocolate bread and a huge tin of molasses cookies.

One of the cronies turns to me and says, "I've never seen so much food going into Jerry's boat. Lotsa beer. But never that much food."

Jerry carts cases of diet Mountain Dew, diet Coke, and La Crosse beer in a wheelbarrow, and I follow in my flip-flops and robe. "Beer's for ballast," Jerry quips as he dumps a case into the cooler and smothers it with ice.

My husband, Larry, suggested running a background check on these guys, but I resisted. I was seeing myself as Katharine Hepburn in the *African Queen*, but Larry was thinking Natalie Wood. Traveling with two river pilots named Tom and Jerry seemed like a safe bet to me. I envisioned a cartoon cat chasing around a savvy mouse. Now I'm not so sure.

I've read stories of pilots who, for one reason or another, needed to lighten their loads. Before the river was managed and dredged, ships often ran aground. About a hundred years ago in the late fall when the river runs low, a packet ship filled with German immigrants got wedged onto a sandbar. In order to get off, the packet boat unloaded the sixty or so immigrants and their families. They unloaded their luggage. Then, as the boat floated off the sandbar, the crew left them in the middle of winter on Island 65 with minimum provisions, never to be heard from again.

The river is filled with hundreds of nameless islands and secluded backwaters, those dark spaces on the navigational maps only experienced river pilots know. Ideal for depositing human remains. If I complain about the coffee or if I don't want to swab the deck, what's to stop them? The eagles would pick me down to the bones. The truth is, I don't know these guys from Adam. I'm going on instinct and, as my husband is quick to point out, I've been wrong before.

~ 3 ~

IT WAS at my nephew Matt's wedding two years ago that the idea of going down the river got into my head. Matt, a nationally ranked wrestler with a cauliflower ear and a bone-crunching grip, was marrying a lovely girl named Gail, a black belt in karate, who could "kill him" with swords, as Matt likes to brag. The wedding was being held in La Crosse on the banks of the Mississippi.

The ceremony looked like a convention for bouncers. Matt's wrestling team served as ushers, and they ate all the shrimp, then went to work on the mushroom caps. It was raining and gray, but as the strains of the wedding march were heard, the sun came out and the river glittered like gold—"a miracle," the guests would later recall. After the reception the wrestlers built a bonfire and we sang "This Land Is Your Land" and "Little Boxes," accompanied by an acoustic guitar and a set of bongos, as the river, dark, mysterious, and beckoning, churned by.

The next day Larry and I went for a walk. It was a clear and crisp May afternoon and we needed to decompress from so much family time. As we strolled along the river, I spotted a houseboat. It was small and white with neat blue trim, shutters, an upper deck, white curtains in the windows—just sitting there, as if expecting company. I liked its name. *Reckless Abandon.* "Let's have a look," I said, and we wandered over.

It was a small vessel, but it had a sweet galley, a nice roof deck, and some cramped sleeping quarters. Gazing through a window, we could see that the whole inside wasn't much bigger than a kitchen in a Manhattan studio apartment. I walked around to the back where a man with a grizzled face sat with a fishing line in one hand, a cigarette in the other. "Is this your houseboat?" I asked.

"Yes it is."

He flung his cigarette into the water and introduced himself as "Smokey" [sic]. "That's cuz I smoke so much, but I'm gonna quit."

"Can we see it?"

"Sure," Smokey said. And he took us inside.

I'd never been inside a houseboat before, but this was cozy. I liked the curtains, the windows, the open feel. "The nice thing about the Mississippi," Smokey told us, "is that you can moor up wherever you go. If the weather gets rough, you can tie up to an island. You know, like Huck Finn, you can just go wherever you want to go."

As I looked out across the river, I tried to imagine what it would be like—going down the river in a houseboat like this one. Or maybe even this one. "Don't let this river fool you," Smokey went on. "She can be a bitch."

"How far can this boat go?" I asked.

He shrugged. "I don't know. As far as she wants, I guess."

"Could she go to Dubuque?"

He gazed down the river.

"I don't know why not." Smokey shrugged. "Never been there."

"Well, what about Hannibal?"

Smokey considered this as he lit another cigarette, which he gripped in his yellowed hands, then puffed between his yellowed teeth. "Never been there either."

"Well, do you ever rent your boat to anyone? Would you ever think of that?"

Smokey smiled through stained and ragged teeth. "Don't know why not, if the price is right."

While Larry stared at me, dumbfounded, I handed Smokey a slip of paper and he wrote down three or four phone numbers: where he worked, where he tended to sleep, where he was supposed to live, and who might know where to find him.

As we walked back to the hotel, Larry said to me, "You aren't seriously thinking about traveling with that guy?"

I shrugged. "I don't know," I said. And under my breath, "Maybe I am."

Six months later I started calling Smokey. For a while, as I planned this journey, I had my heart set on renting his boat. I talked to him a few times. First he had an accident on his Harley and was out of commission. Then he left the ammo plant where he worked the graveyard shift. After that I kept calling and calling the numbers he gave me, but, much to my husband's relief, I never reached him again.

When I made my decision to do this trip, I asked Matt to put up signs at the local marinas: WRITER SEEKS RIVER PILOT WITH HOUSEBOAT TO GO DOWNSTREAM. No one answered my ad. So I flew to La Crosse and Matt and I hung out at the Pettibone Marina on a sweltering July afternoon long enough for the harbormaster to tell us to go talk to Tom Hafner. Tom, he said, lives on a houseboat called the *Samantha Jean* on the other side of French Island. "I don't have his number," the harbormaster said, "but just go over there."

As we drove on to French Island toward Tom's place, Matt pointed to a derelict house where a man kept his dead mother in the freezer for four years. "It wasn't murder," Matt assured me. "He just wanted to collect her Social Security." We both gazed at the ramshackle house with its weedy front yard and collapsed Venetian blinds.

"I guess nobody wants to live there now. But otherwise," he said, with a sigh that did not inspire confidence, "La Crosse is safe. Just don't go to La Plume Island at night. That's where the bodies tend to wash up. It's not that people are murdered at the marinas, but for some reason, maybe it's the current, they wash up there."

We found the *Samantha Jean* moored in a grove of dark trees at the bottom of a slope and I sent Matt ahead on the wobbly dock and called out politely, "Tom? Is Tom Hafner here?"

The boat rattled and water sloshed and soon a huge, forty-something man with a graying beard, bulging biceps, and considerable girth emerged. He seemed to favor one eye, or perhaps it was one ear, more than the other, but the slant of his face gave him a vaguely ominous look. "Howdy," Tom said, crushing my fingers in his. We sat down and the boat rocked again, then seemed to sink. Small waves hit the sides.

A mosquito bit my ankle as Tom offered us a can of diet Mountain Dew, which we declined. He popped one open as I explained that I wanted to go down the Mississippi River in a houseboat and I was looking for someone to teach me how to pilot. "After I learn how to pilot, I was thinking about renting the boat and doing the trip on my own," I said.

Guffawing laughter poured out of Tom and shook the boat. "First, you can't do it on your own. Oh you could putter around a little here and there, but you can't go through the locks and dams on your own, and you've got about twenty of those between here and St. Louis. You need a person to steer and at least one other to hold the lines. Really you need two. You can't tie up on your own. How're you going to anchor by yourself? What're you going to do if you find yourself in fog? With a barge coming upstream? You probably don't know how to navigate, do you?"

He took a gulp of diet Dew, crushed the can, grabbed another. "You probably don't even know how to stay on the main channel. And how're you going to sleep on a riverbank alone? I wouldn't let my girlfriend do that. I wouldn't let my dog do that. Basically, forget about doing it on your own."

I agreed to forget it.

"What you really need," Tom went on as he popped open his second can of diet Dew, "is someone who wants to move a boat. You don't want to hire an outfitter cuz that's gonna cost you an arm and a leg. You know, fuel downstream and back because they gotta come home. You need to find a person who has a boat and wants to take it south. If I had a boat, I'd take you, but I don't. . . ."

I looked at the boat we were standing on. "Well, what about this one?"

"Believe me, I wish I could." He shook his head. "She's not made for travel. Oh, she's fine for around here, but I wouldn't trust her in a storm. What you should do," Tom said thoughtfully, "is talk to Jerry Nelson. Jerry was one of my first tormentors. He got me into my first boat. I'd trust him with my life. Jerry moves boats, big boats sometimes. You could just go stow away on one. Maybe just stick out your thumb and hitch a ride."

~ 4 ~

THE FIRST time I was ever on a river was with my father. We had rented a boat on the Fox and my father steered. I was surprised that he knew how to pilot, but it seemed he had lived a different life before I was born, one I would rarely be privy to. My mother had packed a picnic of fried chicken and potato salad. My brother, John, and I were navigating. As we cruised the river, Dad said things like, "Mark seagull on right; mark tree on left."

We laughed because, of course, we understood even then that you cannot mark seagulls or trees. The seagulls will fly and the trees are everywhere. But we laughed because it was funny. Because my father laughed. We were happy that day, which wasn't always the case.

I hadn't thought about that time on the Fox in years, but it came back to me as Matt and I pulled up to the French Island Yacht Club, where Jerry Nelson moored his boat. The docks were lined with houseboats with colorful awnings and painted trim, screened-in porches, and gas barbecue grills on the back. I admired the window boxes, where plastic flowers bloomed, and the beautifully appointed decks with vinyl furniture, where you could dine as the river drifts by. And they had nifty names like

*Shady Lady* or *Martin's Fling,* and, my personal favorite, *Naughty Buoys.*

We wandered up and down the wooden planks, shouting for Jerry Nelson. After a few moments a tall and fit sixty-year-old man, pale for someone who spent all his time on the water, appeared on the bow of a houseboat. He wore khaki shorts and a Hawaiian shirt. "Are you Jerry Nelson?" I asked.

"Yes I am." He had a quizzical smile and just stared at me. I explained that I was a writer and I wanted to take a journey down the Mississippi. "I'm looking for someone who has a boat he wants to move," I said, parroting what Tom had told me to say. "Someone who could take me down the river."

"Oh," Jerry said. "I see." He stood perfectly still as if he were frozen in space, and Matt and I were motionless beside him. He cocked his head at me in a way that I recognized from my father. I could tell that Jerry, like Tom, was hard of hearing in at least one ear.

I grew up with a deaf man. My father had scarlet fever when he was a boy. Though he could hear music, he often couldn't hear what was being said. Restaurants were particularly difficult. For the first fifteen years of my life, until he had a surgery, he never heard footsteps, the sound of a train's wheels when he rode on it, voices on the telephone. In order to communicate, he shouted. In the end he shouted about many things.

My father was charming, handsome, debonair, and people said he looked like Cary Grant. Greer (as in Greer Garson) and Cary, that's how people referred to my parents. At one time he was considered to be Chicago's most eligible Jewish bachelor. He was very much in demand, a fact that made my mother jealous, not of other women, but of his allure.

But underneath, as my brother and I knew, my father was a very angry man. Seething in ways few could imagine. Street angel, house devil, the Yiddish expression goes. His temper was reserved for those closest to him and limited to peccadilloes, the smallest of things. To lights left on and dishes in the sink. Bread not broken before it was buttered. The offenses varied, but the result was the same.

His anger was never physical. It was only words, but, as I've learned over the years, words can kill. The pitch of his voice would rise. I was always a little afraid of him. We all were. To this day his outbursts are incomprehensible to me. He never apologized. He never acted as if anything was wrong. He'd blow up and call us names, then make us popcorn or take us to play golf, as if nothing had happened.

Now Jerry, with his head cocked the way I'd seen my father's a hundred times, still hadn't moved. I could tell that he was turning something over in his mind. After what seemed like a long while, he said, "Actually, I've got a boat I've been thinking about taking south."

"You do?" I was stunned.

He nodded. "It's an old houseboat. I want to start wintering in Mississippi on the Tenn-Tom. I've got some friends down in Portage Des Sioux who said I could dock with them over the winter, then I'd move her farther south next spring."

Jerry paused again and I took this as my cue. "So you have a boat that could make a trip like this?"

"Well, not all the way, but . . ." He nodded. "Yes, I do."

"This boat?" I asked, pointing to the one we were standing on. It looked big and roomy with nice curtains and an outdoor grill. Jerry shook his head.

"Nope. Another boat."

"Oh. Where is this boat? Can I see her?"

Another pause. "Sure," he said, not moving. "You passed her coming down."

He pointed to the parking lot, then slowly headed that way. I followed him up to where boats in various states of disrepair sat on trailers in dry dock. I had passed her coming down, but hadn't noticed. That's probably because she wasn't much to look at. The paint was peeling from her hull in strips and it looked as if you could poke holes through the wood. A line of greenish brown muck that reminded me of pudding oozed from her baseboards. The railings were rusted away and smashed-up plastic chairs were piled on the stern. She had a FOR SALE sign taped to her back door and scribbled below it in pencil the words *River Queen*.

"She's been out of the water awhile," Jerry offered by way of explanation. Three years in fact, he said as I climbed the rickety ladder onto the deck. The windows were so dirty I couldn't see inside so Jerry popped open the door. It was about 140 degrees in the cabin and the floor was covered with power tools and cardboard boxes filled with junk. Dust and grime coated every available surface. "So what d'ya think?"

I was thinking that I'd seen other houseboats with their window boxes and Weber grills, sun awnings and deck chairs, but my options seemed to be running out. This was truly a wreck of a vessel, but I'd already taken leave of the college where I teach, my family and friends, and, some might add, my senses in order to make this journey in September. I'd squirreled away the money I'd need. If I was to begin in the fall, I had to come up with a plan.

This seemed like a boat I could afford. Definitely within my budget. And she was only going one way. Besides, for whatever reason, perhaps a drug-induced haze, I had a vision of this little ship all white and shiny, carrying me downstream. Somewhere beneath the rust and peeling paint, I thought she had class.

"Will you fix her up? I mean, before our trip?" Jerry looked puzzled as if he wasn't sure what I meant. "You know," I explained. "Clean her up."

"Well," he said. "She could use a paint job. I'll take care of that."

"And maybe get some . . . chairs? And, um"—I gazed at the top deck—"some shade?" He nodded in what I assumed to be agreement. "Would she make it to Memphis?" I asked, trying to hide the skepticism in my voice. She looked as if she wouldn't make it to the first lock and dam.

"Oh, she'll make it. She was built for Lake Michigan where the waves get high. But I'm only going to St. Louis." The wheels in my head started to turn. I didn't want to have to change boats in St. Louis. I wanted this boat to take me farther south.

"Well, I have to get as far as Memphis . . . on this leg." I had decided that I'd go to Memphis, take a break, then finish the trip.

Jerry grumbled. "I don't like the lower Mississippi very much. You ever looked at that part of the river? It can be boring and monotonous. You need to bring a very long book." This coming from Jerry gave me pause.

I had looked at the lower Mississippi. If you turn the map on its side, it looks like somebody's very agitated EKG. As Mark Twain wrote, the lower Mississippi, which begins at Cairo, Illinois, is the "crookedest" river in the world. You go almost twelve hundred miles while the crow flies six hundred. Often on the lower Mississippi you are traveling as much east and west as north and south. And many of those miles had levees that kept you from seeing much beyond the riverbank itself. "But we'll see," Jerry said, nodding his head. "Memphis isn't that much farther."

"Can you go slow?" I asked.

"The only thing I do better than slow," Jerry said, "is stop."

~ 5 ~

IN THE fall of 1965 when I was applying for college, my mother told me to go east. She said that sometimes in this life an opportunity presents itself and you have to grab it. I know when she said this she was wishing she had. Though I had never had any intention of leaving Illinois, it is what I did. I went east and never looked back.

With AAA maps marked in thick blue Magic Marker, my parents drove me to college. They rode in the front and I spent the entire ride staring at my mother's thick red hair, rolled in a tidy French twist. She was once voted Redhead of the Week at the 1933 Chicago World's Fair. There was so much luggage in the backseat that the customs officials in Windsor didn't know I was there. We went to Niagara Falls and put on yellow rain slickers. I stood with my parents on the ledge behind the falls, water spraying our faces. Then they dropped me off in Boston, and they were gone.

Years later I opened a drawer by my father's bedside table looking for a pen. As I began to rifle through, I came upon hearing-aid batteries, assorted Father's Day and birthday cards, photographs of grandchildren as babies, my brother's college graduation diploma from 1973, a *Life* Magazine from 1962.

Then I found the maps. They were old and folded, salvaged from the glove compartment of a car we hadn't owned in years, but as soon as I saw the thick blue lines, I knew that these were the AAA maps with the route that had been drawn for my father. I followed the arrow up past Lake Erie and Niagara Falls, Buffalo, Albany, and finally Boston, where they dropped me off. Another arrow pointed the way back to Chicago. It followed a southern route, one I never took because I never returned, but my father probably kept them because he believed that one day he'd bring me home.

I thought I'd left the Midwest behind. Though I longed for the flatlands of my youth and wrote about them in my novels and stories, returning wasn't in my mind. The river, like childhood, drifted into memory. Years went by. I moved from Boston to New York. My parents kept waiting for me to return, but I had my reasons, and I suppose they were good ones, for not moving home.

While the Midwest always had an allure, I was rarely back for long. A restlessness grew in me I couldn't squelch and I began to wander the world. I moved to Mexico for a couple of years, then to Rome. I took the Trans-Siberian Railway from Beijing to Berlin. I was known by some to be a drifter, though I had an apartment in Manhattan, sometimes a job, and often a cat.

Then, in the spring of 1993, when I lived in Brooklyn, with a family of my own, I was invited to Kansas City, Missouri, to give a talk. This was not supposed to be a momentous, life-altering experience. Just a visit with an old friend, a day of sightseeing, then Sunday brunch with a book group.

Normally I like an aisle seat, but for some reason this flight was heavily booked and I got a window. I was a little crammed in by a large man sitting beside me who turned out to be Cole Younger's great-great-grandson (of the notorious James-Younger gang). He was president of the Cole Younger Historic Society and talked my ear off about his famous relative and how many people he'd killed and banks he'd robbed.

After a while I grew weary of him. As we flew over the Midwest, I turned away. I gazed out the window and what I saw below astonished me. Though I knew the rivers were flooding that summer, I did not anticipate that the two great rivers—the Mississippi and Missouri—had converged into a giant lake. Indeed, there was barely the shape of a river below. Only huge pools of water. Farmhouses had the numbers of their insurance policies painted on the roof. Others had just written the word "Help."

But Kansas City seemed immune. At the airport I was met by my hosts, who took me to my hotel—a charming historic building along one of the tributaries of the Missouri River. The hotel was right in the heart of downtown with a lovely river walk and a gentrified shopping area, and here the river flowed smoothly by with none of the fury and devastation I had witnessed on my flight.

That night I went to Stroud's for fried chicken, then tried to walk it off with a stroll along the Missouri's branch just outside my hotel. It was a clear, warm night and the walk was illumined with old gas lamps, providing a quaint view of downtown Kansas City. By ten o'clock I was tired but also restless.

I couldn't get the river out of my mind. Finally I fell into a deep sleep, but was awakened in the middle of the night by a roar. At first I didn't know where I was. Then I remembered—in a hotel in Kansas City. The roaring came again and it sounded like rushing water.

I had no idea where it was coming from. I walked around the room in the dark, not wanting to turn on the light as the sound grew louder. I went to the window of my hotel and pulled back the curtain. I looked down. I thought because of the darkness and my fatigue, my eyes were playing tricks on me. It did not seem possible that what I was seeing was there.

A torrent filled the street. It was black-and-white and seemed to go in several directions at once. Where the river walk had been was now a coursing flood, dark and roiling. This flood ran down the road, spilling into the side streets. It blocked, as far as I knew, my only exit from the hotel. It was as if that river had suddenly changed course, leaped over a wall, and was now just a few floors below my window.

The noise was deafening, like an engine revving over and over. And I was afraid. This was not some slow river, some "old man" river. This was a churning creature, seemingly with a mind of its own. How far would this water rise? Could I get to the roof? Could I get away? Or would I be swept away in its current? I am a strong swimmer, but I knew I would drown.

I sat at the window, unsure of what to do. The sun appeared, a pale violet in the sky, and the river disappeared from the street and slipped back into its banks, like some monster in a child's bad dream. And I was left to wonder if that raging water had been there at all.

~ 6 ~

IT SEEMS if Jerry was right about anything, it's "slow." The morning is inching toward noon and Tom's still trying to get the manifold installed. I'm starting to think that we are never going to leave. As I'm getting dressed behind the lime green curtain, Tom comes into the galley and grabs a handful of chocolate chip cookies and another diet Dew. I hear him crush an empty can in his bare hands.

While Jerry is on his knees with a caulking gun, trying to attach the toilet bowl to the base, Tom's putting the starboard engine back together. Tom's coming along was part of our "deal," such as it was. Since I'd wanted to do this trip alone, it seemed to me that two people was more than enough. But as we negotiated our journey, Jerry told me he needed Tom. "He's a good mechanic," Jerry said. "And besides, Honeybun wants him along." "Honeybun" is Jerry's wife, Kathy.

"You mean Tom is our . . ."—I hesitated to say the word—"chaperone?"

"Something like that," Jerry replied.

Now I gaze at Tom, yelling at his engines ("Come on, you lazy little girl!") as Jerry tries to make the top of the toilet hold. "Getting there, Sir!" Tom shouts. "We'll heat her up soon."

"Whenever you're ready, Tommyboy."

"You'll be the first to know, Sir."

Jerry gives the toilet a shove. When he's satisfied, he stands up and stares at it for a long time. Then he looks at me and says, "Well, hopefully it won't leak."

I am reluctant to christen it (and besides, we still have no water with which to flush as our water pump isn't hooked up), so I make several more trips up to the boathouse, where the cronies sit, taking this all in. I pause, gazing down at the *River Queen*. Her polished trim glistens in the sun.

In the six weeks since we made our "agreement," which consisted of a handshake and some vague financial arrangements, Jerry and I shared many phone calls in which he'd tell me how the paint job was coming, how they'd gotten the bimini shade up on the flybridge. He'd refurbished the engines and secured the davits for the aft transom, which was to hold the dinghy. In most of these conversations I had no idea what he was talking about.

Then a week ago Jerry phoned to say they'd launched her. "You mean she's in the water?" I asked, ebullient.

He paused as he tended to do. "Not 'in the water,' Mary. We like to say 'on the water.' It's better if a boat's on it than in it. Do you catch my drift?"

Yesterday when I arrived, the *River Queen* was floating on the water, exactly as I'd imagined her, all white and shiny. Her bimini shade was up and the captain's wheel on the flybridge was a brassy brown. She looked shipshape to me. But as I came on board, lugging my duffels and suitcases and backpack with computer and binoculars and yoga mat and Eddie Bauer drinking mug and waterproof matches and all-weather gear, the orange life jacket circa 1950 I borrowed from a neighbor at the last minute, sticks of half-skim mozzarella cheese and twelve individual servings of tuna fish I tossed in "just in case," I saw that things weren't as they seemed.

The deck was a mess of muddy footprints. Inside the cabin was still filled with junk, much of it appearing to be the same I'd first seen. All the surfaces were covered with cables, power tools, boxes of screws and bolts. My "bed" was buried beneath tarps and drills and a blown-up air mattress. A layer of grime, which I correctly believed to be axle grease, was everywhere. The round hollow of a toilet seat lay on the floor. Outside Tom stood, holding engine parts in his blackened hands.

I tried to put on a good face, but I was despondent. I had no idea how this boat would come together in any way in the next twelve hours, let alone be the cozy little houseboat I'd envisioned myself traveling on. But somehow all the clanging and banging have led to something and just before noon, when I was ready to despair, Tom gives a shout. "We're ready to rock 'n' roll!"

"Holy buttocks," Jerry quips. And then in a more serious captain's voice: "Are there any unauthorized personnel on board?" Jerry asks.

"Just Mary," Tom says with his big guffaw.

"Ha ha," I say as I start to untie the lines. I'm fumbling with the ropes when a man approaches.

"I'll take care of that," he says. His name is Dave and he's just appeared on the dock. With a seaman's expertise and a few deft strokes, Dave unloops the line from the cleats and hands it to me as if I know what to do with it. "Well, Jerry," he says as we proceed to start our engines, "good luck."

And the laconic Jerry replies, "Thanks," as he takes the line out of my hands and ties it to the bow. Now Dave starts to push us away from the dock. It appears as if we really are leaving.

"Jerry!" Tom shouts. "I need you to fire them up! Start with a half throttle, okay?"

"Roger," Jerry says.

"Clear!" Tom yells.

"Contact." There is a sputter, then nothing. We begin again, same routine. Another "clear!" "contact." Finally there is a roar, like a great beast waking, a fart of exhaust that fills the cabin and my sleeping nook. I head to the back to close the doors.

"Don't worry about that!" Jerry shouts. "The fumes will go out once we're under way. Clear!" Jerry yells.

"Contact." Now the engines scream to a start. Some of the cronies have come onto the dock with wry smiles. We still have no water, electricity, working toilet, fridge, screens except at the helm, whistle, siren, night-light, or shower, but we appear for now to have two engines. Basically we are a hull, traveling downstream. The cronies and a few extras give us a shove, then start waving as we putter, trailing a plume of smoke and a few backfires, onto the river.

I wave back. We are on the Black, which in a few miles will feed into the Mississippi, and I feel the tug. I am like some feckless explorer setting off to find the New World. I stand at the bow, waving frantically, a mad, wild figurehead. And it is clear to everyone, especially to me, that I have no idea what I am doing.

Tom takes over the wheel on the flybridge and Jerry says he's coming up too. I decide to join them. I go through the cabin to pick up my White Sox cap on my bed. Thrilled to be sailing, I spring out the aft door and smash my head on the steel frame. "Oh-oh," Jerry says as I exit, rubbing my skull. "Low clearance."

On the flybridge Tom's got Samantha Jean sitting in his lap. She growls when she sees me coming and Tom tucks her into the black bomber jacket, covered in dog hair, that takes up the only available plastic chair. "That's her jacket," he tells me. "Don't ever touch that jacket."

"Oh, I wouldn't think of it." Samantha Jean gazes up at me with her rheumy eyes.

"I mean, she wouldn't bite you or anything, but she'd make a big noise."

"No problem," I say.

It is a warm day in late summer as we head south. Jerry's come topside as well and he takes the wheel as we approach a railroad bridge. He scrunches up his face, surveying it. Then shakes his head. "Hey, Tommy, you think I'm gonna make it?"

"I don't think so," I say, but Jerry ignores me.

"You'll clear her," Tom says, "but we should take down the bimini." Quickly we peel back the bimini shade. "You got her." He reaches up and touches the bridge with his fingertips.

Jerry whistles through his teeth. "Way to go, Tommy."

Tom and Jerry have known each other for years. They have worked together. Tom, whose mother died when he was nine and father when he was seventeen, looks up to Jerry as a father. I am the third wheel. Or fourth if you include Samantha Jean.

We approach the Xcel Energy generating plant, where an old pal of Jerry's has been waiting since seven a.m. to take our picture. As he comes out of a small outdoor office with his camera, Tom pretends to moon him and we're off.

After a few moments Jerry says, "You take her above, Tom. I'm going below." Tom slips into the captain's chair, dog in his lap, happy as a clam.

"Is there anything I can do?" I ask.

They both look at me and shrug, wondering what there is I could possibly do. "No," Jerry says, "you can just relax." But I don't want to relax. I want to be busy. I don't want to be a passenger; I want to be part of the crew. On the other hand we've only been sailing for three minutes and I have no idea what there is to do.

I climb below and settle into a seat at the bow. I am squinting in the afternoon sun, the wind at my face as the Black merges with the Mississippi. Here the river is wide and rolling, its surface a blue gray sea. To my right is Minnesota with its hilly, mountainous rises. On my left, Wisconsin is flat, not from glaciers, Jerry tells me; the river just carved this gully for itself.

As we enter the main channel, I begin to weep. It is inexplicable to me because I haven't cried in weeks. But now I weep for my father, who can't see this, and my daughter, who has left home. I cry because I have no idea why I am here or what I am doing. I am sailing into a great unknown with strangers. I do not know what awaits me, and I weep for those times that will never return.

I am crying as Jerry taps on the glass. I pull my White Sox cap down low so he can't see my eyes. "A pair of bald eagles," he says, pointing. "At three o'clock." At first I'm not sure what he means. Are a couple of eagles due to arrive in the afternoon? But then I understand this is seaman's talk.

The sky becomes a cosmic watch, time emblazoned there. Jerry hands me my binoculars. High above I see the eagles, circling one another, dancing in the sky.

# STORM

FOR A time after he died, I heard my father's voice. He came to me when I was swimming or doing yoga. When I was on the subway. Always when I was alone. He'd say normal things, the kinds of messages you'd leave on someone's answering machine. "Hi, Mary. Just checking up on you."

Often he spoke in aphorisms and clichés. "There are no problems, only solutions." "I never make a decision until it happens." "Roll with the punches." "Go with the flow." It wasn't a hallucination or a dream or anything crazy. It was simply his voice.

When I was small, my father was the one who put me to bed. He tucked me in with a story and a song. In the darkness of my room I listened to his tenor's lilt. My mother was never part of these nightly rituals. She'd blow me a kiss from the doorway, her silhouette framed in light. But every night my father sat at the edge of my bed.

The stories varied, but the song was always the same: "The Whiffenpoof Song." "We're poor little lambs who have gone astray . . . poor little lambs who have lost the way." It was a sad song to sing to a child, but I wanted to hear it over and over again.

I hadn't heard my father's voice in a while, not since I started taking the drugs, and I was sorry about that, but now as we head out on the river, it comes back. I hear my father say, "Life is one big compromise. If you can get that into your head, you'll do all right." But what compromises do I need to make now?

"If you listen, you'll learn," he tells me.

We drift by beaches and recreational areas. At Mile 689 Jerry tells me that Wild Kat Landing once had a two-horsepower ferry going from here to Brownsville and that meant "two real hay burners"—two draft horses—turning the wheel. As we round Turtle Island, the cliffs of Minnesota recede. A flock of white pelicans perches on an exposed rock, along with some cormorants. There isn't a soul on the river as it opens wide, and I cannot see its banks.

Houses rise high upon the cliffs, looming there. I see no access roads. No town for miles. As we chug along at a clip of 8.2 miles per hour, Jerry shows me how to read the miles off the daymarkers that dot the banks. "Okay," Jerry says, "take your binoculars and read those numbers there."

I scan the water and I give him the river mile off our next daymarker. It's 686.1. Jerry flips through the thick, bound set of Army Corps of Engineers navigational maps and he shows me that this puts us at Henning Light Daymark at the end of Turtle Island. We will use these daymarkers to figure out our position as we travel down the main channel. As we pass between the buoys, he teaches me the simple adage that I learn like a nursery rhyme: "Red Right Returning."

This means that as we head upstream the red buoy is to starboard. Going downstream, which is what I plan to be doing all the way down the Mississippi, red is to port. Given that I am left-handed and somewhat directionally challenged, this seems simple enough. "Of course," Jerry warns, "the buoys could shift in a storm or the Army Corps of Engineers could've missed a spot they had to dredge and you'll run aground. But basically, you want to stay between the buoys."

As he's talking, I'm reading the Army Corps of Engineers disclaimers that appear on our navigational maps. "Buoy positions represented on these charts are approximate and subject to change depending on river stages and channel obstructions."

And, if that doesn't inspire confidence, "Area in river that generally meets project depth dimensions (i.e. 9 feet or greater) is subject to change as a result of scour or deposition in the river." In other words there are no guarantees that we are going to travel safely. And should we run into trouble, we are advised to contact the office of the United States Coast Guard at a phone number in New Orleans.

Jerry's maneuvering the boat, his eyes set on the river ahead. "I was out on the river once down near Prairie du Chien," Jerry says as I'm searching for daymarkers and buoys, "and I saw this guy in a cruiser." He chuckles to himself. "He was zipping along at a wide part of the river and the buoys were set up so you had to go way west before you could come back east."

I'm watching how he turns the wheel. He's got his eyes set far in the distance at something I can't see. "Red buoy at eleven o'clock," Jerry says, pointing. I'm starting to see the world as a gigantic time device.

"I see it," I say.

"So I'm following the buoys," Jerry goes on, "but this guy in the cruiser, he takes this shortcut right through the middle and I think to myself, 'God, I wish I knew this channel well enough to take the shortcuts like he does' and then all of a sudden I hear this loud splash and I see that the cruiser has landed flat on a sandbar and he's stuck there."

I put down my binoculars. "What'd you do?"

"I would have gone to help, but I'd have gotten stuck there myself. I called the next lock and dam and told him where the guy was. I have no idea how long he sat. I'm sure they had to get a tow to pull him off."

Jerry has a good laugh over this as he points out half a dozen white pelicans resting on another sandbar. "So," he says, "the moral of this story is stay between the buoys."

"Got it," I reply. At Mile 679 we approach our first lock— Genoa Lock and Dam 8. The town of Genoa was once called Bad Axe Landing (and indeed at least four daymarkers south of Genoa are called Bad Axe), but in 1869 a group of homesick

Italian immigrants renamed this place Genoa after their hometown. Other than its name, at least from the river, I don't see anything Italian.

Jerry speaks with authority into his marine radio. "Lockmaster, this is pleasure craft, *Friend Ship,* requesting lockage." A voice replies that seems to be coming from outer space.

Jerry repeats, "This is pleasure craft *Friend Ship,* requesting lockage." Despite my protests Jerry has named our boat *Friend Ship.* I'd have preferred *Reckless Abandon,* but *Friend Ship* it is. *River Queen,* he informed me, is just her brand name. He has made a sign with nautical waterproof letters—FRIEND SHIP— and stuck it on the bow of the flybridge. But she's still the *River Queen* to me.

The lockmaster answers our call. "*Friend Ship,* we're opening the gates. Come on through."

It wasn't long after the Louisiana Purchase in 1803 that the Mississippi River got itself linked to America's sense of itself as a nation and its manifest destiny. Over the next hundred years the need to control the river rather than let it flow as nature intended became more and more apparent. In 1917 an act of Congress put the management of the river under the control of the Secretary of War, and it was considered military territory.

River towns grew and with them factories, commerce, and transportation. The Mississippi was the main artery through which all of this had to flow, and it was up to the Army Corps of Engineers to manage this. The problems of the upper Mississippi were different from those of the lower. The lower river was deeper and more narrow. It tended to build up speed, which also deepens its channel. The upper river had other problems. It was wide and its bottom unpredictable. Steamboats and barges easily caught a snag and sank.

If the lower Mississippi needed its levees, the upper required locks and dams. In 1930 the United States Congress authorized the building of the lock and dam system on the upper Mississippi River. Between 1934 and 1938 twenty-seven were built. Their purpose was not flood control, but navigability. The locks and dams provide a water stairway that descends if you are going downstream, or rises if you are going upstream, a total of 417 feet. The goal is to keep the main channel of the river at a consistent depth of nine feet.

Now we are coming to my first lock and dam. I am as excited as a kid going through a tollbooth for the first time with an E-ZPass. "Tell me what to do," I ask Jerry as eager as I can be.

Jerry hands me a short stick and a pair of blue vinyl gloves that resemble the feet of blue-footed boobies. He explains that my job, along with Tom, is to hold the line that the lockmaster will drop, and keep us from smashing into the cement wall as we drop the normal ten feet. I'll want the gloves, he says, for when I have to push off the wall. "It can get kinda scummy," he says.

"River scum," Tom says, holding up his paws. "I bathe in it."

"I'm sure you do," I tell him.

"Take this line, Mary," Jerry says, handing it to me. "Wrap it once around the railing, then hold it firm. Don't tie it to the railing. Tommy, you remember what happened to that woman up in Trempealeau at Lock and Dam 6?"

"Oh, yeah," Tom says. His voice has an ominous ring. "I remember."

"What happened?"

"Well, she tied up the boat and didn't hold the line and as the water level dropped," Jerry tells me, "the boat was yanked out of the water and she panicked and grabbed a machete to cut the line and managed to slit her own throat."

I'm shaking my head, holding the line more loosely now, poking at the lock wall with my stick. "You're making that up."

"Naw," Tom says, "I heard it too."

"Yeah, she died," Jerry says, deadpan as always. "So just wrap the line loosely and hold the slack. And don't wrap it around your wrist." As Jerry shows me how to hold the line, I see for the first time that he is missing the tops of three fingers on his right hand.

Tom gives me a nod. "Oh, you don't ever want to do that."

With my short stick and rope I push off the wall. I am barefoot and as I pull the line, I step forward and smash my foot into the cap on the hole that contains the anchor line. The pain in my toes is terrible and I'm hopping as we leave the lock. "Safe journey," the lockmaster cries as we sail on to the river past Thief Slough.

After the lock and dam the day feels long. I want something to happen, something more exciting than banging my toes. Is this all it's going to be? Just floating along? For days, weeks at a time? We pass an eagle's nest. A hundred white pelicans sit on a sandbar to port side. Jerry says they started showing up around 1997 and never left. Overhead they soar with a wingspan of eight or nine feet.

The day has misted over and there is an otherworldly beauty. I am stunned by the breadth and width of this river, an expansiveness as far as I can see. Here it has carved its way through sheer rock, which juts up on the right side. Weeping willows line the bank. There is a kind of slowness that I wouldn't exactly call monotony. It is as if everything is happening in slow motion.

I'm not a boat person. I like to be in water, but not on it. I love to swim. I like the freedom to float, to come and go as I please. I've been on ferry boats in Greece and Fire Island and I've sailed the Galápagos on a cruise ship, but we stopped every few hours. Already I am feeling the confines of this space. I don't do so well in elevators, crowds, and, I suppose, I could now include boats.

But I have opted to do this and must make do. "Life is one big compromise," my father's voice tells me. "Go with the flow." I'm not sure my father ever went with the flow, but what choice do I have? For now I am content, sitting on the bow, the sun and a warm breeze on my face. Since I haven't spent much time on a boat before, I decide to familiarize myself with nautical terms. Perhaps because I am a writer I like to know the language when I go anywhere. I want to know what all the words mean. It gives me a greater sense of calm and control. Where do I tie something on the gunwale? Is the bilge the same as the hold? Do we have a lazaret?

I've brought a glossary with me and I start with A. "Above deck" means "On to the deck" not "over it." For that I am instructed to see "Aloft." But there is no entry for "Aloft." When I read that the command "dead astern" means "directly aft," I'm at a loss. I become tangled on the problem of knots. I see that knots are what you tie, but they are also the speed at which you travel. This seems a paradox I cannot resolve.

As I ponder it, I am aware of the wind rising, a shift in the air. Still the sky is sunny ahead. The golden light of late afternoon sparkles on the water. But now the wind whips across the bow. Little whitecaps pop from the surface. I shiver and wonder if there might be an approaching storm.

I turn to ask Jerry if we are expecting bad weather and see the blackness behind us. The sky has turned to night. I have had nightmares of skies like this. And now this charcoal blanket is swirling over our heads. I point and Jerry, who is at the helm, turns at the same moment. "Holy shit," he says.

Tom, on the phone with his sister, shouts, "Hey, my sis says there's a big one coming."

Jerry looks behind him. "You don't have to tell me." Tom snaps his phone shut and suddenly all the slow motion turns to fast forward. "Tom, take the wheel!" Jerry shouts. "Mary, come topside. Now!"

This is clearly a direct order, but in the wind I can barely climb the ladder and I'm holding on with a very tight fist. I am, however, no longer bored. Quite the contrary. As I struggle up the ladder, I'm thinking to myself, "I've been on the river four hours and I'm going to die." As Jerry and I inch our way on top, Tom, who is already topside, scoops up Samantha Jean and tucks her into his jacket. "I'm taking her below." And I'm not clear if he means the ship or his dog, but I'd place my bets on the dog. In the next gust she could blow away.

The wind and blackness are upon us as we struggle to secure the flybridge. The bimini is flapping like an enormous bird, caught by its feet and fighting to take off, as we rush to get it down. As I am tugging on the bimini, I turn, and in the distance, the blackness begins to swirl and I think this must be a tornado. My heart freezes. But it is just coal dust rising from barges behind us.

I am gazing back at the swirling dust when the surface of the river suddenly rises like a great white ghost in some grade-B horror flick. A rather poorly executed special effect at that. A horizontal wall of water about twenty feet high and 150 feet wide careens toward our boat. I shout at Jerry as he grapples with the vinyl bimini. "What is that?"

He looks up and we see this same movement of water ahead of us, coming across the bow. "Get on your hands and knees!" Jerry shouts. "Crawl off the deck! Get back inside!"

"But don't you need my help?" I yell back.

"I need you to crawl off this deck! Now!"

As Jerry bends, struggling against the wind, I squat, battling the gusts. I don't crawl exactly, but I stoop way down. Clutching my glasses, worried that they will fly away, I fight my way to the ladder. The air whirls and the sky turns blacker than night. At the base of the ladder, I grab hold of the railings. The boat is pitching as we plow into the waves, and the deck is wet and slippery.

I make my way to the cabin and Tom, without taking his eyes off the river, pulls open the door. Samantha Jean is buried under a blanket, hyperventilating, and Tom has his eyes dead set on the horizon. Ahead of us there's a hint of sunshine, but we are engulfed in the driving rain and blackness above. We can barely see what's right in front of us. Tom's eyes begin to dart back and forth across the surface. On the flybridge I can see Jerry's legs as he fights to tie the bimini down.

It is clear that we cannot make it to either bank in this squall. We just have to take the hits as they come. Waves crash across the bow as we are pummeled with rain. I think Jerry's going to be blown into the river as he staggers along the railing, making his way below. Without a word between them Tom steps aside and Jerry takes the wheel. He aims the *River Queen* into the rising swells as we race the storm.

Whitecaps build and Jerry keeps pointing us into the waves. The boat rocks. We hear something snap and Tom looks around, shaking his head. We do not speak as Jerry drives in and out of the chop. For twenty minutes or more the world around us is black as night, and we are being tossed and hurled, then suddenly we come into brightness and the river smooths out as calm as it was before.

"It's moved east," Tom says.

Jerry nods. "It's behind us now."

Tom's cell phone rings and we learn from his sister that a funnel cloud touched down forty miles north of daymarker 660 where we first saw the storm. "Too close for comfort," Jerry says.

We assess our damage. The pipe holding up our satellite dish has snapped in two. (I am actually somewhat relieved by this, for I feared beer-drinking bouts of *Monday Night Football.*) The screens over the windshield have blown away and Jerry is particularly upset about these because they have to be custom made. The plastic deck chairs got banged around and all Tom's things topside are soaked. "We got off easy," Tom says.

We stay in the cabin as the boat is drying out in a blaze of afternoon sun. "Well, I'm glad that that's over," Jerry says. "In all my years on the river I've never seen that before."

"You're kidding?" I can't believe this is true.

Tom is shaking his head. "And I hope I never see it again. . . ." They are focused on whatever that wall of water was that chased us. "Never seen anything like that. The way the wind picked the river right up."

"So it wasn't good, right . . . ?"

They look at me as Tom pops a diet Dew and Jerry sticks a beer into his silver aluminum mug. "Nope, not good," Jerry mutters, taking a sip. I am starting to think that I could liken boating to what my ob-gyn once said about delivering babies. He said that 99 percent of the time it's routine and dull. And that 1 percent of the time you are scared out of your wits. Now I understand what he means.

"Was it a tornado?"

"Well," Jerry says, "technically it was a tornado, but a tornado never touches down on a river. I don't know why. It will hop right over the river, but it doesn't touch down."

"So it was . . . a waterspout?"

They look at each other and nod. "It was something like that. The important thing is we're more or less in one piece." Though Jerry is still upset about the windshield screens.

Before us the river is a glossy sheet, calm as if nothing ever happened. Like a man with a bad temper that flares, then recedes. It is hard to believe that half an hour ago these waters rose and came chasing after us. Now our course is smooth with gentle bends. A stream of gold sunlight, pouring down from heaven, lights our way.

# ISLANDS

~ 8 ~

IN THE 1830s a boy named John Banvard left New York and set out for the West. His father had recently died and Banvard, who was just fifteen, was forced to seek his fortune on his own. At that time the frontier wasn't Wyoming or California; it was the Mississippi River. Despite Lewis and Clark's journey to the sea thirty years before, anything beyond the river was still considered mysterious, uncertain, and wild.

In Kentucky, Banvard became an itinerant performer, impresario, set designer, and painter. Then, as a young man, for two years he floated in solitude down the river on a raft, sketching the eastern bank from St. Louis to New Orleans. When he returned, he built a barn and put his renderings of log cabins and steamboats, cottonwoods and river town life on an enormous canvas, which he mounted on rollers.

As the rollers turned, Banvard recounted his often tall tales of pirates and deprivation and the characters he encountered. With his "Three Mile" painting, as it came to be known, he captivated audiences from the rough-hewn crew of sailors in Louisville to Queen Victoria. For a time his panoramic vision made him the richest, most famous artist in the world.

People came night after night. After the success of the eastern bank, he returned to the river and painted the western bank. He added music and light, creating the world's first

# Islands 39

multimedia show. He traveled all over the world, spinning stories of the river.

With the invention of the motion picture camera, Banvard's fortunes changed, and in time his panoramas were forgotten. He was buried in a pauper's grave, and his paintings, except for a few small panels, were lost forever, though some are believed to be used in the insulation of old houses in Watertown, South Dakota, where he lived his final years.

Ever since I read about Banvard, I wondered what made him so taken with the river. Was it the death of his father? Or just the need to make his way in the world? Was it escape or necessity? Or a bit of both? In the end I came to think of it as his obsession—one I am trying to understand. Just as I'm trying to understand my own. I imagine Banvard on his raft, drawing the river, making up his tales. Perhaps traveling not all that much slower than we are.

❦

"The first rule of boating," Jerry says, is "keep your nose into the current and the wind." It's after the storm and I'm standing next to him at the helm as the lecture begins.

"What's the second rule?" I ask.

"Don't forget the first rule," he says, his voice, as always, bone dry. He explains that in a storm you go into the swells nose first. "You don't want to go straight into the trough. Don't let the boat broach," he tells me, making a flipping movement with his hands, which I assume to be a broach. "You don't want that to happen."

He's got his eyes on the horizon and he's moving the wheel with his thumbs. "You want to keep the rudder indicator at zero, or as close to it as you can," he says, pointing to a round instrument with a needle that moves to either side of zero. "You know, even keel. Just move the wheel easily along. Point her toward your farthest buoy. Here," he says, not even looking my way, "you try."

"Now?"

"Now's as good a time as any." Jerry steps aside and nervously I take the wheel. I'm looking at the rudder indicator as I move to the right or left, but I'm having trouble keeping it at zero. For whatever reason the boat seems to be steering me. It's a little like walking a dog that weighs a thousand times more than you do. Heel, heel, I want to say. I am surprised at the tug of the river, at how hard it is to hold a straight line.

"Okay," Tom says, "now she wants to go this way, but don't let her. Don't let her get away from you."

"You want to keep a straight course between your buoys," Jerry tells me. "You see the buoys? Set your bow toward a distant buoy." I'm attempting to see the buoys and hold a straight course and not go crashing into the riverbank. But I was never very good at patting my head, rubbing my tummy, while jumping up and down on one foot at the same time either. "Keep your eyes on the horizon," he tells me.

Jerry takes a clothespin and clips it on to the windshield. "Here," he says. "Aim your nose at this."

I try, but it's useless. My eyes seem to be crossing and the clothespin is more a distraction than anything else. "Head for that red buoy," Jerry says, "then straighten her out." I keep trying to hold the rudder indicator at zero and aim for the red, but I can't seem able to do the two things at once.

"You see that?" Jerry says, pointing at the blue gray surface of the river. I see nothing. "Over there where the water ripples. Those lines tell you there's something there. . . ." I sigh because to me the water ripples everywhere. "That's a wing dam. You wanta watch out for that."

I am watching for something I cannot see and I do not even know what it is. I have no idea how to read the surface in order to know what lies beneath. This is what Captain Horace Bixby once tried to teach a young and apparently not very swift cub pilot named Samuel Clemens. "You only learn the shape of the river," Bixby in *Life on the Mississippi* warns a disbelieving Clemens, who will soon take his pseudonym from the river and become Mark Twain, "and you learn it with such absolute certainty that you can always steer by the shape that's in your head, never mind the one that's before your eyes."

I don't have any river in my head yet. I hardly have it in front of my eyes. I cannot tell a wing dam, whatever that is, from the normal flow. A deadhead could leap up and grab our rudder and I wouldn't know. I'm a person who tends to see mirages anyway. But here mirages are everywhere. The surface seems to ripple in the same way no matter what, unless the wind has raised it out of its bed. But for the next half hour I manage to stay between the red and green buoys, avoid a few logs drifting by, and not rip the bottom out of our hull.

The river is not the same as when Twain was a cub. Now there are the locks and dams. The Army Corps of Engineers manages and dredges the main channel and the corps has provided fairly accurate navigational maps. But this does not mean we can't run aground or ruin our keel on what we do not see. We can still get caught on a snag or battered in the shoals.

Take the main channel. If I look at the maps and follow the buoys and daymarkers, I should pretty much be able to stay within the channel. Apparently I cannot. There are times when the river turns into a maze of competing rivulets, when what looks as if it should be the main channel is really a poorly dredged chute. I've come to such a spot where there appear to be several ways to go. "Look for your buoys," Jerry says.

To my right the river is vast, but the buoys appear to the left down a narrower chute. "But this is where it's wide."

Jerry shakes his head. "Doesn't matter. That's the main channel. That's where it's dredged." He points to an instrument. "This is your depth finder. We've got a draft of 3.5 feet. I'd like twice that beneath us."

As we approach Lock and Dam 9, Jerry takes over and Tom gives me a high five. "You did great," he says, nearly breaking my hand. "Except you covered about five river miles in ten."

"What do you mean by that?"

And he makes a zigzagging motion with his hand.

As we enter Lock and Dam 9, it's pouring again. A dark cloud has snuck above us, the remnants of our earlier storm, but the green light is a go and we breeze in. We are the only craft and have the lock to ourselves. It seems as if the lockmaster, who putters up to us on a little yellow golfcart in matching yellow rain gear, has little to do. There's no traffic here.

I'm in my flip-flops and my New York City Marathon rain slicker, which was left at our house by a visitor years ago. Despite the rain, I remain excited as I hold the lines in my blue plastic gloves. As our boat descends and the water rushes out of the lock, I cling to my rope and push us off the wall.

My assignment this time is to prevent the bent-over satellite dish from smashing into the cement lock wall as we descend the ten-foot drop in the lock. But the rain is cascading and the deck is slippery and I'm having trouble getting a grip. It is actually not that easy to keep the dish from crashing into the wall. Jerry's very nervous about this. And I'm getting soaked. The wind blasts under my slicker, threatening to raise me like a dandelion spore. I improvise and slip beneath the satellite dish, which provides a kind of umbrella as I keep my blue-gloved fingers pressed to the wall.

Tom, who thinks this is very clever, gives me a thumbs-up.

"You're going to teach me how to have fun again, aren't you, Mary?"

I am surprised by this comment. It seems as if Tom is nothing *but* fun. "I thought you were going to teach me!" I call back.

As we sail out of the lock and dam, we leave the storm behind. There is demarcation in the sky where the bad weather ends. Blackness, then light. Again it strikes me as almost a special effect, an almost unnatural line. I have never seen the weather so clearly defined. Suddenly it is a warm evening, without a cloud or trace of storm as we enter the east channel. "That's Scrogum Island on port side," Jerry says.

"Say what?" Tom laughs.

"Scrogum, Tom. Not Scrotum."

~ 9 ~

TIME ON the river is a relative thing. Not like any other kind of time. We're traveling at about eight miles per hour and three of those come from the river's natural flow. Your average marathoner can do better than that. At this speed I can see the underside of a bird's wing. The eyes of a disenchanted woman, hanging laundry up to dry. Children taunting a mongrel at the river's edge. The bait, wiggling on a fisherman's pole. The grimace of an old man, his life behind him now. It's more poem than story, but the long, narrative kind.

River time, as far as I can tell from my now brief experience, bears no resemblance to land time. When you're driving down the highway, you can say, well, if I'm driving sixty miles per hour and I've got one hundred and eighty miles to go, I'll be there in three hours. You can calculate, give someone an ETA.

But here you can't really account for time at all. A boater might tell you it takes two hours to get from Hannibal, Missouri, to Rockport, Illinois, which is a stretch of fifteen river miles or so, but if you've got a lock and dam in there, you might luck out and float through in ten minutes, or, if there's a double barge in front of you, two hours. Or four. You might do better tying up for the night. It's anyone's guess.

Given our late start, two locks and dams, one tornado, and me weaving across the river for an hour, we did pretty well. We traveled on our first day sixty-six miles in about eight hours. Jerry says there is a dock at St. Feriole Island, where we can spend the night, and, after a long day, I am ready for dry land.

We arrive at this little "courtesy" municipal dock, an appendage to an old 1930s levee, where Jerry says we'll tie up. "Really?" I ask. "Are we allowed?" I'm not expecting a red carpet and a marching band, but I thought we might be pulling into a marina with lights. And possibly a shower.

"Well, if we aren't, someone will let us know," Jerry says with a wave of his hand.

"We'll get a parking ticket," Tom quips.

"Besides if we get away early enough, they won't come and

charge longside." This feels a little dicey to me, but then I'm a person who is uncomfortable with library fines. I mumble something, but Jerry ignores me. He's annoyed because a fishing boat has tied up in the middle of the dock, but after some maneuvering, we sidle alongside. It turns out to be a very peaceful place with just the gentle ripple of water and wind. Two kids fish off the pier.

Jerry pauses to admire the levee, an old stone wall that's fifty years old. "Don't make'm like that anymore," he says. It is our first mooring, and, as we secure our lines, Tom executes a fancy looping motion with the rope. He makes circles with his fingers as he pulls the line around like some cowboy doing lariat tricks. He gives a tug on the knot and practically lifts the boat out of the water. "That should hold," he says.

"How'd you do that?" I ask, but he just gives a shrug. Then he picks up the rope and does it again around my ankle. "Easy," he says, giving my leg a yank. The boys want to clean up, which in this case means take bottled water and splash it on their faces. But I want terra firma under my feet. Just eight hours on the river and I'm wobbly as a colt.

In the dusk I cut across a small park, illumined with amber lights and dotted with picnic tables, facing the river. A cool breeze blows as I scamper across the railroad tracks and head to The Depot, which was once the old railroad station and now, after all the floods, is the only restaurant in town.

"Hotel California" is playing. I take a table near the back and wait for the boys. Tom's gone to walk Samantha, and Jerry says he's going to get gussied up. There's a pool table, and several dead animals hanging from the wall. There's also a female bartender and four people at the bar. A woman with bleached blond hair, sitting at the bar, is laughing loudly, and a few moments later when Tom and Jerry arrive she comes over to take our order.

"So what'll you have . . . ?" the blond woman asks.

Jerry asks what's on draft and Tom orders his usual—a diet Dew. I'm contemplating a vodka tonic when she says, "You want the same thing as your husband?" pointing to Jerry.

"That's not my husband," I say as Tom gives a big cough under his breath. Jerry's got his face buried in the menu.

"I'm hungry," I say and they both agree. "I'll have a cheese-burger, medium rare."

Tom pipes in. "I'll have two but cook 'em well. . . ." He gazes at me sheepishly because he knows I'm paying for dinner, which is part of our agreement. "One's for Sam."

The blond woman stares at us, perplexed. "Oh, I don't work here," she explains, slurring her words. "I just thought you guys looked like you needed a drink."

Johnny Cash comes on with "I Walk the Line" as our real waitress—a large woman in a very small miniskirt—comes to take our actual order. Neither Tom nor Jerry can bring themselves to look at her. Afterward Tom says, "That was the biggest miniskirt in the world." Jerry laughs his head off. I grimace and look away as the drunken woman, who is now dancing with a man at the bar, gives me a wave.

Our burgers arrive. They are pretty tasteless and Jerry makes a face. "Tastes like your foot's asleep," I say and they howl.

"Did you make that up, Mary?" Jerry asks.

"No, my dad. He said things like that all the time. If he didn't like something, he'd say it tastes like the bottom of an owl's foot."

"The bottom of an owl's foot. Well, that's a hoot." Tom groans and Jerry goes on, not skipping a beat. "Where'd that come from?"

I shrug. I actually think it is a Yiddish expression, but I don't want to say so. I have not told them that I am Jewish. We haven't discussed our politics. This is the heartland after all and some things may be better left unsaid. "Oh, my dad. He always said things like that."

"Musta been a funny guy."

"Yeah," I nod, thinking of my father's dry sense of humor. "You know, he lived along the river in the 1920s. In Hannibal, Missouri, and Quincy, Illinois."

They nod, chomping on their burgers. We have thus far ex-changed little personal information and it is the first time I have mentioned my father. "He said he spent time on an island some-where in between. On a farm."

Jerry nods, picking at his fries. "I see."

Just before I was to leave on this journey, I was going through my sets of stacked drawers. I have a dozen of these and each one is labeled for something I am doing. I toss ideas and notes into them. Scribblings on cocktail napkins or yellow pads. Story jottings. One is labeled "Mississippi" and in this drawer I found road maps, dining information. How to rent a paddleboat. News stories from the 1993 floods. Maps, scribblings, articles I've clipped for one reason or another. Some are obscure to me even now. Between "Prairie Islands on the Missouri" and "Mormon Town Flourishes in Illinois," I found a crumpled sheet of yellow paper. I opened it and read what I knew was my father's shaky hand.

Last spring I asked him to tell me what he could about the river and the places he'd lived as a young man. He was over 102 years old, but he still had his smarts. The more I thought about the river, the more I wanted to ask him. I was sitting, poised with yellow pad and pencil, but he was nodding off to sleep and gave me a wave. I went on an errand and when I returned, I found he'd scribbled something down.

It read, "We had a structural engineer who had twenty acres in the middle of the river. He had a couple dozen cows and milked them every day. They canned and sold the milk unpasteurized to drink. Wife and son ran the farm. This was seventy years ago. We used to boat in summer and sled in winter to cross the river to his farm."

That was all. I had many more things I wanted to ask him. Where is this island? Who owns it now? Does it have a name? But he was sleeping when I returned and I had places to go. I had to leave. I kissed his forehead, combed back his hair. And I never saw him again.

"Good fries," Tom says.

"My dad's part of the reason why I've come on this trip," I tell them. They both nod, then push their plates away.

"Let's get some shut-eye," Tom says.

"Do you want to shoot a round of pool?" I ask. I'm not sure I really want to shoot pool, but I'm not ready to return to the boat either. But they decline.

"Been a long day," Jerry says.

We make our way back to the boat. The amber lights glow along the walk across the railroad tracks, through the grove of trees and picnic tables, back to the river. A crescent moon casts its reflection on the slow-moving water of the east channel.

It is our first night together. I wait for Jerry to pull his bed out, but he just lies down on the narrow sofa in his sleeping bag at the helm. Tom has staked out a place on the flybridge under the stars. Once on his air mattress he puts on his headphones, tucks Samantha Jean in ("She's my bed warmer," he says), and goes to sleep.

I draw the lime green curtain, which is all that separates me from these men. It is the only privacy and safety I have in the world right now and it is flimsy to the touch. Since we are bedding down, I go to the bathroom. I use bottled water to wash, brush my teeth, and flush. When I am finished, I can't open the door. It budges about an inch, but that's all.

I struggle, then try to figure out what is wrong. It seems that the shower door has come ajar just enough so that I am unable to open the bathroom door. The two doors have become locked in some kind of triangulated death grip.

I start to call. "Jerry," I say softly. Then louder. I know he is hard of hearing and if he is sleeping on his good ear, he won't hear me. I know this because, as a girl, I used to cry out to my father in the night and he never heard me either. I call again, more loudly now. "Jerry!"

Then I begin to bang. Tom is also deaf in one ear and, if he has his headphones on, which he does, he won't hear me at all. I bang and bang. Then I start to shout. Samantha must hear me because she barks and like a chain reaction that wakes Tom, who shouts to Jerry. "What is it?" Jerry calls out, startled.

"I'm stuck in the bathroom."

"Where are you?"

"The bathroom!" I scream.

He shuffles over and starts fiddling with the doors that have become entwined. "Hmm," he says, "this could be a problem."

"It is a problem," I tell him, but he doesn't reply. He unhinges the stuck doors, slams the shower door closed, and without a word turns back toward his couch, stretches out, and goes to sleep.

I pull back my curtain, grateful to that little dog who saved me from spending the night in the head. After reading for a few moments by the light of a flashlight, I lie there, adrift on the river, aching for sleep. My heart beats like a hummingbird's in my chest. I gulp down an anxiety pill and wait for it to work.

What did Emily Dickinson write? "Hope is the thing with feathers/that perches in the soul." Inside of me it feels as if it is trying to fly away. Shallow breathing is fear, I've heard my yoga teacher say. For months I've woken with this pounding of my heart. At home I take my husband's hand and place it on my chest. I make him keep it there until the racing stops.

But some nights if he is tired, I don't want to wake him. I worry I'm becoming a burden. I get up and walk around. When I am this way, I can't read or think or write or answer mail. I'll go to the blue chair in our kitchen by the window. This chair was my father's. He sat and read in it all the time. He watched the news. When he moved from Chicago to Milwaukee, he sent it to me. I can sit in it for hours and just stare outside. I've watched the sun come up in that chair.

~ 10 ~

MY FATHER was living in Sharon, Pennsylvania, when a gypsy predicted his fate. He was dating a "shiksa," a woman he knew he'd never marry, and she had a nine-year-old daughter. He told me once that he was most fond of the little girl. The woman wanted my father to go with her to a soothsayer to have her fortune told. She persuaded my father to take her, perhaps hoping the soothsayer would tell my father to marry her. He agreed to drive her, but said he wouldn't go inside.

He drove this woman to a neighborhood of tenements and slums and waited in the car. The woman went in and a few minutes later she emerged, distraught. "She wants to see you," the woman said. Reluctantly my father went in.

The fortune-teller was a large black woman and she told my father that he would receive a letter from someone he loved. In that letter would be a request and my father would accept the offer. He would return to Chicago. He would meet a woman, marry her, have two children, and live near a lake. She also told my father that she'd had nothing to say to the woman who had brought him here. That nothing in her life was ever going to change.

A week later my father received a letter from his brother, Sidney, whose hospital robe I still wear. The letter told him that his architectural business was failing and begged my father to return to the Midwest and become partners with him. My father accepted and left the woman and her nine-year-old daughter behind.

After Christmas my Aunt Ruth, who was married to Sidney, went to Saks Fifth Avenue to return a peach-colored nightgown her husband had given her for the holidays.

The woman who would become my mother was selling lingerie. I picture her helping women pull up corsets, slip heavy breasts into industrial-strength bras. I imagine her telling a bride-to-be that a particular nightie will do the trick. My mother had studied fashion design at the Art Institute of Chicago. She received a scholarship after a designer from Saks recognized her talent but had to drop out during the Depression when her father wouldn't give her the nickel she needed for bus fare.

My mother truly had an artist's flair. She could do anything with her hands. I recall her quilting my bedspreads late into the night. She spent seven years on these. Or painting a portrait of a woman—half her face black and the rest of it blue. She explained to me that the black was a shadow. Just a few years ago we went to an exhibit of Picasso portraits at the Museum of Modern Art. My mother swept through the gallery. "Now that one, you see, it's very good." She pointed to a charcoal sketch.

"He was very free when he did that. He didn't overthink it." A small crowd soon gathered around us. They thought my mother was a guide of some kind.

But she never finished school. She returned to Saks and had been selling lingerie ever since. And now a woman she seemed to recognize came in to return a peach-colored nightgown. They had gone to grammar school together, but hadn't seen one another in twenty years. "My brother-in-law has just moved back into town," my Aunt Ruth said. "Shall I give him your number?"

It took a while for my father to call. When he finally did, he said, "I was going through my pants before I sent them to the cleaner and I found your number." Hardly the most romantic opener, and perhaps it should have been a sign, but my mother was glad he called. A week later they went on their first date. My mother was not a young woman, in her thirties, living at home with my grandmother, her brother-in-law and sister. She had been waiting for a long time for her life to begin. And he was a forty-four-year-old bachelor. My mother wondered at first if something wasn't wrong with him.

Before leaving on her date, she told my grandmother, "If I don't like him, I'll be home by ten." At a quarter to ten my father told her he was tired and took her home. When she walked in at ten o'clock, my grandmother said, "Oh, you didn't like him."

"I'm going to marry him," my mother replied.

He called her on Sunday from a skating rink and asked if she liked to skate. She loved to skate, she said. In truth she had skated only once before in her life, but she went down to the rink anyway and sprained her ankle. The following weekend he took her to dinner and she ate soft-shell crabs. When she vomited all the way home, she was sure she'd never hear from him again.

He didn't call the next day, and she knew it was over. She'd spend every New Year's Eve for the rest of her life sitting with her sister and brother-in-law, childless as they were, embittered and alone. Then in the evening the phone rang and my father said, "I'm sorry I didn't call earlier, but I thought you'd need to rest."

He offered to drive her to work on Monday morning and she accepted. When he picked her up, my grandfather sat in the front seat. Every morning after that my father picked her up with his father in front. Then one Friday night he invited her home to dinner. My mother told me that Grandma Morris didn't care if she was a two-headed monster with green hair. She was thrilled that "Sonny" was bringing a girl home. In her more bitter moments my mother would quip that she was the only Russian Jewish woman my father had met who could "pass" among his fancy German Jewish friends.

The following Monday when my father picked her up, his father got out of the car and moved into the backseat. They didn't really know each other. I'm sure if they had, there would have been second thoughts, but they were married six weeks later. And I was born thirteen months to the day after that. They had another child and, as the soothsayer predicted, built a house near the shores of Lake Michigan.

~ 11 ~

It is odd to move through the world without caffeine. It produces in me a strange, sleepwalking state, as if I'm wrapped in gauze. Though I'm feeling rather Zenlike the next morning as I rise. I am not sure when I was last coffee-free. Perhaps in eighth grade. I am used to waking to the smell of dark beans brewing, the promise of an infusion to start the day.

But as I rise the next morning there is none to be had. Certainly not on board. We still can't boil water and I'm sure the people who run The Depot are recovering from the night before. I pad onto the deck where Jerry is staring at the newspaper from two days before. "Good morning, Mary," he says.

I give him a nod, then grab a water bottle from our cooler, which is now filled with floating shards of ice like an Arctic spring. In the head I pop my prescribed medications. I pee into my jar and brush my teeth with bottled water. Then, leaving Jerry muttering about yesterday's news and Tom nestled topside on his air mattress, cooing sweet talk to Samantha Jean, I'm off.

It is a pleasant morning after the storm as I cut across the park, and for the moment I have no regrets. Albeit drugged, I made it through the night. I wasn't raped or killed. The boys perpetrated no crimes against me as far as I could tell. To my complete surprise I slept rather well and enjoyed the gentle rocking of the river, which I found preferable to an electric storm.

There is a crispness in the air. A hint of fall. It's the kind of midwestern morning I remember. A gentle breeze blows as I wander past a grove of trees on St. Feriole Island. From the plaques that line this island I learn that this was once an important gathering place for French-Canadian fur traders and Native trappers. It was inhabited until 1965 when floodwaters crested at 25.38 feet and inundated the island with more than five feet of water. One hundred families were moved inland under the federal relocation program. Now the Mississippi continues to flood periodically (in 2001 the island experienced a double crest flood with a height of 23.75 feet), and St. Feriole Island has become a park.

I pause in the grove where I take in deep breaths. It seems that a tornado does wonders for the quality of the air. I walk on, stopping to explore a large yellow brick building, abandoned and gutted, which was an elegant old hotel for decades. In its next incarnation it became a slaughterhouse owned by Armour until it was closed in 1965. I gaze into its gutted lobby, trying to imagine animals, bludgeoned to death in this vast, hollow space. I move on. Just beyond the grove and across the tracks sits the Villa Louis—"the house on the mound." The Villa Louis is an elegant old home that has in recent years been refurbished and returned to its former splendor. I was hoping to visit, but it's just past eight and a sign informs me that the villa doesn't open until ten, at which time Jerry wants to sail. I've brought my journal and my watercolors with me and I am content to plant myself on a stone block in front of the villa and scribble and paint for an hour or so.

I have kept these journals for years—as I wandered the dusty streets and marketplaces of Central America, as I traveled across Siberia. I wrote in them when I lived in Paris and when I was under house arrest in Havana. On the inside cover I always write "Reward," but I have never lost one, though once in Spain a young man raced off a train to give a journal back to me and I kissed his hand. And on the Vltava in Prague a boat vendor accepted one as collateral so my daughter and I could rent a pedalboat.

Mainly these are working journals, but inside of them I also keep a diary and paint. I cut and paste boarding passes, snapshots, local flora. What happens around me, what is said. The bizarre, the inane, the weather, the everyday. I write it all down here. I jot in the margins and paint the pages in the colors of my moods.

My first journal was a gift from my father. He gave it to me on September 12, 1967, before I sailed to France. This was thirty-eight years to the day before I left on this journey. He had my name embossed in gold and inside he wrote, among other things, "This book with its blank pages is for you to bring to life."

My father never visited me that year. He was loathe to travel beyond the safe confines of his world as he defined it. At the airport his eyes filled with tears as he rushed back to his car and waved good-bye. Inside the journal he gave me I wrote of revolution. I hung out in the Latin Quarter with French students, determined to overthrow the state. When May 1968 began I found myself at the barricades, embracing the struggle. My last words in that journal were "Shit on them all." It was my rebellious year.

My daughter, Kate, purchased for me the journal I am using now. She bought it when we were in Florence just weeks before I was to begin this Mississippi journey and Kate was heading off to college. We had always been close. In baby pictures you can't tell us apart. We love olives, chocolate, and burned onions. I don't know anyone else who loves these three things. And now she was leaving. Who would borrow my silver belt, my cashmere shells? With whom would I play Balderdash or work out at the gym?

But, despite our similarities, Kate and I had our issues. She was pulling away and I was desperate to hold on. I was petrified of her leaving and that made her all the more ready to go. We quarreled about this over the years as I think many mothers and daughters do. But I left my parents' home and never went back. I assumed she would too.

I feared this trip to Florence would be our last hurrah. We had ambitious plans for our time together, but wound up spending most of our afternoons hanging out at a café in the Piazza della Republica. One morning I spilled espresso all over my journal and was upset. The pages turned wrinkled and brown.

Later we went to see an exhibit of drawings by Michelangelo. On the wall were framed pages of brown manuscript with drawings and writings in Michelangelo's own hand. "What's this?" I asked my daughter.

"Oh, just some other artist's coffee-stained journal," she replied. We went into a paper store and Kate bought me a new journal for my river voyage. "To my favorite traveler," she inscribed on the inside cover. "You make everything beautiful." On one of its creamy pages I begin to sketch. I'm not very good at this, but I enjoy passing the time. I'm trying to draw the villa. I do landscapes, still lifes, sleeping cats. I almost never paint when I'm at home, but I've done this for years when I'm on the road.

I'm not sure how long I've been here when a car pulls up and a man and a woman get out. They are nicely dressed, which I am not, and they look at me and smile. "What're you up to?" the man says.

I'm embarrassed now. "Oh, I just like the building."

He glances at my painting and nods approvingly. "Well, do you know what you're sitting on?"

"Oh, no, I don't." I jump up, thinking that the cement block I'm seated on is some kind of heirloom.

"You see," he goes on, "the carriages would pull up next to this stone block so that the ladies wouldn't have to show their ankles when they stepped down. It was considered indiscreet. Come back later. You can take a tour."

"Oh, I'd love a tour. It looks so beautiful. But I'm on a boat and we're only here for a short while. We have to sail." Even as I say this, I'm aware that "sail" isn't the right word, but how do I call what we do? Float, putter, drift? Careen? Nothing seems quite right.

"Oh, yeah? Where are you sailing?"

"Down the Mississippi," I tell them. "I'm writing a book about it."

They seem intrigued. "Well," the man says, "we're expecting the wives of the governors of Illinois and Iowa at ten, but I think we could arrange a special tour for you right now, don't you think, Linda?" He turns to the woman.

"I don't see why not," she says. And he unlocks the gate and I follow them inside. They open the doors to the villa and Linda Travis leads me around. We walk into the entryway with its chandelier and blue-papered walls as Linda lovingly shows me the grain painting of the woodwork, the Lincrusta walls, the brocatelle curtains.

She explains how this house came of age during the arts and crafts movement and also during the time of Frank Lloyd Wright. Both Wright and William Morris took a more simplified and organic approach to decor. Ninety percent of the house has been returned to its original form. Linda shares with me the resurrection of this private house into a public museum, complete with the family portraits, dolls, original silver and crystal, largely because family members returned their inherited possessions for the restoration of their ancestral home.

But I am more taken with the story of its former owners, Nina and Louis Dousman, a handsome, stylish St. Louis couple. Louis Dousman built the Villa Louis and they lived here with their five children. They were a loving family until Louis died suddenly of what appears to have been appendicitis at the age of thirty-seven. Nina was then advised to sell many of the assets, including Louis's beloved racehorses. Nina married again and moved to New York. But after the failure of that marriage, she returned to St. Feriole Island to raise her children at the Villa Louis.

This house is also a story of the river and its changing fortunes, for Villa Louis had its heyday during the time of steamboats and fur trading. Prairie du Chien, the mainland city that lays claim to this island, was once a major trade center. But as the river economy shifted, the city came to depend more on farming and the local industries of clam fishing, button manufacturing, and a woolen mill. As fortunes fell, so did those of the Dousman family, and eventually they left this island behind.

As Linda Travis guides me, I linger at the cots where children slept. The bed where Nina dreamed alone. I wander slowly through the rooms where servants lived. I gaze at the kitchen where butter was churned. The garden with its artesian fountain. The cook's garden with its heirloom bulbs. I am consumed by the fate of families, by vicissitudes of everyday life. Love and its loss haunt these walls.

My father built the house where I grew up on the banks of Lake Michigan. It was on the North Shore of Chicago in a town of ravines and bluffs and old Indian trails. When our house was being built, he often took me there. I was perhaps three or four, but the smell of sawdust and fresh paint still makes me think of home. My father would walk around with a set of blueprints, telling the contractor where to move the bathroom, where to put a door.

One day he was talking to his contractor upstairs in the unfinished frame of the house and I wandered off on the floor below. I found a double-edged razor blade, which I'd never seen before, and I sliced my arm. When I showed him, my father shuddered. "Oh my God," he said. He wrapped my arm in his handkerchief, as blood dripped into the wood, leaving a stain. Eventually it was covered in tile. Even though I haven't lived in that house in almost forty years, I like to think that this part of me remains.

I loved that house. I loved its white brick and green shutters, its garden and its proximity to the lake. Its address, 105, remains my lucky number to this day. If I get on a flight, and it's #105, I know I'll be safe. My father loved that house as well. After all, he designed it. He watched it being built.

My father told made-up stories about a brook and a bridge, about a lady who lived inside a pumpkin, and one about a little snowflake. He told them to me night after night. He embellished them and made them better and I loved the lilting sound of his voice. Each story had a theme, which boiled down to this: Never leave home. Don't go away. Bad things happen if you don't stay near. I suppose he should know. He hated travel, and, as I look back, I think there was something agoraphobic about him. He couldn't stand anything he couldn't control.

Every winter my parents did go to Florida for a "getaway" week without us, but my mother began to complain. He never wanted to do anything. He wouldn't go in the water. He'd just sit on the beach. One year she told him that if he didn't go in the water with her, she wouldn't come down to Florida again.

So my father went into the sea. He was up to his knees when he felt something stinging him around the legs. He bent down and soon it was all over him, all around him. He was engulfed in the sticky blue tentacles of a Portuguese man-of-war. At the emergency room the doctors told him it was the worst jellyfish attack they'd ever seen.

After that he never went near the water. For the rest of his life he stayed high up on the sand in shoes with kneesocks, a baseball cap, and sunglasses, his eyes scanning the sea for predators. In his later years they wintered in Florida. When I went to visit and would go for a swim, he'd sit on the seawall with binoculars, scanning the water for sharks.

The truth was he never wanted to go anywhere. He loved the house he built. He loved the cherry tree in the yard. He would have lived his whole life there if he could have. But my mother wanted to move. She raised her children in the suburbs, which she abhorred. She worked for the PTA and been a leader of my Girl Scout troop. She marched in the Flag Day parades. Now she wanted the gritty streets of Chicago and its shops, not the tree-lined roads and lake below the bluffs that my father adored. She wanted to pound the pavement in her high heels.

Reluctantly he sold the house. The day we moved out, when I'd just returned from France, I woke to the sound of my father mowing the lawn. They moved into the city, into a skyscraper he and his brother had designed. A few weeks later my mother gave my dog away to a checkout girl at the A & P. He barked too much in the apartment, my mother said. Then she sold our piano, and my father never played again. He used to walk around the apartment with nothing to do, saying that selling that piano was the "dumbest thing" he ever did.

In his later years he seemed happiest in his lounge chair, in front of the television, alone. When he turned one hundred and they moved to Milwaukee to be closer to my brother, my father, using an old Prohibition term, described this solitary part of his life as "a dry run."

I leave the Villa Louis and head over to the gift shop where "Bridge Over Troubled Water" plays poignantly. I'm looking at souvenirs, postcards, snapshots of the Dousmans. I'm grazing on a short history of the villa when I notice the time. It is past ten and Jerry was very clear about leaving at ten. I've never been known for my promptness. I'm sure there are complex reasons for this. My father ran a tight ship himself and he was fanatical about being on time. Hours before we had to be anywhere he'd start: "Are you getting ready? Are you going to be on time?"

I seem to have rebelled in this regard. It was one of the silent wars I waged, the only way I knew how to combat my father's rages, which were not so silent. I would linger in jeans and T-shirt until just before we had to walk out the door. I had this timed perfectly in fact, enough to drive my father wild. "You aren't going to get ready, are you?" he'd say. Then I'd appear, on the dot, all dressed, makeup, stockings, heels, just as they were heading for the door.

Given the fact that Jerry was once "Air Force" and given his somewhat protomilitary style, I decide to hightail it. I scurry out of the gift shop, sorry to leave this peaceful place behind. Heading past the villa, I catch a glimpse of Linda and her cohorts, now in turn-of-the-century reenactment garb, greeting the wives of the governors of Iowa and Illinois. But I must rush on. Ahead of me the railroad tracks that run between the river and the Villa Louis cut a slice through St. Feriole Island.

A freight train chugs my way. It stretches as far as I can see, car after car. If this train reaches the intersection before I do, I'm going to be literally on the wrong side of the tracks for a while. If the train has to stop on the island, it could be a much longer wait.

But the freight is approaching at about the speed our houseboat travels and I'm pretty sure I can beat it. I dash down the street, past the duck pond and the Villa Louis gardens. I rush toward the tracks as the train comes near. It can't be going more than five miles per hour and is perhaps fifty yards away. I can see the engineer's dark eyes. I give him a wave and he replies with a long, warning blast.

It is a sound of youth, a memory rising. When I think of childhood, I think of horse chestnuts, girls walking together to school, the trains. Camel hair coats and saddle shoes. The sound of my father leaving for work and coming home. The Chicago Northwestern he took twice a day. F. Scott Fitzgerald would agree. At the end of *The Great Gatsby* he wrote, "That's my Middle West. Not the wheat or the prairies or the lost Swede towns, but the thrilling returning trains of my youth."

I hear the whistles. The 8:08; the 5:15. My father punctual as the railroad that carried him. On nice days he walked to the station, his arrivals and departures perfectly timed. More often my mother drove to pick him up or drop him off. When I had a bicycle accident and had to go to the emergency room, she made me get in the car with her so that he could see I was all right, even though I was bandaged like a mummy from head to toe. I can see his train pulling in. I see him, clicking his tongue, shaking his head when he sees me.

Still I think I can make it. I run like a rabbit, my backpack and paints and journal bouncing behind me, and the engineer honks again. Breathless I race to the other side and it still takes the train another minute or two to get to the crossing. As he passes, the engineer waves at me, pretending to scold. Then he honks once more.

‿◦

The train chugs across the island, coming to a halt as I dash through the small park. The wind off the river is cool and fresh.

The air smells of cut grass and leaves. On the dock beside our boat an old man is fishing. A worm hangs from his hook and I hear Jerry say, "Hey, where'd you get that worm?"

The man laughs, staring at his rod. He has no teeth.

"In your own backyard?"

As I approach I can see that the man is perhaps retarded or just very old and dotty. But he and Jerry are yukking it up. Now Jerry turns to me. "So, Mary, we now have a toilet and a fridge." He pauses for effect. "I hope you can tell one from the other."

I give him a smile. "I think I can." Apparently he isn't annoyed at my lateness. Indeed he seems quite relaxed.

It is clear that while I was at the Villa Louis, Tom and Jerry were working on the boat. The head is now operating and the water pump is hooked up. This does not mean that water actually flows, but it does mean that if we switch on the pump, we'll get a trickle of cold water, though Jerry controls the switch at the helm and seems reluctant to use it. A shower appears to be a distant dream, but they tell me that they also have hooked up the gas. We can now boil water. I am oddly ecstatic.

I make my first cup of coffee on board. As the water boils, I drop in a Folgers Coffee Single ("tea bag") which Jerry brought from home, and watch the water turn a light shade of beige. I've always believed that it isn't coffee if you can see the bottom of your cup. I can definitely see mine. I add two more tea bags until it turns murky as the river we're on, then I go on deck to sip it.

As I'm standing in the sunshine, enjoying my first Folgers aboard ship, Tom points to a half-built structure on the bluff a hundred yards south of where we're docked. "See that place?" he says. "They were going to open a restaurant or something, but a guy hung himself in it last winter and now no one wants to use it."

Somehow this shatters the peace of my morning. We all pause, unsure of how to respond. Then Jerry says, "So, was he well-hung?"

There is the usual guffaw. "Reminds me of that house where the man kept his mother in the freezer," I say, deciding I can play the death-and-doom game as well as anyone.

"Oh, god," Tom says, "that's in my backyard. The day I moved in they were moving her out. I wanted to get the guy a sticker that says 'My Mom's Cooler Than Your Mom.'"

I start to laugh, then gag on my coffee.

"Aw," Tom says, "Mary's all choked up."

"Okay," Jerry says, staring at the river, "rock 'n' roll."

"I'm gonna warm up that cold-blooded thing." Tom heads back to his engines.

"Roger," Jerry says, giving the key a turn.

"Clear."

"Contact. Jer, keep your rpms up for a moment if you could." Jerry seems to be resisting and Tom calls out to him again, "Keep them up. I need you to give me more."

At last the engines sputter to a start and we're off. Tom comes onto the bow and stands right in front of my view. Jerry says, "Tom, get out of the way. I can't see the buoys."

"What do you mean?" He gives his girth a pat. "You can't see the boys?"

I pull a chair to the side so I can see too and it scrapes against the floor. "Violation!" Jerry shouts. ("Violation" means you have done something very bad.) I'm a little stunned by his outburst. I can see this as a "technical error," which is boatspeak for a boo-boo, but hardly a violation. Still Jerry snaps at me. "Pick that chair up and move it next time. We spent a lot of time painting that deck."

"Aye aye," I say, giving a false salute, though I am annoyed at being shouted at for a minor infraction. In fact I do not like to be shouted at at all. There is no place to go on this boat, really, if one is in a bad mood or wants to be alone. I sit at the bow. I can feel Jerry's eyes, staring at my back. I spread out my journal and paints on the wooden worktable I have claimed as my own. It is an unstable, three-legged job with a peeling linoleum surface and Jerry says he'll use it as firewood first chance he gets.

I'm just getting set up when a huge shadow looms, blocking out the sun. I gaze up and see Tom. "Excuse me," he says, "but I need some of my things." Tom stows all his personal items in the hold on the bow and he has to move my table to retrieve his razor, an extra jacket for Samantha Jean, any of his things.

Before I can say a word, Tom hoists my table, which is covered with scissors, glue, water bottle, journal, paints, and moves it out of his way. Amazingly nothing spills. He opens the hatch and disappears into the hold. Moments later he's heaving shorts, razor, and various personal effects onto the deck. "I won't be long," he says.

We are living in close quarters, to say the least. Jerry and I are basically sleeping in the same room. Tom isn't, but only by default. He's camping out on the flybridge under the stars. I have no idea how or where we'll all sleep in a storm. There is no space for clutter, for things not put away. All our clothes, our drug kits, anything personal must be stowed.

Tom keeps his bedding and air mattress in the dinghy and secures them with bungee cords, but the rest of his things are in the hold. Jerry stows his stuff in the cubby above the couch where he sleeps and in the cabin hold, along with the cases of beer and diet Dew and diet Coke that aren't on chill, our screens which haven't been installed, and whatever else is down there. It seems to be a kind of bottomless pit.

But Jerry doesn't seem to have much. A few Hawaiian shirts, caps, a couple pairs of shorts, jeans. I've brought the most stuff. I guess I was thinking closet, drawers. Just shy of "cruise." Wishful thinking, obviously, on my part. In the cubby above my bed I stow my underwear, T-shirts, and shorts. I also keep my emergency items there, such as my flashlight and batteries, my earplugs so I can read if the engines are roaring, and the jelly jar I brought in which to pee, not knowing what the sanitary conditions would be.

While Tom's organizing his things, I go into the cabin to put mine away. I make my bed, which consists mainly of folding my sleeping bag, then start to tear my duffel apart. In the duffel I keep my jeans, my flannels, a slicker and all-weather gear, several nice shirts, and a pair of khakis, which I'm sure I won't have occasion to wear. There are no hooks, nothing to hang anything

on, except the showerhead. I begin what will become a daily ritual of folding and refolding my things.

I take my shirts and sweaters and sweatshirt and sweatpants,
and lay them out on the bed. I begin to fold. I roll up my T-shirts
and flannel pants, my slicker. Shoes I tuck in rows under the bed.
What would my father say about all of this? He'd shake his head,
give me that sardonic smile. He'd look at a crumpled blouse,
jeans with a tear in the thigh. "You aren't going to wear that, are
you?" he'd say. Meaning, I guess I'm not.

My father was an impeccable dresser and he cared a great
deal (inordinately I might add) about how people looked. If their
nails were buffed, their shoes shined. I would not call him a
dandy or even dapper. He was just a very well-dressed man. He
had exquisite taste in fine herringbone or tweed jackets, cashmere coats and scarves, cashmere sweaters and fedoras. He had
his silk ties made specially in Hong Kong and they all had
matching handkerchiefs, which he folded carefully into his
breast pocket.

The one thing about my father's style that amused me were
his toupees. When I was five or six years old, my parents were invited to a Suppressed Desire Ball. Guests were to invent costumes
that depicted their secret wish, their heart's desire. My mother
went into a kind of trance. She bought blue satin and gossamer
cloth. She cut out pictures of the Eiffel Tower, the Taj Mahal. On
a mannequin in our basement my mother fashioned for herself a
costume of the world.

My mother could do anything with her hands, but she used
her talent mainly to design strange Halloween costumes for her
children. In my life I have been a giant squid, a house of cards,
and a money tree. She spent six weeks on her costume for the
ball, but it was my father who won first prize. My bald father
borrowed a wig from his barber and went as a man with hair.
The judge said his was the simplest and most imaginative.

Afterward my father began wearing his wigs all the time. As
he grew older, his toupees aged with him. They grew grayer,
whiter, thinner. In his closet he kept several wig stands and, as a

joke, someone painted my father's face on one of them. At night with a grimace he'd unglue the toupee from his head and put it on his likeness.

As a girl I teased him. If he was engrossed in something, I'd put on one of his toupees and wear it around the house until he noticed and told me to put that "damn thing" away.

Now I cannot bear the thought of my father's toupees or where they might be. I can't stand thinking about his clothes at a church auction, a rummage sale. Donated. Being picked over. Tossed aside. Strangers in my father's suits.

I loved the smell of my father. His talc and his cologne. Old Spice, I think. When I walk by a man on the street who smells this way, I want to follow him. I loved watching him dress, doing his tie. When I first met my husband, this fascinated me. I could sit beside the mirror forever and watch all the loops that are required in a man's tie.

My husband still wears the yellow and cranberry and green sweaters my father handed down to him one by one, but what about the rest of his things? The toupees? The wig holder painted with my father's face? "Do you want to know?" my brother asks when we speak on the phone.

"No," I say back, "don't tell me. Don't tell me a thing."

The wig stand, he will tell me later, he put in the trash.

## GHOST RIVER

~ 12 ~

"Nothing remains to me now but my life," Joliet wrote after a shipwreck swallowed the maps and journals that recorded his discovery of the Mississippi. As we approach river marker 630.6 Jerry calls me out to the bow and points to a narrow, unnavigable rivulet, clotted with fallen trees, merging with the Mississippi. I gaze at the trees, lying with their roots in the air. Pushovers, Jerry calls them. Trees that grow in shallow water, shaky soil. Trees you could just walk up to and give a shove.

Gazing at the navigational maps where Jerry's got his finger planted, I see that we have reached the choked mouth of the Wisconsin River. A disappointing trickle, barely noticeable, hardly the place I envisioned. But it was here, just three miles below St. Feriole Island, that Joliet and a Jesuit priest, Father Marquette, first entered the river that the Indians up north called The Big Water.

Tribal leaders warned them that this river was filled with "monsters that devoured men and canoes together." Along its banks warriors who would "break their heads with no cause" roamed. They would face a searing heat that would turn them black and kill them. Marquette thanked them for their advice but "told them I would not follow it because the salvation of souls was at stake, for which I would be delighted to give my life."

In May of 1673 Father Jacques Marquette and the French Canadian explorer and geographer Louis Joliet, armed with compass and astrolabe, left Illinois country in birch bark canoes and traveled along the northern rim of Lake Michigan until they came to the limits of the French penetration into the continent. On the tenth of June they paddled up a sluggish stream, which was the Fox, until they reached the portage, where their guides, refusing to go on, left them. They carried their canoes until they found the broad and beautiful Wisconsin River and on the seventeenth of June Marquette and Joliet entered the Mississippi "with a Joy that I cannot Express," Marquette wrote in his journal.

Marquette and Joliet began making careful notes about the current and depth of the river, on the fish and game along its course. They saw wildcats and what they described as "swans without wings" and "monstrous fish" (probably giant blue catfish), but it was the "wild cattle" that excited them. Herds of bison darkened the prairies and the plains and Marquette and Joliet were the first Europeans to see them.

Now just after noon on our second lazy day we arrive at the place where Marquette and Joliet first saw the Mississippi. As we pass the mouth of the Wisconsin, we come to an open stretch, bordered with savannah-like wetlands that could be found in Africa or the Amazon. If I didn't know where I was, I'd think I was in another country. A flock of snowy egrets rises. A lone white pelican soars over our heads. Blue heron, fish dangling from their mouths, glide over the surface of the smooth water. It is a wild, seemingly undiscovered place and I feel what the early explorers must have felt.

As Jerry guides our ship, I stand beside him. Other than our vessel and these birds, the river is breathtakingly empty. There's not a house or man-made structure on either side. We are at this juncture on a beautiful day and there isn't a pleasure craft or a barge in sight. Not a tow or a fishing boat. I am seeing the river as Marquette and Joliet saw it. Perhaps as no one has in hundreds of years or more. Deserted, abandoned, frighteningly so. As we pass the confluence, we are traveling down this ghost river alone.

~ 13 ~

ON A Saturday in August two weeks before I was to depart, Kate sulked in her room. She had been gearing up to head for college, but the previous night she'd walked into our piano bench (which the child of a friend had moved into the middle of the living room) and smashed her foot. Her toes turned a shade of eggplant, tinged with green. As she sorted out her clothes, Kate hobbled around on a pair of crutches she'd found discarded near our house.

Somehow this accident was my fault. I was responsible for the piano bench being in the middle of the floor. But I was also the reason why she was walking through the living room in the first place. It seemed we had an infestation of Japanese water beetles. I had never seen the beetles because they are nocturnal, but so is Kate. And I had not called the exterminator. Kate was going through the living room to avoid the kitchen where the water beetles roamed when in the darkness she walked into the bench.

She was to leave in two days for a college orientation program that involved hiking along the Appalachian Trail, which now seemed dubious. I would be leaving myself for the river just ten days after her. How odd it felt to be going our separate ways after all these years. When she was born, I had this dream. I dreamed that on her first day of her life she was a baby and on the second day she crawled. On her third day she left for school and by the fourth she was gone. I thought of this dream as I helped her pack for college. I had no idea where the time had gone.

Our belongings were spread across two rooms and working their way downstairs. I was distraught, trying to stay upbeat, at a loss for things to say. "Honey, would you like to take the drying rack?" I asked and she gave me one of those anatomically impossible looks only teenagers can muster, which roughly translates to "You aren't serious, are you?"

I had the news on, but I wasn't really watching. I was studying Kate's housing assignment from Smith College. The letter that had just arrived informed us that Kate Morris would be living in Morris House, named for deceased alum Kate Morris. I was trying to determine if this was a sick joke or the makings of a horror film when the phone rang. I wanted to ignore it, but Kate picked it up. I heard her chat for a moment and assumed it was for her as it usually was. Then she called out: "For you."

It was one of my childhood pals. I have a group I've known since kindergarten and we check up on one another from time to time. My friend Laurie wanted to know if I was still planning on taking the trip down the Mississippi River. I looked at my duffel, my sleeping bag, my all-weather gear. "Of course I'm still going. Why wouldn't I?"

"Well, you know, with that storm . . ."

I hadn't been paying much attention to the news. I'd been shopping for school supplies and soap and underwear and duffel bags. I'd been dealing with Kate's foot, helping her sort out her things, taking pictures down that had hung on her bulletin board for the past ten years. I'd been trying to borrow a life vest from our neighbors across the street. "What storm?"

"That hurricane. Katrina."

I knew that a storm had hit Florida, but I hadn't heard much more. I didn't know that it had crossed the Gulf and was heading toward New Orleans. Or that it was a Category 5. And, most startlingly to me, I hadn't gotten the news yet that New Orleans was being evacuated. I stopped what I was doing and went into the den. For the first time I saw the long line of cars heading up Highway 10.

My arrival time in New Orleans was over two months away. I had a river pilot, named Greg Sadowski, a friend of Jerry's, who was planning to take me the rest of my journey from St. Louis or Memphis on a cruiser. I assumed New Orleans would be all right by then. But the Doomsday forecasters were chatting away. Worst-case scenarios abounded and if I were to listen to these, I'd never get past Memphis. Predictions were being tossed around of skyscrapers toppling, a thirty-foot storm surge that wouldn't subside for three months destroying everyone's homes and businesses. There was talk of toxic gumbo, a concoction of oil, gas, sewage, and coffins, which in the Big Easy rest aboveground.

Kate came into the den, holding her parka. "Mom," she said, "should I pack my winter clothes?"

"I don't know," I told her, now glued to the television. "I'm listening to this."

In my heart I believed that this storm would veer or dissipate as they tended to do. I understand the entertainment value of a big storm, an unsolved murder, a crisis of proportions beyond imagining. I was hoping that much of this was news hype. Still, I was beginning to wonder if I would leave on this journey. If it hadn't just been ill-fated from the start.

But late that night, after we'd packed Kate's winter clothes and closed her trunk, I switched on my computer and saw an e-mail pop up from my nephew, Matt. I opened it and there she was. The *River Queen*. Still on her trailer in dry dock, but looking whiter and brighter. I saw plastic chairs on her deck and on the fly deck. A shade up top. I was hoping for good weather. A peaceful passage under the stars.

✄

In the morning it appeared New Orleans had been spared. The worst of the storm hit Gulfport and Biloxi. The tragedy of Mississippi was profound, but it seemed as if the Big Easy could relax. I breathed a sigh of relief as well. In a few days Kate would be at college, though not hiking, and I would be on my boat, heading downstream. I went back to packing and planning, to tying up loose ends.

That evening I met a friend in a café, and she arrived distraught. Her parents had gone to New Orleans for the weekend on a lark (they had some frequent flyer miles they needed to use) and she was waiting to hear from them.

"They fled a little while ago," she told me.

"They fled . . . ?"

"Yes, you didn't hear? The levee broke."

"It broke?"

"Yes, about an hour ago. . . ."

When I left her, I headed home, where I watched the horror unfold. Water streamed in from the breached levee along the 17th Street Canal, causing the worst urban flood in United States history. People, who had lost everything, stuck in the Superdome and beneath a highway overpass, were now being called refugees. The pictures were wrenching. Mothers clasping babies, who were screaming for milk. An old woman in a wheelchair, a sheet over her head. Blacks, the poor, the disenfranchised. Those with nowhere to go.

I began trying to reach Greg Sadowski. When we last spoke, he was moving a huge, brand-new boat to New Orleans. But the circuits were busy and I couldn't get through.

The following Saturday Larry and I piled Kate's things into the car and drove her up to school. In the car she listened to her iPod, then slept with her dog. How do others do this? I wondered. Say good-bye to the people and places they love most in the world. But having watched those images from Katrina, clearly we were the lucky ones. When we arrived at Smith, we unloaded the car. We dumped everything into her room, then spent an hour or two helping her unpack. But after a while, it was clear she wanted to do this with her roommate, who had yet to arrive.

We found a housemate to take a picture of us on the porch of Morris House under a banner that read: "Morris: The Best Place to Live." Then Larry and I said good-bye and got in the car. Kate was ready for us to leave, so we did. We drove about a hundred yards to the end of her street, where her father and I sat on a park bench and wept. Then we got back in the car and drove home.

~ 14 ~

SILENTLY A towboat named *Genesis* tugs a barge past an old limestone quarry. This is the first sign of life we've seen in a while and, along with the name, this moment has an almost biblical feel. The pilot gives a long wave as he rides by and we wave back. The barge he pulls is "riding high," which means he's empty. "High profile," Jerry explains. Until now I have only understood this as it relates to celebrities. "Look at the watermarks," he says. "You can tell if they're empty or full." Then he shakes his head.

The quarry itself is still. No work is being done. We pass other barges that are showing a low profile, clearly full, but neglected at the river's edge. With the Port of New Orleans closed, these barges have nowhere to go. Jerry stands by the railing, shaking his head. As we slip past them, he stares, then goes back inside to look at his maps.

Jerry spends much of his time staring at things. He stares at the motor. He stares at maps. He gazes at birds, the sky, the movement of the waves. He looks deep into the hold and at the sink. If something isn't working, he gapes at it. Or if it presents or is going to present a problem, he stares. Often he just stands on the deck and gawks at whatever is behind him or ahead.

Sometimes he is just looking at the river. He'll be gazing and then make a pronouncement, almost for no reason, as if to himself, "Take her to port. There's a wing dam." Or a snag. A log. A piece of debris. I don't know how he sees any of these things. Jerry reads the ripples and the places where the water turns smooth. He'll say, "See that line in the water? You want to avoid that." But I'll see nothing beyond the ripples the surface makes. If a boat is coming toward us, Jerry keeps his eye on its wake. He stares through his binoculars or camera lens. He is like a heron, eyes on the water, before making his move.

Once the *Genesis* is behind us, it's open river again. Jerry's piloting, eyes straight ahead, and I'm standing beside him. Then he steps aside. "You wanta give it a try?" he says. I'm not sure if I do, but he lets me take the wheel. Somehow it doesn't feel right. The current is stronger than it was the other day. It's as if I've caught a giant fish and I'm trying to reel it in. Or it's trying to pull me out.

Jerry keeps reaching over and bringing me back to zero. "You
gotta keep her steady," he says, and I think I hear some impa-
tience in his voice. Or perhaps fear for his boat. But she keeps getting away from me and I find myself jerking her back. Jerry
shakes his head and I think I hear him going "tsk tsk."

"I don't think I'm very good at this," I say.

"Naw, it's just that this wheel has a lot of play. You have to
move it for an inch or two before it connects to the boat."

"I can see that," I say. But my steering feels like the nautical
equivalent of a poorly dubbed film. One of those spaghetti west-
erns where the words coming out have no relation to the movement of lips. There's a delay between when I turn the wheel and
when the boat actually moves. And I'm having trouble anticipat-
ing it as we edge closer to the riverbank.

"Point her straight," Jerry says. "Look at your depth finder." I
look at the depth finder, which reads 5.5 feet. We have a draft of 3.5
feet and Jerry is happier with more river beneath us. "You're getting into the shallows. Keep her nose toward that red buoy ahead."

It's been years since I've taken driver's ed, but I'm sure I
couldn't learn to drive a car now. In fact I've been trying to learn
to drive our stick shift that we acquired from a friend at a price
we couldn't refuse. Last summer I managed to lock gears on the
Long Island Expressway at sixty miles per hour as I shifted into
fifth. I haven't gotten behind the wheel since, and anyway, my
daughter won't let me. Nor will she ride with me. It was Larry
who drove her all the way to college and me home.

Steering this boat might also fall under the "old dog, new
tricks" category, I'm thinking, as Jerry reaches for the wheel and
gives it a yank. "Keep your focus," he snaps. I've definitely gone
too close to shore. A glance at the depth indicator shows we're
only in 5 feet of water. As I jerk her around, she pitches to an
awkward angle, though hardly enough to capsize. Topside I hear
Tom squeal, "Roller-coaster ride."

"I'll take over," Jerry says, his voice flat with what I can only
interpret as disapproval.

"I was just trying to stay near the green buoy."

"Yes, but we've got a wing dam there." He points at a ripple that looks like all the rest of the river. Another one of those mirages I don't see. I'm a flop. I know I am as Jerry shouts up to Tom on the flybridge, "Tommysan, take her topside."

"Aye aye, Sir."

I'm feeling like the hometown team that just lost. There's a small public humiliation here. I also realize I'm hungry. Food will provide a change of subject. It's close to noon and, outside of coffee, I haven't eaten all day. "Lunch anyone?" I ask.

"Affirmative," Jerry says as he scribbles in his log. I can only imagine what he's writing. "Girl can't steer." "Female unreliable." Words to that effect.

"Ah, well, shall I make something?"

"That'd be great." It's clear he isn't offering to help. I have a sense that certain tasks on board are going to fall along gender lines and galley work will be mine. But I like to cook and pride myself on it. "Stick to what you know," that voice in my head says. It is the way to a man's heart, after all.

I assess our larder, something there wasn't much reason to do before we had the gas and refrigerator hooked up, and make note of what we have. In the cubby above the sink I find two cans of Campbell's Chunky Chili With Beans—the Sizzlin' Steak version. Two cans of Chunky Chili No Beans—the Hold The Beans version. Two cans Chunky Chili With Beans—Tantalizin' Turkey. Two cans of cut spinach. One can of sliced beets. I make a silent vow. My mantra becomes this: I will never eat out of a can. I will hold on to whatever decency I can muster on this journey by not eating from cans.

I continue my inventory. Two boxes of Folgers "tea bags"— one caffeinated, one decaf, for me. Two jars of peanut butter. One jar of reduced fat Hellmann's, mustard, ketchup, salt, pepper, paper plates, paper towels, plastic knives and forks. A giant bag of Cheerios, Kellogg's Raisin Bran (for me). The fridge has eggs, cheese, some lunch meats, and dozens of cans of diet Dew, diet Coke, and vast quantities of beer. Above the fridge Tom has his stash of Wonder Bread, Chips Ahoy, which he eats by the fistful, and assorted Snickers, Milky Ways, and a two-pound box of malted milk balls, none of which I will get even a nibble of.

I open all the cupboards, looking for pots and pans. "They're inside the oven," Jerry says without looking around. In the oven I find a small Teflon frying pan, a tiny pot for boiling water, and an omelette pan with a fifty-cent tag on it from Goodwill. These are my working utensils.

I have brought with me a few cans of tuna fish, a green apple, a package of smoked chicken, some cheese sticks. I cut up the chicken and make a small salad for myself with the green apple that's starting to go bad. I put it into a Tupperware bowl and give it a shake.

For the boys I make smoked chicken sandwiches on Wonder Bread with mustard and mayo. I put chips on paper plates and slip Tom's to him through the small window above the helm where he pilots on the flybridge. I cut a piece of Wisconsin cheddar and slip it to Samantha Jean, who rips it out of my hand.

Afterward I go up to collect the trash. "How was your sandwich?" I ask Tom.

"Too much mustard," he says, shaking his head. "Don't give me any mustard next time."

✺

After lunch, I plant myself at my battered wooden table on the bow. An old loneliness settles in. I call Larry, but he's not home. I'm longing to talk to Kate. It's only her second week at college and I had promised myself I wouldn't phone her. I wanted to give her time. But now I want to hear her voice. I give a call and get her voice mail. Or rather I get the rap music of a group unknown to me. After a few choruses I hear my daughter's voice. "It's Kate. I'm not around . . ." Where is she? I wonder. At the library, studying. Or in her room. It is so odd that I do not know the books she is reading, the face of the girl she hangs out with down the hall. Does she see that it's me calling? Is she screening her calls?

I leave a brief message, then open my journal. I begin working on a painting of the riverbank, the islands ahead. I dab a little blue, wash in some green. Soon it starts to look like something. I create dark pines, the reflection in the water. I layer in more colors—some purple and red. I let them bleed and blend.

When I am satisfied, I reach for my glue. As I grasp it, the small painting blows away. Both Jerry and I see it go. It flies into the air and is about to sail into the river when it hits the gunwale and is pinned by the wind against the side.

"Thank you, *River Queen*," Jerry says, heaving a big sigh.

I ask him why.

"Because any other boat and that'd blow away. . . . She's got good sides, this old boat." Then he adds, "But next time put a book or something on top of it."

I'm starting to see that things don't just fall on a boat. They fly, they skid. They soar and slide. They are carried by the wind. They disappear for good. If they are lightweight, like your letter home or your paintbrush, they will be gone in a heartbeat. Every object that isn't heavy must be weighted down. Each piece of paper has to have a book, a set of keys, a coffee mug sitting on it. Every coffee mug must have a lid.

To look at a map you have to remove whatever is holding it down. To read the poem you have just written you must take it out of the notebook where you've tucked it for safekeeping. Nearly empty drinking glasses will spill their remains, paper plates will hurl like Frisbees into space. The third rule of boating seems to be this: Anything that can fly away will. If something matters to you, hold on to it for dear life.

~ 15 ~

THE MILWAUKEE Heart Hospital sat in an industrial park parallel to the main highway that heads north to Green Bay. It was off a major road that felt more like a service road, surrounded by warehouses, towers for high-tension wires, some malls that sit far back from the road. We recognized it right away by the giant red heart that looms from its main wall.

It had taken us ten hours to get here, due to storms all across the Midwest—whirling, black thunderclouds. In the summer there are often these storms in Wisconsin—ones that can lead to tornados farther inland, away from the lake. The big, beating down, scary kind.

It was literally a dark and stormy night. The sky had a greenish glint, the kind no midwesterner wants to see because of what it might bring. The parking lot had five cars in it and the only sign of life was a flock of Canada geese that padded across the newly seeded lawn.

"What is this?" I asked my husband. "*The Twilight Zone?*" He shook his head.

"It's a hospital," he replied.

"But there's no one here." It was a brand-new thirty-bed hospital, state of the art, in the middle of nowhere, that had, it appeared, no patients except for my father. My father, Sol Henry Morris, was almost 102 years old. He was so old that when we had his prescriptions filled, the druggist had to call them in because the computer would default and think my father was only two. It seems that you cannot administer blood pressure medication to a two-year-old.

In his youth he used to walk miles every day and attributed much of his longevity to exercise and temperate habits. "Nothing in Excess" was his motto. We attributed it to his rotten disposition. (Articles have linked longevity to bad tempers.) Whatever the causes, my father was as old as a land tortoise. His age has always been a cause of both fascination and concern.

I suppose there are reasons why my father didn't marry until he was forty-four. Or my mother, for that matter, until she was thirty-four. He spoke with nostalgia for the friends, the speakeasies of old Chicago, and the girls of his youth. He admitted to me once that his bachelor days were better than his married days. I had the old photos to prove it.

For years my father joked about his age. As he got older and older, he looked twenty years younger than his chronological age. Once he repeated his motto "Nothing in Excess" to a group of aging widows as the secret to his longevity, but apparently they misunderstood and heard "No Sex." When he saw their troubled faces, he corrected the error.

Whatever his secret, my father was very old. He remembered the invention of the automobile, the airplane, moving pictures. He saw one of the first automobiles rumble down a Chicago side street. He was a young man during the Jazz Age. He grew up between the wars. He was still in his twenties when the stock market crashed. He was too old to fight in World War II, though he tried to volunteer.

Doctors studied him. At ninety-five he had the physical stamina of someone seventy. Indeed, people took him for seventy. Until he was a hundred, he remained handsome and strong. He was the oldest patient his urologist or cardiologist or pulmonologist had ever had and keeping him alive became their private calling. To me my father simply seemed invincible.

But the day before my arrival in Milwaukee, my brother called to say, "If you want to see him, you'd better come now." If my mother had called, I would have assumed it was a tactic to get me to come home. She has done such things before. But not John.

As we approached the hospital, fork lightning skirted close to the high-tension towers. The glass doors slid open, cool air blew our way. Before I could say a word, the elderly receptionist looked up. "Oh," she said, "you're here to see Mr. Morris." She knew who we were coming to see. How was this possible?

Except for the sounds of whirring machines, the hospital was eerily still. There were no voices, no footsteps, no one crying out in pain. In fact there was nothing. No signs of life. I held tightly to Larry's sleeve. We took the elevator and got off on the second floor and found ourselves in a circular corridor filled with empty hospital beds, empty rooms, waiting rooms, conference rooms, offices. Travel pictures of the Pyramids of Egypt and Mount Rushmore hung on the wall.

We followed the circle until we came to a corridor filled with light. In the first room lay an enormous woman with tubes coming out of everywhere, machines pumping away. At her bedside was a man, silently sobbing. In the next room lay a thin, young woman, also connected with tubes.

At the nurse's station two or three nurses and what I assumed were a few doctors were working. One of the doctors was talking on the phone. He rattled off organs: Kidneys, heart, liver. No one looked up at us. No one paid any attention to us at all. Across from the nurse's station a large man lay almost naked on a gurney. Tattoos covered his arms and chest. Snakes, women, a wolf. A rose bloomed on his chest.

In the next room I found my father. He was sitting up in bed, eating vanilla ice cream and watching television. On the screen in black-and-white a woman stood on a dock beside a swamp. A group of men who appeared to be scientists were with her. Beneath the dock a creature that looked like a man in an iguana suit swam, trying to grab the woman. Its claws reached out of the water toward her feet, but the woman, unaware, walked off the dock unharmed. And the creature disappeared back into the darkness from whence it came.

My father, engrossed in *Creature from the Black Lagoon*, didn't see us come in. Then he looked up. "Hi, kids," he said, "thanks for dropping by." He put down his dish. "Lousy ice cream," he went on. "They're gonna kill me in here. Lousy food. Lousy service." He talked about the Milwaukee Heart Hospital as if it had three Michelin stars and was about to lose one. "See my doctor?" He pointed to the nurse's station where I did see his doctor on the phone. "He's running some kind of racket. All he does is talk on the phone. Making deals."

"Actually, Dad, I think he's arranging for organ donations," I told him. My father's eyes widened. "I think all the other patients in the hospital are brain-dead," I said. "You're the only one who's alive."

This gave him pause and the complaints stopped. Just then my father's doctor came in. He explained to me quite simply that last night my father had zero kidney function. We both looked at my father, eating his ice cream, watching television. "Basically," Dr. Brown said, "if I had his kidney function, I'd be in an irreversible coma right now."

My father put his hand to his ear. "What's going on?" he asked. "Are you talking about me?" He smiled his whimsical smile. On the television the woman dove into the lagoon and swam as the creature, circling beneath her, tried to pull her down.

~ 16 ~

TOM'S ON the flybridge, talking to Samantha Jean. He's telling her to be a good girl and stay in her jacket. "No, don't give me those sad eyes, Sam." I can hear him as I step across the starboard engine, which has its hatch open, and climb what Tom calls the "Jesus" ladder. This is because if you're about to sail off of it in a storm, you'd yell "Jesus!"

But Samantha Jean is standing up, begging with her big brown eyes.

When Tom sees me coming, he gives a special stern look to his dog. "Okay, Girl," he says, "big leap," and the dog catapults into his arms. "Now you stay in Daddy's lap." I give Samantha Jean wide berth and sit on the bench across from Tom, but the dog follows me with her gaze.

It's only day two on the river and early afternoon at that, but it feels as if we've been sailing forever. I'm looking for a change of scene. I like it up here on the flybridge, though Tom, unlike Jerry, will talk my head off. In a way it's just another side of loneliness, but the vistas are wide and the breeze cool. And I'm ready for a little company.

Tom steers, hugging his dog to him. "Sammy likes the boat because it's a nice smooth ride. See how relaxed she is?"

I look across at Samantha Jean and smile. "Yes, she seems relaxed." For now, I want to add.

"Oh, yeah, this is her vacation too." He nuzzles his face against hers. "Look how smooth the ride is. You know, this *River Queen*, look how nice she handles," Tom tells me, staring straight ahead. "She's like the Thunderbird of houseboats. You know, an old skirt and cardigan sweater. Ten-cent hamburgers. They don't make them like this anymore."

"They don't?"

"Naw, she's a vintage boat. About 1969 or so. You don't see many of these around."

"I knew she had class," I say, running my hand along the shiny trim. I didn't know that the boat I fell in love with was a vintage, that she came of age as I did. A girl of the sixties. I am starting to understand her appeal.

"Yep," Tom says, "you don't see many boats built the way she is. Do we, Baby?" Tom says to Samantha Jean, who licks his nose. "Don't build 'em like this anymore. We sanded her three times before we painted her with the fiberglass paint. Up until midnight doing that." We are silent for a moment as I think of the work Tom and Jerry put into this boat to get her on the water. I'm taking in the wide river, the sunlight streaming down. Tom's hands move the wheel gently and it is a smooth, easy ride.

Then, he looks at me with that slightly ominous eye. As if reading my mind, he says, offering me the wheel, "You wanta take over?"

"Naw, it's okay." The river is open without a vessel in sight, but I am hesitant. "I didn't do so well this morning," I say, thinking back to Jerry losing patience with me.

"Aw, you'll get the hang of it," he says as he buries Samantha Jean in her black bomber jacket. "Don't you even think about getting out of there." Then he relinquishes his captain's chair to me. I settle into the high chair with the cushioned seat for the first time and almost topple over backward.

"Oops." Tom catches me. "Don't lean back." (Later we will retire this chair.) As I reach for the wheel, I'm having visions of destruction and mayhem. As with our stick shift back home, I'm sure I'll never learn how to drive this thing. "Keel over" has taken on new meaning for me. "Just like a woman driver," my father would say.

But as I take the wheel and begin to steer, the boat responds to my touch. This wheel seems to have less play than the one below. If I turn, the boat turns with me. When I straighten her, she goes straight. I feel her move with me in a watery dance à deux. I move her back and forth and she glides. Also I can see the river much better from this vantage point. I see why Tom likes it up here on the fly.

I ask him for the binoculars and he hands them to me. The sun warms my face as I scan the river. Tom stares straight ahead. "Just hold her steady now," he says. "Keep an eye on your buoys." I seem to be able to do this better from above. At least I am able to keep us off the riverbanks.

Once Tom sees I'm handling her well, he turns his attention to his dog, who, despite orders, has left her bomber jacket and whines at his feet. He gazes down at her as if she's just a stubborn child, which in a way she is. "Okay, Sammy, you win, big jump," and once again the little dog leaps into his brawny arms. "I can never say no to her."

The river makes a wide turn and I follow the bend. Then I've got a straight shot down and it's easy. "I'm sorry Kim couldn't come with us," I tell him. We haven't really had a chance to talk privately and I've been wanting to tell him that. "Oh, it's all right. It would've been fun if she came, but it's fine. This trip is really about me having time with Samantha Jean." Tom cradles the little dog in his huge arms. "She had breast cancer, you know."

"Kim?"

"No, Samantha. But Kim helped me find the vet who would operate on her. I figured she could lose a tit or two. She's got about a dozen." He rubs Samantha Jean's belly. "Anyway, Kim helped me save her life and I'll never forget that." Tom explains to me how he has two dogs by two mothers. Samantha Jean was given to him by one of his girlfriends. "But when I thought I was gonna lose Sammy I got Monster Dog. He's a Jack Russell and drives Sammy crazy. So it's good for her to be on this trip. Gives her some time with just me."

Apparently Monster Dog's mother works in a petting zoo. "I don't date her anymore," Tom says, "but I go back to see the snakes. Ralph and Ezra. I call Ezra King Tut. I can get him to stand five feet high in the air. Just a trick I taught him. Sammy doesn't like it when I touch the snakes."

Tom gazes down at Samantha Jean, giving her belly a big rub. "Oh, you're not jealous of old King Tut, now, are you, Girl? Come on, Sammy, doggy hug. Doggy hug." And Samantha wraps her paws around his neck and plants a wet one on his lips.

Tom's just rambling and I'm not really listening. I'm piloting the boat. I still don't see the ripples in the water, but with my binoculars I scan the banks as any seaworthy captain would. And I am holding eighteen thousand pounds of ship on a steady course. "Do you ever think of getting married?" I ask him. "To Kim or anyone?"

"Oh, I think about it," Tom says. Then he caresses Samantha Jean's paw. "But you know in a way I already am."

"You mean . . . ," I gaze at the dog with her wiry hair, her beady eyes.

He's still stroking her paw. "I kinda am." I reach out to stroke Samantha Jean's paw as well and she looks up at me and growls so I turn back to the wheel.

✒

At Lock and Dam 10 we luck out. A huge fuel barge is just coming through, heading north. "We'd have been sitting here for two hours," Jerry says, poking his head through the cabin window, "if she was just locking in." His jaw drops when he sees me at the wheel, but he doesn't miss a beat. "I'll take her below."

"Aye aye, Sir." I'm getting good at my "aye ayes."

When I feel him take the wheel, I let go. Jerry maneuvers us into position and the lockmaster, a woman this time, greets us. "Are you Barb?" Jerry asks, friendly as always.

"I sure is," Barb replies.

"Well, pleased to meet you," Jerry replies.

It's a standard six-hundred-foot-long lock, 110 feet wide, and once again we have it to ourselves. I tug the rope, holding the line, and in ten minutes we're through. Guttenberg, Iowa, which is right ahead, has a fuel dock. Jerry doesn't want to stop at this little marina, but I'd like to visit the town.

I convince him. "What if we don't make Dubuque by to-night? We need fuel, don't we?" He shakes his head, clicks his tongue. He points out that even if we run out of gas we'd still be sailing downstream at three miles per hour. Then he shakes his head again. "Not safe, though. You don't want to travel that way."

Just ahead is the fueling dock and we pull in. There's no one there, but there is a telephone and across it a note that reads "For Gas, Dial Randy," and an extension. Randy answers and says he's up at the hotel and, a few moments later, a young man with sear-ing blue eyes who reminds me of Brad Pitt appears. A little too good looking, I think, for this tired river town.

But Randy is all smiles, an all-American kid, and we kibbitz with him a bit. As he's pumping, Tom's got Samantha Jean in the waves. "Hey!" Randy shouts. "You don't wanta walk in the shore barefoot there. The clam shells are razor-sharp!"

He seems like a nice kid, I think, though I'm looking at the gas prices, which I'm going to have to pay, and I feel a lump in my throat. $3.86 a gallon. I now know that we get a mile a gallon and that this fuel bill will be almost four hundred dollars. I gasp when our automobile gas at home comes to thirty dollars, but this seems like a lot more than I bargained for.

"So, where you guys headed?" he asks as he pumps fuel into our gas tanks.

"St. Louis," Jerry says.

"Maybe Memphis," I quip.

"Wow, that's gonna cost you," Randy replies. "But it sounds like a great trip."

Once we've fueled up and I pay for the gas, which may as well be liquid gold, I head into town. I walk past Lock 10 Hair and Tanning Salon and pass a sweet place where I'd love to stay called The Courthouse Inn. A few blocks off the main drag I come to a supermarket where I pick up some ground beef that's looking a little brown, salad fixings in a plastic bag, a bottle of merlot, pale pink tomatoes, and onions that look like they've seen better days, green peppers, bowtie pasta. I am determined to cook a meal for these guys in my three little pots.

It's a beautiful day and I don't feel like rushing back to the ship. I'm enjoying having earth beneath my feet. I pop into the Café Mississippi for a cold drink. The bartender, a young college-age girl, is at the bar, smoking. She pours me a club soda, which is flat. But the view of the river is gorgeous. "Pretty town," I say to her as I sip my club soda.

"Yeah. Kinda small," she says, taking a drag. "And getting smaller." She stubs out her cigarette and hands me my check for seventy-five cents. If only our boat could run on club soda. I leave two dollars on the bar.

On the way back to the boat my phone rings. It's Kate calling. "Hey there," I say, picking up on the second ring. I am thrilled to hear her voice that sounds so grown up. Friends often confuse her with me on the phone. She tells me about her poetry class where there are students who have already been published in antholo-gies, her roommate with whom she is now "joined at the hip," and a bizarre initiation dinner in which she had to dress in pots and pans. We're laughing away as I head back to the dock. She's on her way to a class right now. "I'll call you back later," she says.

"You know where to find me," I reply.

Tom who's working on deck sees me say good-bye. "So was that your daughter?"

"Yes, it was," I tell him proudly. "Wanta see her picture?"

I have brought with me a small album with pictures of our family—of Larry, our house, our dog, and snapshots of Kate. Last summer she worked at the New York Aquarium with marine mammals. I have a picture of her on her last day of work. She's leaning over a pool and a beluga whale is jumping out of the water, nuzzling her cheek.

Later that afternoon my cell phone rings once more. "Is that the Whale Kisser again?" Tom asks.

"Who?" I have no idea who he's talking about.

"Your daughter," he laughs. "The Whale Kisser."

I glance at my caller ID. "Yes, it is."

It was my father who told me to have this child. I was thirty-nine years old and traveling through China with my companion of five years. Jeremy and I had walked the Forbidden City and sailed through the now-destroyed gorges on the Yangtze. We had climbed to the Potala Palace in Tibet. But Jeremy, a renowned legal scholar, had to leave me in Shanghai. He was returning to New York, then flying on to New Zealand to deliver a series of lectures on the rights of the Maori. After months of trying to get him to alter his plans, I decided to continue across Asia on the Trans-Siberian Railway alone.

I was in search of family roots on the outskirts of Kiev.

The year was 1986. Just as this Mississippi journey was marked by Katrina, my trip to Kiev was marked by disaster as well. The nuclear accident in Chernobyl occurred two weeks before we left and my venture into Ukraine was looking dim at best. But it was still my intention to persevere. On the six-day train ride to Moscow I was sick and lethargic, the result I assumed of too much vodka, which flowed quite freely on that train, and travel. But by Leningrad I knew. Jeremy and I were going to have a child. I was looking at forty. We'd been together five years. It never occurred to me that we would not marry.

I reached him with the good news. "I'm pregnant," I told him. "I'm going to have a child."

The transatlantic silence was shattering. "Are you sure?" he finally asked.

"I'm sure," I told him.

"Well, a child is a wonderful thing."

"I was thinking we should make it legal."

There was another long pause. Finally he replied, "Legal in what sense?" He had written over thirty books on international law. He had pleaded cases before the World Court. Surely he knew what legal meant.

It was during the months of "white nights" in Leningrad. Like Raskolnikov, plagued by anguish and guilt, I walked the canals. Clearly Jeremy had no intention of marrying and I knew I could not have this child on my own. I wandered into a bar, filled with the most beautiful women I'd ever seen. They were like mannequins with their dark eye shadow, their pointy breasts. They were prostitutes, waiting for men from Finland, and they thought I was trying to hone in on their weekend business. I wandered out and walked some more. Half the night I walked, then went back to my hotel room, a study in curtains and lace, and called my mother.

In tears I told her I was pregnant. I said that Jeremy didn't want the baby and I was coming home to have an abortion. "Are you sure this is right?" she asked me. "Are you sure it's what you want to do?"

"What else can I do?" I sobbed into the phone. And I made her promise, "Don't tell my father. You have to swear."

"I swear," she said.

Half an hour later the phone rang. It was my father. "Mary," Dad said, "I hear you have a problem."

I cried uncontrollably when I heard his voice. "Yes, I have a problem."

"Well," he said, his tone surprisingly modulated, "in my opinion there are no problems. Only solutions." Always his aphorisms. "You know," he went on, "men come and go." He paused as if he knew of what he spoke—as if he was thinking about something he didn't want to say. "But a child is forever."

"Can you live with that?" I asked tentatively. I had never spoken with my father like this before. I peered out of the window at the sunny streets of Leningrad at four a.m.

"I can live with a lot worse," he said.

# MIST

~ 17 ~

IT IS night as we reach Lock and Dam 11 just north of Dubuque. There's no traffic and the lockmaster lets us float free. Normally I like floating free with no ropes, but, as we drop down into six feet of blackness, there's an eerie feeling as if we are sinking into a dark hole. For the first time in days there's silence on board. Jerry has rigged up a beacon on the flybridge, but the river is onyx as we sail into Dubuque.

It has been a very long day and we're tired as we float beneath a railroad bridge and past the huge floodgates of the city. As we ride through them, these gates loom above us and seem to lead into a netherworld. Before us sits Diamond Jo Casino, illumined as fireworks, with calliope music seeping from its decks, and paddleboats, used now only to take tourists for rides. But as we enter the harbor and look around, it's clear that there is no marina. There are no pleasure craft here at all. Jerry has a memory of the marina being between the floodgates, but as we gaze around, it's not. "Do you see anything?" Jerry asks Tom, who stands with me on the bow.

"No, Sir, I don't."

I don't either and I'm crestfallen. I was very much hoping for a shower and some amenities and I feel the irritation rising. I check the map and see that the Dubuque Marina is at river mile 582.0, which was a few miles upstream, just below the lock and

dam, and we missed it. I show Jerry the map. "Can't we go back?"
I ask.

"It's too late," Jerry says, clearly annoyed. "I'm not going upstream in the dark."

"Well, what're you going to do?"

Jerry scans the harbor into which we've sailed. Tied beside
Diamond Jo Casino is a commercial paddle wheeler called *The
Spirit of Dubuque*. "I know the people who own that paddleboat,
a guy named Walt. I've met him a few times," Jerry says. "We'll
tie up here."

"Here?" I stare at him, amazed. There is nothing here except
the casino and this paddleboat.

"What do you think, Tommysan?"

Tom shrugs. "I'm tired. I think we can get power off that boat.
If not, I'll use the 'genie.'" This is what he calls his generator.

"I want to find the marina."

"Well, it's too late now," Jerry snaps as he maneuvers beside
the big paddleboat. So it will be another night of no water, but it
seems as if Tom can rig us up for light. We secure our fenders as
Jerry pulls in beside the empty paddleboat. I can see a walk along
the levee. It is dark, but the walkway is lit. Lovers sit on the wall,
smoking, drinking beer, kissing. But I have no idea how to get
there.

As Tom and Jerry tie up, I'm trying to figure out how to get
off the boat. Jerry says that the only way is to inch along the
outer railing of the paddleboat, go down the gangplank to the
walkway, climb under a chain-link fence, and go past security
into the back door of the casino.

This whole endeavor has a slightly criminal feel. With Jerry's
help, I make my way around the outer railing of the paddleboat,
the river black and murky beneath me. Plastic bottles and debris
float in greasy muck ten feet from where I hover. I shimmy along
the railing, reach the gangplank, slip along it, follow the narrow
walkway, and slide under the security chain, expecting to be
stopped at any moment.

As I make my way to the casino, I pass a young man in gray slacks and a cranberry shirt. He is smoking a cigarette and slips under the chain, heading toward our boat, I assume to arrest us for trespassing. As I enter the casino via the service entrance, a huge bouncer stands at the escalator. He's wearing a shiny gray suit and is built like a vault. I ask him where I can get dinner. He tells me that the restaurants are closed, but that I can get deli sandwiches on the top floor.

I don't want deli sandwiches. I want food. Something hot that doesn't come between two slices of white bread, preferably home cooked. I ask the hostess and she informs me that the restaurant closed at nine. It is 9:10. "You mean I can't get anything to eat on this huge floating casino?"

She shakes her frizzy red head and says with a sweet midwestern twang, one it took me thirty years in New York to lose, "You can get deli sandwiches on three. You can get breakfast at about five. And, of course, the bars are all open until two."

Wow, I think, you can't eat, but you can drink for the next five hours. Now that should help you drop some serious change. I call Tom and Jerry on my cell and inform them there's no food to be had, just booze and slots. "Well," Jerry says, "there's a hotel right there. Why don't you just go spend the night there? You might like that better."

I'm standing in the parking lot, staring up at the generic hotel that looms ahead of me. My feelings are definitely hurt. "Are you asking me to leave the boat?"

Jerry hesitates. "No, I'm not asking you to leave. I just thought you might be more comfortable."

"I don't want to do that."

"We're going to order pizza," Jerry says.

"Where're you going to have it delivered?"

"Oh, Tom's got that all figured out. They'll bring it to the parking lot of the Hampton Inn, which is nearby. Shall we order something for you?"

I hate pizza. I hate all that doughy stuff. I want a meal, shower, amenities. "Order me a veggie pizza, okay? Lots of veggies."

Jerry agrees and I tell him I'll touch base with him in half an hour. I'm going upstairs to have a drink. Three young Asian men get carded as they try to get into the casino, but it seems I'm of age and the bouncer lets me go upstairs without an ID, which I don't have with me anyway.

As I enter the casino, I am stunned by the flashing lights, the hordes of people, the clinking sounds of the one-armed bandits. Tumbling change. The roll of the dice. The spin of the roulette wheel. Croupiers in purple jackets are closing all bets. I sit down at the bar, which is essentially a paneling with about half a dozen games of electronic poker.

An elderly woman a few barstools down is sitting with a pile of quarters, an ashtray full of cigarettes, focusing on her game. The bartender with a bad toupee asks me what I'd like. I ask what he's got in white wine and he tells me chardonnay. "I'll have that." He takes a cardboard container out of his cooler and pours me an eight-ounce glass of wine through a spout.

A blond-haired woman, thin, in a white baseball cap and white capris, plunks herself down two stools up from me. She orders a double Scotch and the bartender seems to hesitate. I can see that she is completely sloshed. He brings her her drink, which she sips as she wins at solitaire and bends the bartender's ear. He listens attentively. Something bad has happened to her. He's nodding compassionately. A man comes by who seems to be with her. He is young and handsome and she shoves him away.

He gives a shrug and goes off and she slides over to the stool next to me to play electronic poker. Her cigarette rests in the ashtray and smoke blows in my face. I'm feeling lonely and she doesn't seem as if she's having the best night of her life either so I ask if she's all right. "No," she says, her words slurring like she's a bad actress in a bit part, "I am not all right."

"I'm sorry to hear that," I tell her. "Is there anything I can do?"

She shakes her head. "There's nothing nobody can do. My best friend died last week. . . ."

"Oh, I am really sorry. . . ."

"My stepfather. But he was my best friend in the whole world."

I tell her I am really really sorry about this. I am about to tell her that I just lost my father, thinking we could commiserate, but she goes on, "And then I had surgery on Tuesday, the day after he died."

I was surprised to see that she was smashed and playing electronic poker so soon after surgery. "Are you okay?"

"Yeah." She brings her face close to mine. "Hemorrhoids," she says. I smell the whiskey on her breath. "The pain is excruciating." Then she turns back to her poker game.

Once Dubuque had more millionaires than any other city in the world. Grand houses on the bluff attest to this wealth. These were men who got rich on the river trade—men who fought the railroads and the bridges that now cross the river. And failed. There is a sense here of a town that thrived and is now coming to terms with its ordinariness and its down-home roots. Leaving the casino, and hoping to find a restaurant open, I stroll across the Third Street Bridge. Most of the closed shops sell candles and potpourri. I pick up the local newspaper, which has four sections— News, Sports, Classified, and Religion.

The bleakness of the downtown depresses me. Several stores are vacant. As with many midwestern cities, it seems as if all the life has been leached out to the malls. It's just ten o'clock and the whole place is shut down. I was hoping I'd find something open, but it looks like it's pizza for the night.

I make my way back across the bridge to the main entrance of Diamond Jo Casino. I go in, then out the back, the way I'd come—through the service door, past the laundry. Why security lets me go this way is beyond me. Once again I'm waiting to be arrested for trespassing when I meet the guy who I passed coming in. He's still puffing on a cigarette, but this time he gives me a hi. "So, are you with Captain Jerry?" he asks, holding up the chain so I can slip under.

Captain Jerry now, is it? "Yes, I am," I tell him, surprised he knows who we are.

"Oh, he's a great guy. Well, enjoy your night."

"Sure. And you enjoy yours." I give him a little wave and wonder if he's being sarcastic, though I must admit sarcasm seems to be an alien mode in the heartland, reserved for the distant coasts. I wander down the levee to the gangplank that takes me on to *The Spirit of Dubuque*. Then, I shimmy once more along the railing until Jerry sees me coming and holds out his hand, making sure I don't drop into the river. Nice way to travel, I think. But I hear the sound of a "genie" and know we are hooked up with power and light.

"So, what'd you say to that guy?" I ask Jerry as he hoists me on board.

"Oh, I just dropped a few names. Offered him a beer." Apparently the mere mention of Walt's name got us hooked up for electricity and a place to moor. Jerry is on the deck, sipping a beer, proud as a lord in his fiefdom. He stares at the levee and at Tom who is making his way, pizza boxes in his hand, as he does a funny side step along the levee wall down to the gangplank.

"Captain Jerry," Tom says, holding up the pizza boxes.

Tom hands me mine. As I open it, all I see is a thick crusted thing with lettuce and tomato sauce, slathered in deep fried taco chips. I stare in dismay. "What is this?" I ask him.

"You wanted veggies, didn't you?" Tom says.

~ 18 ~

AT STRAHOV Monastery in the city of Prague there is a room full of ancient globes. They are kept behind ropes and an iron gate, but I have long had my eye on them. Last summer I was able to get into this room. I wanted to see what the world looked like to the mapmakers almost four hundred years ago. With my fingers I twirled globes from 1630, 1645.

These are some of the oldest globes in the world. London and Rome already exist. But America is a vast, undiscovered land. In between Europe and the New World is a sea filled with serpents, long-tailed monsters, winged demons with claws, ready to grapple a sailing ship down, born of some mad, dark traveler's tales.

America itself is terra incognito. Virgin territory that exists no more. When I looked at the oldest globes, the Mississippi, if it is there at all, is a mere trickle, a barely visible line that doesn't cut a continent in two. Only DeSoto in 1524 has seen it. But it made little impact on him or his men. He made note of it, seemed unimpressed, and promptly died. No one had described it. At the time when these globes were made, America is as un-blemished as a baby's cheek.

This is how it looks to me that morning as we sail out of Dubuque. A white mist rises as we chug through the floodgates the way we came. No one has arrested us or put us in the stocks. It is the coldest it's been and I wrap myself up in Kate's flannel moon and stars blanket I've brought with me. I've got on an all-weather jacket, but still I'm shivering up on the bow.

This scene is out of *Brigadoon* as the river widens and the mist engulfs us. A flock of egrets darts along the surface, dipping in and out of the fog. I am aware of a clattering noise but don't pay it much heed. I'm deciding it is time for a home-cooked meal. The taco pizza almost did me in.

The coolness of the morning makes me think of Bolognese. I've got the bottle of merlot that will go nicely, though Jerry has put it on chill. As we start our day downriver, I go into the cabin to brown the meat with a little butter. I've yet to find olive oil in any of the stores. As the meat cooks, I dice two tomatoes. I pour off the excess fat and stir the meat, then add the tomatoes and adjust the seasoning.

The clattering grows louder. Tom is piloting from the fly-bridge where I assume he must be freezing. As I am putting my tomatoes into the pot, I hear Tom give Jerry a holler. "Will you take over below, Sir? I'm going to go smell my engines." Tom is always smelling his engines, sniffing the air, listening like a bird to the ground. He can hear the slightest strain to a motor when the fuel isn't quite moving along. He talks to his engines the way I imagined he'd talk to a lover, or to his dog. "Come on, Girl. Do it for me. Don't let me down."

This time we hear a big bang and Jerry goes, "Cowabunga. What're you doing, Tom?"

"Just wanta move the fuel along, Sir."

"What's wrong with the fuel?"

I finish slicing the onion and put it all in the pot to simmer. Then take my place back at the bow, shivering once more as I sip coffee and write in my journal. I feel a kind of stutter to the boat as if it is moving in fits and starts. The engine seems to be making burping noises.

A blue heron rises from the bank. I turn to show Jerry and see him and Tom bent over the *Chrysler Marine Engine Service Manual.* They are studying a drawing and I can decipher the upside-down words FUEL PUMP. Somehow I suspect that when you see your river pilots staring into the engine service manual, this cannot be a good sign.

"God. I hate those little marinas," Jerry says.

"Yep," Tom says. "Never should've stopped there."

"And they know we aren't going to go back upstream and yell at them." I'm hiding my head, starting to feel very guilty as I recall the Guttenberg marina where I persuaded Jerry to stop. Jerry explains that, perhaps inadvertently, they sold us watered-down gas, which creates pockets of air in the engine, and that has destroyed our fuel pumps and so on. "We'll go on one engine until we get through the next lock and dam. Then we'll have to fix it."

Tom is working on his engine and I'm stirring my sauce. "Tom, I'm going to take the throttle," but Tom can't hear him with the engines running.

Tom shouts back. "The plugs don't seem to be wet, Sir." But Jerry doesn't hear this.

"Mary, will you please relay?"

"Jerry's going to take the throttle."

"Tell him the plugs aren't wet."

"The plugs aren't wet," I say. For a few moments I shout messages between them as we sputter into Bellevue Lock and Dam 12. Jerry says we won't float free. "You don't float with one engine," he says, shaking his head. "Not enough control of the boat." We go to our positions. Me to the front with my small stick, Tom to the back. Here we'll drop down six feet.

"We should get through okay," Jerry says. "As they say in Oslo, no sweat."

Jerry asks the lockmaster if he could tell us the nearest place for boat and automobile parts. "Just a sec," the lockmaster says. "I'll give it to you as you're heading out."

On our way out the lockmaster attaches a slip of paper to a long, pointed stick. "What do you call that stick?" I ask him as we let go of our lines.

"Oh, we call it a hand-me-down long stick." And the boys have a good laugh over that one.

Just below the lock and dam we spot the Bellevue gas dock, and Tom says, "I could use a shower." I'm nodding in agreement. Three days seems like about my legal limit. "But if I have to," Tom goes on, "I'll jump right in. I've been christened in these waters all my life."

I'd prefer hot water—which is starting to become a bit of an obsession—not a cold, muddy river, but I don't say so. A sign for "broasted" chicken catches our eyes and Tom and I both sigh. I don't even know what "broasted" means, but I make a mental note to bring some back for lunch. We're looking for a landing where there's a marina and also an auto body shop since our engines are Chrysler and can be serviced by auto parts.

We pull up to the funky metal Bellevue Courtesy Dock. It appears that this place is also a trailer park because there are perhaps a dozen or so trailers, most with some kind of dinghy attached. A man named George who seems to be the proprietor helps us tie up. "You looking for gas?" he asks.

"Nope," Jerry says. "We don't need gas, but we've got engine trouble. What we need are parts."

George nods. "You'll find a place in town. Well, let me know if I can help you out. Showers are three dollars apiece. You're welcome to use my phone. Your cell phones aren't going to work around here."

"Well, we appreciate that," Jerry replies.

After we're tied up, George disappears back into his trailer park and Tom and Jerry go to work on our shopping list and I sneak a peek. Heet for gas tank (to suck up the water), spark plugs 2 sets of NGK, six bottles of carburetor cleaning additive, 3 fuel pumps, hoses and clamps, DIL filters, half quart of 50 Valvoline.

I'm stuck at "3 fuel pumps." How many fuel pumps does an engine need? Definitely not good. I take my sauce off the burner and put it in the fridge. I guess we won't be dining for a while. "My treat for the showers," I say. No one argues this time. In fact no one seems to be paying much attention to me at all. I assume I will have time for a very long hot shower. Several if I wish. We are in cell phone limbo (as we will be on much of our journey) and Jerry needs to call for a cab. He's gazing into the engine as Tom starts ripping it apart. "I'll go find George," I offer.

I head into the trailer park where people have set up their campers with signs that read YOU DON'T HAVE TO BE IRISH TO HAVE ATTITUDE. BUT IT HELPS; DANGER NO SWIMMING; or DON'T BOTHER ASKING. I'M IN CHARGE. There are statues of the Virgin, American flags flying. One trailer is landscaped entirely in plastic flowers and shrubs.

As I'm looking for George, I run into a woman from Iowa whose license plate reads IOWA SHROOMS. Dee has got her camper set up on the water's edge. She's got her hummingbird feeders up and her barbecue. Dee has on three or four layers of pancake makeup and her hair is all fixed in one motionless swirl with spray. "Hey there," Dee says. "You just taking a rest?"

"Actually we have engine trouble. . . . I'm trying to find a phone, then I'm going to take a shower."

"Really. I didn't know they had showers here. . . . How d'ya like that. Been here a month fishing and didn't even know I could get a shower. Got everything I need in my camper though." She points to her pull-out breakfast nook, her barbecue and hummingbird feeders where several hummingbirds are flitting along. "You with that houseboat?" Dee asks.

"Yeah, I think we'll be here for a while. My captain is trying to get a cab to take him into town so he can buy parts."

"Well," Dee says, her pancake makeup cracking a little, "my husband can take you. He'll be glad to."

I find Jerry, who is happy for the ride. He says he'll be back soon. I pack up my towel and my cosmetic bag and I go to find the shower. It is located in a pump house off the side and despite the wooden floor and cobwebs and the chill in the air, it isn't bad. The most important thing is that it has good water pressure. I take a very long hot shower, relishing the flow of water down my back. When I return, Tom goes up to take his. He drags his wheely suitcase with Samantha Jean tucked under his arm. "She needs a bath too." He says he'll throw her in the shower with him. I tell him I'll watch the boat.

Tom's got the starboard engine lying in pieces along the stern and, as I gaze at them, I'm not optimistic about what's ahead. Since I can't make any calls, I have time on my hands. It's a cold morning, almost raw, and the river is a monotonous shade of gray. It takes Tom what feels like forever to return from his shower. "I'm going for a walk," I tell him.

"Oh, take your time." I hate it when they say this because I know he means we've got a long layover.

"I'll bring you back some of that chicken," I say.

I decide to go sightseeing in scenic Bellevue. To a New Yorker, Bellevue is our most famous insane asylum, but this place seems pretty stable to me. I leave the trailer park and head up the road where I see a Phillips 66 station and a sign that reads CAR WASH, GAS $2.64, LUBE JOB, LAUNDROMAT, OLD-FASHIONED ICE CREAM CONES, SPECIAL ON AMMO. Then I head to the Richmond Café for that broasted chicken.

When I walk into the Richmond Café, the music video to "Mississippi Girl" is playing. I see two gay guys sitting, having lunch. This wouldn't surprise me, of course, in New York, but it does in Bellevue, Iowa. In fact it looks as if the whole restaurant is filled with guys, right out of *Brokeback Mountain*, eating burgers and fries. At least I think they are gay. Then I realize that the two men I first spotted are just both wearing the same sleeveless T's with the name of the cement company they work for across the front.

All the men in the restaurant are in uniforms bearing names like TRUE VALUE, TACKY JACK'S SURE WAX, and PROFESSIONAL RESCUE INNOVATORS. All the women are wearing rhinestone crosses and taking their mothers to lunch. Everyone in the Richmond Café is either in a company uniform or wearing a rhinestone cross or both. And now I'm pretty sure no one is gay.

"All Jacked Up" comes on the Country Music Channel as I order a hot meal. Chicken, a baked potato, a salad. Sitting there I am suddenly incredibly dizzy. The table, the booth are all moving. I feel as if the boat has entered me. I think it is a combination of the river and the drug cocktail I'm taking. I decide to try to ease off my pills.

Walking around Bellevue, there are smiley faces, Jesus and Mary statues, and names on the door such as HELMUT and SCHRODER. Two men in brown shirts get out of a van and smile at me and say hello as if they have been recently returned by aliens.

As I head back to the boat down a side street, a freight train passes me so closely that I can reach out and touch it. The engineer waves. I wave back. I find this river custom so quaint, yet so odd at the same time. I try to imagine waving at bus drivers, at subway conductors, at strangers on the street. But here we just wave and wave. On the river a fuel barge heads north. Nothing is moving south.

I return up the beach with two bags of chicken, fries, sodas for the boys. I know we must be very delayed because Jerry has gone for a shower. Tom is groaning at his engine. "Come on, Baby. Come on, Girl."

The man who drove Jerry into town stands, rocking on his heels nearby, watching our progress. "Your husband looks like a good mechanic," he says. I look at Tom in his Harley T-shirt, his belly spilling over his pants, as Samantha Jean, her tongue hanging out, peers down at him from the flybridge where he's stowed her. "That's not my husband," I say.

Tom grunts, tugging at engine parts, tossing some into the trash. I am completely skeptical and Jerry, who's back and all cleaned up from his shower, is calmly sipping a beer. But somehow after four hours of throwing out damaged parts and putting in new parts and greasing and lubricating and testing the fuel, it seems we are ready to roll. The chill has left the day and with waves and a push off from the dock we are moving again.

It is good to feel the motion of the river beneath us, the boat chugging along. A huge flock of white pelicans does its strange interweaving dance. Bald eagles perch in the treetops. I had anticipated that the river would grow more industrial below Dubuque, that there would be more signs of man, on the river or along the banks, but it is remarkably devoid of human traces.

I want to stop at Savanna, Illinois, but given the hours we've lost, we have to pass it. We won't make a landing or a marina by dark if we stop anywhere now. We come to a railroad bridge and Jerry is worried about clearance. "Can we make this, Tommy?" he asks.

"I couldn't jump up and touch that, Sir," Tom says.

Tom is right. We sail smoothly beneath the bridge. "Rock 'n' roll," Jerry replies.

The cloudy gray skies open up and it starts to pour. For several miles we are in a driving rain. Jerry calls ahead to the marina at Clinton to see if we can get slippage for the night, but no one answers the phone. "We'll figure something out," he says, shaking his head.

We go by a fuel barge, the *Penny Eckstein*. One crewman, holding an umbrella with one hand, is barbecuing on a small Weber grill on deck. We come up on two islands that have their trees stripped bare. Thousands of cormorants roost in the naked branches. The trees are filled with nests the birds have made from the leaves and bark. We drift past the islands in silence, except for the chatter of the birds. It feels as if ghosts could dwell here.

~ 19 ~

MY FATHER died on May 14, just four months ago, which happens to be my birthday. Or at least he died at the very end of it. We had gone to the theater that night, Larry, Kate, and I, and were walking home along Fourth Avenue in Brooklyn. It was close to midnight and a woman was dragging a suitcase toward me. I stepped aside to let her pass and she kicked me in the gut, knocking me into the street. She screamed obscenities as her punch took my breath away.

Larry and Kate helped me as I staggered home, shocked by the blow. When the phone rang an hour later with my brother calling to tell me that our father was dead, I already knew. I felt certain he breathed his last as that woman kicked me into the street. As I spoke to my brother, I could hear my mother shouting in the background. Not in sadness or grief. And she certainly was making no effort to console me. "Tell her there's no funeral!" she yelled. "Tell her we aren't doing anything at all!"

I never spoke to my mother that night, but I know that she never shed a tear. She had reasons, I suppose, for being bitter. He had sold buildings he shouldn't have sold. They hadn't shared a bedroom in thirty years. He never took her anywhere. Once I asked her if it was his temper that had ruined the marriage for her and she said, "No, it was his indifference."

It had not been a loving union, to say the least, but, after all, it had lasted almost sixty years and produced two children. He was my father and, at the very least, she might have acknowledged my need to mourn him. That night Larry and I stayed up late, discussing what to do. When Kate got up, we told her the news, and she wrapped herself in a blanket and wept.

Kate knew her own history. We had believed in full disclosure. She understood that my father had given me permission to have her and she had loved him in her own way. The last time she saw my father, she went with me to take him to the doctor. On the way back he tried to open the window, but accidentally opened the car door. As his frail body threatened to fly out, Kate caught his arm, pulling him back in. "Hey, Grandpa, where're you going?"

Since there would be no funeral, there was no reason to rush home. My nephews wouldn't be arriving before the weekend. And Kate had her prom on Thursday and the preprom party was to be at our house. It would be difficult to cancel. In the end we decided to sit shiva in Brooklyn, then fly to the Midwest at the end of the week.

For three days our house was filled with friends and food. A shiva candle burned. Flowers were everywhere. Neighbors dropped in. The rabbi stopped by to say Kaddish. Our house and our lives felt full. Then it was prom. When the three stretch Humvee limos pulled up in front of our house, children stopped playing in the streets. Our neighbors on all sides—the elderly Italians, the man who had just lost his wife, the neighbors we'd been arguing with over their construction—all came out to pay their respects. Everyone paused as fifty teenagers in bright satiny blue and red and lemon yellow dresses with stiletto heels and boys in tuxes, sporting white saddle shoes and aviator glasses, piled out of our house and into the limousines. There was palpable silence until an elderly neighbor blurted, "What kind of funeral are they having?"

We flew to Milwaukee on Friday. Against my mother's wishes, I had arranged for a short viewing and Kaddish before my father was to be cremated. When they wheeled him out, my mother poked his skin. "He's cold and he's in a cardboard box."

"That's because he's going to be cremated," I told her.

My mother sat uncomfortably through the Kaddish, then told her caregiver to take her home. Before she left, she went up to his body. "Good-bye, Sol," she said. "It was fifty-nine good years. Good-bye. Now get me out of here."

Perhaps it was dementia. Or some mind-altering drugs she was on for pain in her back and knees. Perhaps it was just the years of being unhappy and dissatisfied. A talented woman with a degree in fashion design who sewed costumes for her children. "Smile," she'd say to him at the end of the day. "It takes 359 muscles to frown, but only two to smile."

No tears were lost here. But I loved him. Perhaps because he believed in me. "Reach for the stars," my father always told me. "You'll never get there. But you gotta reach." Neither my mother nor my brother wanted his ashes so I asked that they be sent to my house. I was out when the ashes arrived and the chiropractor next door signed for them instead.

Joan Didion, delving into the loss of her husband, John Gregory Dunne, who died suddenly at the kitchen table, midsentence, writes that there are two kinds of grief. There is the uncomplicated kind when a person dies, is buried, and grieved. Then there is what the experts call complicated grief. This is brought on by an unresolved relationship, disagreement over final wishes, or delay of the funeral.

Delay of the funeral. I think about this when I think of my father and his ashes, tucked behind my piano where I cannot bear to move or lift the box. I have not touched it since I placed it there. When I consider the options, I realize I do not know my father's wishes. They were never made clear. Perhaps he too thought he'd never die.

My brother wants to scatter the ashes at Sportsman's golf course in western Illinois where Dad spent his Saturdays. My mother doesn't care what happens to them, though downtown Chicago in front of the building he built at Oak and Michigan makes the most sense to her. I rather like having him with me in Brooklyn. I think for some reason, even behind a piano that isn't played very often, he is happiest here.

I have heard of an Amazon tribe that makes a soup out of the ashes of its elders. A year to the day after their death the tribe ingests this bitter broth. Briefly I consider this possibility, but it would be a lonely soup and I fear I'd be partaking of it alone.

~ 20 ~

IN THE early evening as we sail into Clinton, Iowa, the rain stops and the sky is a burst of violet and rose. The *Mississippi Belle,* a huge casino paddleboat, is moored in the harbor, its lights blazing and music blaring. At first I am disappointed at the thought of sleeping beside another casino, but Jerry heads beyond the casino toward the small marina. We drift into a quiet cove, passing houseboats with names like *The Bottom Dollar* and *Blue Tonic,* and come to a courtesy dock and tie up next to a boat named *Sol,* which, of course, in Spanish means "sun," but it was also my father's name.

The dock is in an inlet, filled with mallards and egrets, and I am grateful to be here. As we tie up, once again I watch Tom and Jerry doing their knots. They make crazy loops, circling, tugging, winding in side-winding bends like the river, in and out of itself. "Jerry," I say, "I want to learn how to do that." He gives me one of his stares. "I want a rope lesson."

"What do you mean?"

"I want to learn to tie up the ropes."

Jerry nods, taking a sip from his beer mug. "Well, the first thing you need to know, Mary, is that as soon as a rope comes on a boat it's a line."

I smile. "Thank you, Captain," I mutter under my breath. "I'd like a line lesson. I want to learn how to tie up."

"Sure, we'll teach you." He raises a professorial finger in my face. "One thing at a time."

Tom shows me where to plug into the electricity on the dock and I drag the cable and plug it in. The sky turns scarlet as a bouquet of roses and I sit on the dock, feeding stale bread, of which we seem to have a good amount, to the ducks. I've done this since

I was a girl. On every family vacation I'd wait at the kitchen door of restaurants and take stale rolls and bread crusts to the duck ponds. I have spent entire vacations rubbing hard loaves of bread against the trunks of trees that lean across the water. My father used to complain that we'd gone to Idaho to do what I could do a few feet from home.

I've got about a dozen ducks squawking at my feet when Jerry sits down beside me. As I'm tossing bread, he's snapping pictures. I look at his hand as he clicks. "Jerry," I say, "can I ask you something?"

"Sure," he says.

"How'd your lose your fingers?"

"What fingers?" He laughs. "Oh, those." He holds up his right hand with its finger stubs. "Well, I lost the tops of two when I was a boy. The third one I lost when I was working on a houseboat a few years ago."

"When you were a boy?"

"Yeah." He's staring out at the river now. "You know, my dad was a fireman and he had a workshop in the basement. He made furniture and stuff. Anyway he was at work one day and I went down and used his saw."

"Oh, my god. . . . How old were you?"

"I was about four."

"Four? Wasn't anyone watching you?"

"You know, these things happen. Kid'll get away from you in a minute. I think my mom was home. I know my dad felt awful about it."

"I'm sure he did. . . ."

"It was a technical violation," he says with his usual laugh. "Funny how these things happen. You know, same thing happened to my son, Chris. He swallowed a bottle of Liquid-Plumr when he was two. Don't know how he got into it."

"He swallowed Liquid-Plumr?"

"Oh, yeah, god it was terrible. His eyes were rolling back in his head. He smelled like a tank of gasoline. I didn't think he was gonna make it. The doctors didn't either. You know most kids when they do something like that . . ." Jerry was shaking his head, whistling through his teeth.

"Well, was he alone . . . ?"

"You know, these things just happen sometimes. But, Chris, well, he's lucky to be alive. Burned his whole esophagus. But . . ." Jerry tosses his hands in the air. "That's a whole other story."

We sit, tossing bread to the ducks. The sun is setting behind us and soon it is dark.

"How about some dinner?" I ask him.

"Sure," he says. "Sounds like a good idea."

We go into the cabin to fix dinner and Tom's got the satellite dish working. CNN is on and George Bush is standing with the head of FEMA, Michael Brown. Bush is saying something about how he stands by Michael Brown and FEMA's response. I stand in silence, listening to Bush defend Michael Brown. Jerry glances at the television. "What an idiot," Jerry says under his breath, flicking open a beer.

"Really?" I ask.

He rolls his eyes. "Oh really," he says. "Don't get me started," he says.

"Actually I'd like to . . ." He just gives me a wave of the hand.

It is dark as we sit on the bow and I proudly serve up my Bolognese with farfalle. "Wow, this looks great," Tom says, popping perhaps his tenth diet Dew of the day. "What's that white stuff?"

He's pointing at the pasta and I tell him it's like spaghetti except it fits into our little pot. "It's called 'bow ties,'" I explain.

"Doesn't look like spaghetti to me," he says. I've set the table with our best paper plates, napkins, whatever utensils I can find. "Mind if I get some bread?" Tom asks.

"Of course I don't mind."

He fills his bowl, heaping the bow ties with Bolognese, which he then spoons on to a piece of Wonder Bread and eats as a sandwich, gulping down his diet Dew. He has one or two more of these sandwiches, declares them good, and gives what's left in his bowl to Samantha Jean. When Samantha Jean is done with my

Bolognese, Tom takes her for a walk on the levee. Then, without saying goodnight, he crawls up to his resting place on the flybridge and settles onto his air mattress. He puts on his headphones and goes right to sleep.

But I never seem to go right to sleep. Even in this gentle cove, my heart beats too fast. After the dishes, I crawl into bed. I work on a crossword puzzle I've brought with me. "Has to do with ribs." I'm thinking "barbecue," but I get it wrong. Later I'll discover it's "babyback." Same number of letters. I hate trick questions. For tank top I put halter, but it's gas cap. Another trick. I hear Jerry's heavy breathing. I resist at first, then pop an Ativan and, when I don't seem to get groggy, an Ambien and finally fall off into my drugged sleep.

In the morning we are off early. I am sorry to leave this quiet cove. The river is smooth as glass and we seem to skim its surface as we sail. At Mile 507 we come to the confluence with the Wapsipinicon River, which translated means "the river where you find white potatoes." We don't find any. River pilots call this the "Wapsi" and just below the confluence we come to the Wapsi River Light 506.4.

At Mile 498 the river makes a sharp left-hand bend. For the next 43 miles we will be traveling west. There is an Indian legend about this bend. It is said that the Mississippi was on its way to the Gulf of Mexico, but, after passing through the northern bluff country, the river did not wish to go on. It turned for another long look before continuing its journey south.

# CURRENT

JORGE LUIS Borges wrote that there are only four plots in all of literature. The story of the love of two people, the love of three people, the struggle for power, and the journey. I feel as if I have been through the stories of love and the struggles for power. Now it is time once again for the journey.

My teacher John Gardner reduced it to two: You go on a journey or the stranger comes to town.

Or as Stanley Elkin said about science fiction: You go there or they come here.

In any case the journey figures in.

I'm thinking about this while I'm listening to Bix Beiderbecke. We're approaching his hometown of Davenport, Iowa, and "Riverboat Shuffle" is playing on my laptop. I'm thinking about the sweet sound of Bix's solo when the song switches to a lively "It's a treat to beat your feet on the Mississippi Mud. What a dance, do they do, people look around and I'm telling you . . ." Jerry's snapping his fingers and Tom's grooving to the beat.

The tempo shifts to "Slow River" as elegant Victorian houses rise above the floodplain on the hillside. There's a hint of old money and better days here. "Slow River" is a lazier tune than "Mississippi Mud," but it's still high-pitched and breezy. No blues, no heartbreak here. Bix plays a soft, playful horn, reminiscent of an adolescent boy's voice, just starting to deepen, still cracking from time to time.

He was a white boy with a horn, and like many of his great black contemporaries, he couldn't read a note. He was a piano prodigy, but for some ungodly reason, at least in his own family's view, he was drawn to the river and its jazz. He was born the year after my father, and if Bix had lived past the age of thirty, I'm wondering what he might have done. I'm sure my father heard him play at the "black and tans" on the South Side or with the Wolverines on the Indiana Dunes.

But no matter how far Bix wandered from Davenport, the river was in his blood. At the turn of the century when he was a boy, "steamboat fever" was all the rage. Mark Twain published his *Life on the Mississippi* in 1883 and *The Adventures of Huckleberry Finn* two years later. In the 1890s the Streckfus family, one of the biggest names in steamboats, settled across the river from Davenport in Rock Island, Illinois, but Streckfus men tended to marry Davenport women and Davenport was considered to be a gracious, cultured place. The city soon became home to Streckfus Steamboats, a line of excursion boats that, along with its moonlight cruises, offered jazz.

When Bix was a boy, these steamers docked at night off Davenport and hot music reverberated off the decks, up and down the river. No one knows for certain when Bix Beiderbecke first heard hot music played; if he wandered down to the shore when steamers were there. But one thing is certain. When Bix was fifteen, his brother, Charles, returning from World War I, brought home a recording of the Original Dixieland Jazz Band. From then on "Tiger Rag" and "Skeleton Jungle" rocked the sedate Beiderbecke home.

Down in New Orleans, Captain John Streckfus, an amateur musician himself, hired a man named Fate Marable to put together a river band. Searching for talent, Marable paused one day on the corner of Rampart and Perdido, where he listened to an illiterate street musician and hired him on the spot. To play with

Marable's band, Louis Armstrong had to learn to read notes, which he forced himself to do, though basically Louis always played by ear. He blew on the trumpet with Marable's band as it traveled as far north as Pittsburgh and Davenport. Some have speculated, based on Bix's sound, that he and Louis Armstrong must have crossed paths.

By listening, Bix learned to play. Though he couldn't read music, he amazed listeners with what he could do with that horn. As a jazz friend once said, Bix played like a black boy, but he was white and the crackers could listen to him and feel okay. It's hard to know just how the music came to him. It just did, though his father never approved.

His parents believed that music was for church and community gatherings and they sent him to the Lake Forest Academy, just a stone's throw in Illinois from where I grew up, so Bix could get some discipline and a good education. Instead, Bix got his education on the South Side of Chicago, where he went night after night to listen and blow on his horn. He started recording and, dutifully, he sent his records to his parents. A few years later when he was dying of alcoholism, Bix returned to his family's home. He found all of his records in a closet. They had never been opened.

Davenport is famous for other things. The first railroad bridge over the Mississippi was built here in 1856 though it was almost immediately struck by a steamboat and collapsed. The first chiropractic adjustment was performed in 1895 in Davenport by D. D. Palmer on Harvey Lillard, who claimed it restored his hearing. And Dred Scott, the famous slave who sued for his freedom, lived on Second Street with his wife, Harriet. In fact there are so many historic buildings that one has a placard that reads ON THIS LOCATION IN 1897 NOTHING HAPPENED.

But I'm on a Bix pilgrimage. We dock at the Lindsay Park Yacht Club for fuel and a pump out and I head off on a shopping expedition. At a grocery store nearby I purchase steaks, chicken, bratwursts for the freezer. Green beans and corn. I see that they've got something called hedge balls on sale with the pumpkins and the gourds for sixty-nine cents apiece. It's a weird shade of lime with wrinkled skin and I have to dodge them on my walks through Prospect Park in Brooklyn. My husband likes to smash them into trees. I've been passing up a gold mine.

I drop my groceries back at the boat, then amble through the town of East Davenport. It is a quaint town with ice-cream shops and little cafés. An old-fashioned candy store sells penny candy. When Kate was small and we spent our summers in Vermont, we always bought penny candy from a general store. She'd take a paper sack and fill it with candy on her own. Now I pick out gummy bears, cinnamon balls, button candy, chocolate coins. I buy a pound and have it shipped to my daughter at school.

After the fuel up and pump out, we move the boat half a mile downriver where a friend of Jerry's named Wakim has a boat shop on the levee. Wakim has told us we are welcome to tie up there for the night. The boat shop is filled with huge boats in slings, having their hulls polished, holes repaired. Someone who works in the boat shop is waiting for us. We learn that not only can we tie up for the night but they've left the keys to a pickup truck. We can go shopping.

But I'm going to spend the day searching for Bix and the night at a hotel, which I booked for some reason on the outskirts of town. Tom agrees to drop me off at the hotel. We drive quickly out of town along Highway 61—an ancient American route— now home to strip malls. We pass the Wal-Marts and Walgreens, a Target and Home Depot. One warehouse store after another.

Clearly I'm in the heartland now. Giant billboards loom. One displays a complacent-looking fetus and huge letters that read LIFE BEGINS AT CONCEPTION. A big black one says ONE NATION UNDER ME, SIGNED GOD. A bumper sticker reads JESUS DRIVES THIS TRUCK.

✖◦

I've always rather enjoyed cemeteries. In fact I'm wishing my father was buried in one instead of sitting in a black plastic box behind my piano, but that's another story. In college in Cambridge, Massachusetts, I liked to read in the Mount Auburn Cemetery. In

Los Angeles I enjoyed a drive around Forest Lawn and wondered if Gene Autry was really buried with his horse. I've had some good times at the Greenwood Cemetery near my house in Brooklyn. All in all I find cemeteries restful places to be, for the living and the dead.

The Oakland Cemetery is a place of rolling hills and huge plots of old Davenport families. But after walking around in the blazing sun for almost an hour, going up and down hills, past statues of sad little angels and bubbling fountains, I can't find Bix's grave. There is a sign at the office that says if the office is closed I should call Doug. And a number. I guess this means if a loved one dies on the weekend or at night, this is whom you phone.

I call the number and a man with a deep voice answers. I'm immediately embarrassed. I've had my share of funeral operators lately, those who traffic in the dead, and I feel their sacrifice is underappreciated. I want to say, "this is not an emergency," but then is death ever? Instead I tell the man on the other end that I am looking for a grave. "Bix . . ." I stumble. "The cornet player. Bix Beiderbecke."

I fear I am having an "Alas, poor Yorick" moment. Never having spoken to a gravedigger before, I'm nervous and mispronounce the last name as "Biderbeck," but Doug corrects me. "You mean Beiderbecke."

"Yes," I say. Obviously he's been asked this question before. I tell him where I am in the cemetery (at the base of a hill near a large headstone for someone named Davenport) and he instructs me to go past the pond, back up the hill. Look on my right. I follow Doug's instructions and in a few moments come upon the large family memorial Beiderbecke. On the ground the smaller headstone: LEON "BIX" BEIDERBECKE 1903–1931.

He lived twenty-eight years and became, as so many jazz performers did who died young from drugs and alcohol, a legend. At his grave is a bouquet of plastic purple violets, a small painting of a man at a piano with the word *Stardust* across the painting, and a homemade sign that reads "Bix Bix Bix." Other than this, the grave is unadorned.

Bix is buried with the same family who refused to listen to his records, beside his mother, father, sister, and brother and dozens of other Beiderbeckes who never listened to his music or cared for him or the life he led. He would be astonished to know that an annual "Bix Lives" July festival is one of the things that keeps Davenport on the map.

I pay my homage, then pass by the old Coliseum Ballroom, where such jazz legends as Bix and Louis Armstrong and Guy Lombardo played. It's a yellow stucco building with high arches at the entryway, and I walk into this dark old ballroom with a wooden stage and balcony of wooden seats. The "Col" has been taken over by a Mexican American organization and a group of girls with long black hair and budding breasts are preparing for a *quinceaños* celebration.

They pay no attention to me as I wander through the wood-paneled ballroom. Posters of great jazz performances cover the walls. The Hispanic girls are lined up with their arms raised. First they form an arch under which the girl being honored will pass. Then they break into dance. Music blares from their boom box. But I think if I close my eyes and pretend the macarena isn't playing, I'll hear another tune.

A big band in full tux plugs away. Someone wild is at the keyboard. A high-pitched trumpet comes in for a chorus or two of "Davenport Blues." I look up on that stage and see Bix, pants too short, white socks showing, raising his horn. The bathtub gin flows. The cops with cash in their pockets look away. Or lean their backs against the wall to listen. A sweet, sweet sound fills the room.

The Beiderbecke family home, a big white (though now with yellow trim) Victorian, is at 1934 Grand Street and I ask the cab I've hired to take me there. We drive up to an ordinary house on an ordinary street with a public school across the street that Bix attended. Out front a woman tends her bed of annuals. She's got a trowel and she's pulling up weeds. As we pull up, she looks at me and I can tell she is used to this. People make pilgrimages here all the time. I get out and stand in front of her house and she keeps planting her annuals.

How did this happen? I ask myself as I gaze at the tidy home, the front porch swing. How did this house and this street produce this man? I recalled my own rebellions, my desire to get away. I tried to flee when I went to college, but I've carried on my own tug of war with home. I am reminded of a neighbor of mine who broke her arm. She seemed calm as she was taken to the emergency room, but on the forms she wrote down the address of the house she grew up in where she hadn't set foot in forty years.

For years after we moved out of my childhood home, I had dreams of that house. They are always more or less the same. I am walking somewhere—in a jungle, down a Paris street or a country road. Suddenly it starts to snow. In the snow there are footsteps. I follow them and they lead me home.

>O

When my father was born in the fall of 1902, Chicago still had a great deal of prairie. I like to imagine my father playing in empty lots of wheatgrass, blowing as the clouds drifted across the open sky. But once I asked him what it was like and he told me that the prairie was brown, windy, and dry. When his brother, Sidney, was born, he remembered running across it to the next neighbor. Where he ran is now Rogers Park.

As a child I pretended I was a pioneer girl. I had a dozen brothers, never sisters, who were always being wounded or shot. I was the only one who could remove an arrowhead, heal a wound. I found the paths no one could find. I blazed the trail and brought deer meat home on my back. The truth was I never liked being inside very much. I was desperate to get away.

It was not a happy home. But our misery was a private one, nothing anyone ever showed to the world. My childhood was a minefield I navigated with mixed results. To my father every-thing was a lethal weapon. A pencil, a kitchen knife, a drinking glass could all become the instruments of my demise. If I walked with a sharpened pencil, I risked tripping over some unseen object and stabbing myself in the eye. Kitchen knives could mysteriously be launched. A glass could fly out of your hand and smash into your skull.

It was rare that something—a bicycle, a soda bottle, a baseball—did not pose a threat. My life goal became an obvious one: I had to survive. The problem was that these things not only incited his worry, they also set off his wrath. The house was booby trapped and he was the monster, lurking behind its doors, ready to catch us off guard. I can recall the way his rages came over him. A man of dark skin and dark eyes, it seemed as if a fire was lit from within. His words flew out of his mouth like flames.

His paranoia about the physical world projected itself onto the social order. At any moment one could fall from grace. Table manners ensured against such a fate. The list was a mile long. How pieces had to be chewed, soup sipped, cutlery put on the edges of plates once eating was done. I had to get into the habit of being a lady. Perfection was a kind of norm. But children are not very good at perfection. They are snotty, dirty little beasts, reluctant to fit the mold.

My father's outbursts were confined to our four walls. Only waiters who didn't make his vodka tonic just right or busboys who didn't clear fast enough got a hint of his rages. He called us names. He told us we were stupid or selfish or spoiled brats. Once when I was visiting from college, I came home for dinner half an hour late. The meal was already eaten, the table cleared, and my father began to yell at me. He yelled until my brother stood between us and told him to stop.

But his anger rarely left home. Toward the end of his life, though, my father grew careless. Once he was in the car, driving a friend of my mother's named Scarlet to a concert. Scarlet said something that my father didn't like and he began calling her names. He called her a liar, the worst kind of person, every name in the book.

The next day my mother called me in tears. "A terrible thing happened," she said.

"What's that, Mom?" I asked.

"Your father lost his temper with Scarlet Leyton. I'm sure she'll never speak to me again. He's never done that before."

I paused. "What do you mean, Mom? He's never done it before? He did it every night."

"But he never did it with people before," she said.

"People," I said. "Aren't we people?"

"Oh, you know what I mean."

In the end, looking back, I think that my father was an incredibly anxious person. In fact I think that in this day and age he'd be diagnosed with an anxiety disorder and medicated. Shortly before he died, a friend of mine had a serious panic attack. His daughter, thinking he was having a heart attack, called me, and I rushed to his house. I had never seen anyone writhing or screaming in so much pain.

Afterward I went online and read a description of someone who suffers panic attacks. Fear of restaurants, fear of travel. Anxious in situations he cannot control. Nervous, claustrophic. Cannot be hemmed in. Uses temper to control his anxiety, often around seemingly meaningless things. And I found myself reading a description of my father.

I remember the circus. We went every year, but my father always had to leave before it was over. He didn't want to get stuck in traffic, in the rush. He couldn't stand being caught in the crowd. We'd be gathering up our things just as the huge cage was being assembled in the center ring. The cages that I knew contained the great cats were wheeled in, but I never saw the lion act because it was always at the end.

On Saturdays he would drive me for horseback riding and wait in the car. He'd take us to the movies, but never come inside. I sat through *Peter Pan* and *Moby Dick*, knowing my father was dozing in the parking lot. Even as I grew older and I was kissing boys in theaters, it was my father I envisioned, waiting in the car.

Once our new puppy chewed through the upholstery of a quilted chair. My mother noticed it late in the day and my father's train was due home in an hour. My mother, with her degree in fashion design, got on her hands and knees. She wore a shirtwaist dress and an apron and her legs sprawled across the floor. I watched her move needle and thread as she requilted that chair.

Then she raced to the station to meet his train.

✦

A cabdriver takes me to the Lonestar Steakhouse out on Highway 61. He asks what I'm doing in Davenport and I tell him I'm writing a book about the Mississippi River. "Wow," he says, "that's cool. You know when I was a boy my father told me once that he walked across the Mississippi. And I said 'Dad, you aren't Jesus.' And he told me he walked across it at its source where it's only a few feet wide."

At the Lonestar I'm on high mullet hairdo alert. It seems they are everywhere. "Well, how're you doing tonight?" my waitress, Tammy, says. "You all by your lonesome?" I've got the happiest waitress in the world and she tries to sell me something called the Texas Rose, which is a whole onion, fanned open and deep-fried. I pass on the Texas Rose and I order a glass of cabernet and a small New York strip steak. They do have sixteen-ounce steaks on the menu, which she tries to convince me will give me more for my buck, but I say no.

After that Tammy loses interest in me. I sit, sipping my cabernet, staring at the humongous footballs and beer cans that cover every inch of the ceiling. On the wall a stuffed Texas longhorn peers down at me. Tammy delivers a bucket of beer to a table with two mullets. A couple gets up and starts doing the Texas two-step in the middle of the floor.

I go back to my hotel. Thirsty, I get up in the middle of the night and find the water bottle I keep by the side of my bed. I take a big swig, but the taste is orange Fanta, which I assume was left by a previous guest.

The next morning in the hotel breakfast room I'm lining up my pills as an old waitress with a blue rinse and a tag that reads NANCY pours my coffee. I ask her how things are going and she says, "Could be better."

When I ask her to fill me up again, I say, "How so?"

"It's just not a good time around here," Nancy says. I can see she's old and tired and doesn't want to be working on her feet.

"Things slow on the river?" I say.

Nancy nods, her face a rut of frowns. "We're fifty inches of rain short. My son's a farmer. He's got four farms. Owns two and farms the other two. He lost his whole corn crop. Lost everything. Between 9/11 and Katrina and now this drought . . ." She shakes her head. "If you ask me, I think this country's just about through."

Nancy brings me my eggs, which I eat slowly. She doesn't talk to me again.

~ 22 ~

I'M BACK at the boat before nine and the boys look happy to see me. We're heading south again. But before we do, Jerry says I can pilot up- and downriver, get the feel of going upstream, and try out some wide turns. So far I've only piloted on a straight shot so this will be new for me.

It's a warm day and I slip into a pair of pink capris and a pink spandex top, which I haven't worn yet. They are also the only clean clothes I have left. When I emerge from my nook, Tom gives a whistle. "Oh-oh," he says. "Lady in Pink."

"Violation," Jerry says.

It's a big river here with just some pleasure craft as I maneuver under an old railroad swing bridge. I ease the wheel gently and execute my first turn around Stubbs' Eddy, named for James R. Stubbs, who returned from the army in 1834 and lived for twelve years in a cave on Arsenal Island with an assortment of animals, including a pet pig. Since the outside curve of a river bend is known as an eddy, steamboat men, travelers, and locals came to call this bend in the river Stubbs' Eddy.

As I'm making my turn, a cruiser, zipping along at about thirty miles per hour, slows to about two and gives me wide berth. "Hey, watch out for the Lady in Pink," Tom howls.

"He just didn't know what you were doing," Jerry says. "He wanted to avoid any unplanned directional maneuver."

"Well, I know what I'm doing," I reply defiantly. Just then a sailboat cuts me off and I have to veer. I assume I've got the right of way, but Jerry shakes his head. "The boat with the least control always has the right of way," he tells me.

"Well, in this case . . . ," Tom says, chuckling as the sailboat tacks away. "Hey, he's not taking any chances."

"Okay, guys, got it." I continue making my turn.

"You don't mind if I joke with you a bit?" Tom says, rather sheepishly.

"What the hell. It's open season," I reply. I'm heading for my second pass under the swing bridge when I notice that there are hundreds of people on the levee. In the water nearby boats are anchored. It is the anchored boats that give it away. "Hey, Jerry," I say. "I think there's a concert."

"What makes you think so?"

"Well, see all those people and the boats? The boats are listening to music from the water. That's why they're tied up there." I can see that they are dubious, but I know from summers spent in Prague, where I used to get into a pedalboat with a picnic to hear concerts for free.

Jerry takes the wheel as he always does when we maneuver in tight situations. As we get closer, they see I'm right. Sure enough, it's a concert, but it's electric blues. I have a feeling they won't want to stop.

"It's blues," Tom says.

"Let's rock," Jerry says. He brings the *River Queen* into position near the levee. If it's an old levee, he says we've got only six feet of draft, but he checks our depth and when he likes the way we're lined up, says, "Okay, Tom, let's drop anchor."

Tom tosses an anchor in. "You want me to leave her slack?"

"Don't drop the line!" Jerry shouts. "Let me move her back before she sets."

Tom's staring at the water. "That's pretty nice for one anchor. You want another for a lovie-dovie?"

"Hey," I ask Jerry, "have you ever thrown an anchor without a rope on it?"

Jerry looks at me as if I'm crazy. "No," he says. We've got some B. B. King playing on the levee and the boys settle back with beers and diet Dew. I take a diet Coke for myself and start dancing on the flybridge. "Well," Jerry says, "we scorched a mile and a half today."

"Come On, Baby, Let the Good Times Roll" is playing and the crowd is rocking. A couple, dressed in all-white linen, is dancing on the levee. He's wearing a white cap. I've come up on the flybridge with a bag of green beans in my hand to clean them in the shade. "What's that?" Tom asks when he sees the bag.

"Green beans," I say, holding it up.

He looks off as the music comes on loud and strong and pretty soon I'm dancing away and the couple sees me. They give a wave. The young man takes off his cap and salutes me. A cruiser comes up fast and a brown-haired woman in a bikini stands up and shakes her tits in time to the "boom boom" of the song at the crowd, which begins hooting and applauding. Tom's applauding and Jerry's just shaking his head. The hooter gives one last shake for good measure, then speeds away.

There's a break in the music and I settle under the bimini and start breaking the tips off the beans. Tom stares at me for a few moments. "What're you doing?" he asks.

"Um, I'm cleaning these beans for supper."

"Well, you should do that in the galley, not on the fly."

"Ah, well, I wanted to get some air and shade." I point to the bimini, but I see that Tom is clearly annoyed.

"That's not something you do on the flybridge." And he gets up and heads below.

I'm stunned that I've upset him with my green beans. After all, he eats on the flybridge. Why can't I prepare my beans? But it seems I've broken some code of the sea. Perhaps it's bad luck having a woman on board. Or having green beans on board. Obviously I have offended some sailors' sense of propriety or evoked some age-old superstition. I'm recalling Jonah. Perhaps now is when they cast me into the drink.

The music starts again and I put the green beans away. The couple in linen are dancing and waving me on and I can't resist. I'm rocking alone, shaking to the blues, when suddenly I hear a splash. It sounds as if a rhino has leaped into the river. Gazing down I see Tom swimming and splashing while Samantha Jean starts to have a heart attack with me on the flybridge.

His mood of moments before is altered as he frolics and dives and knocks himself out. He disappears under the water, then comes shooting out again. He lies, splayed on his back, floating. Then after a while he wants to get back on the boat, but he's having some trouble reboarding. I must admit to some small sense of satisfaction as Tom flails around by the swim platform but can't quite heave his hefty self on board. As he swims to the bow and tries to board from there, I'm gloating. This must have something to do with karma.

He shouts up to Jerry. "Sir," he says, "could you lower the bow step, please?"

But Jerry refuses. "Your failure to prepare is not my priority," he says sternly, walking away. Jerry looks up at me. "That is an unauthorized swim." I can't tell if he's kidding or not.

I give him a shrug, but I see that Tom is panting, struggling now to stay afloat. "Come on, Jer."

Jerry shakes his head. But Tom is pleading and, finally, with a melodramatic wave of the hands, Jerry lowers the bow step for Tom. "Thank you, Captain," Tom says as Jerry tosses a towel into his gut.

I switch to an afternoon beer, a rarity for me, as we groove to "Last night I got caught in a hurricane/when I asked her what her name was, she just said desire/Last night I got hit by a speeding truck . . ." I am lost in the lyrics, swaying on board, but the day is getting later and we need to find a place to beach for the night.

It's time to pull up anchor. "Let's move her forward a bit before bringing her up," Jerry says to a dripping-wet Tom, his belly shaking. "I don't want her to sink in deeper."

Tom hauls the anchor out, and, as he does, a giant razor clam clings to it. "Wow," he says. "Look at that." He holds it up and it is a very big clam, maybe eight inches long. "I've never clammed with an anchor before." He starts prying it off the line and gives me a look. "Now don't clam up on me."

To the tune of "Evil Woman" I groan as I struggle to help him with the line. Our little spat has ended. Tom jiggles the line until the clam drops back into the river. As we stow the anchors and start downriver, Jerry muses, "Maybe we should'a saved that clam and Mary could've put it in her journal."

The river opens up and the urban landscape drifts behind us once again. We pass a silent grain elevator on the side of the road. I'm thinking it's Sunday, but Jerry says it's the drought. "She'd be working today if she had anything to do." A barge going north soaks us with its wake. Some of its rafts have coal on them. One is filled with portable toilets.

I want to see where we're headed and start flipping through the river planner I bought in La Crosse. But this planner ends a mile south of Davenport and we're past that point. Now I'm making it up as I go along.

~ 23 ~

BUFFALO BEACH presents itself around a wide bend. The sun is setting and we've decided to tie up here for the night. But passengers on two cruisers are having a party at Clark's Landing, where we're heading. Just south is another, more deserted, beach on a woodsy spit of land and I've got my heart set on that one. "Can't we go there?" I ask Jerry.

"Be quiet," Jerry snaps. "Let me get us in." He is nervous and focused and, I've learned, can get more than a little ornery in those moments. He points the nose of the *River Queen* straight for the beach, checking the draft of the boat, and cuts the throttle. At last I hear that sound of the boat coming up on the shore and, when Jerry is sure we are secure here, he explains, "There are rocks and wing dams over there. See them?"

I look, but see nothing. Just more ripples in the water that all look the same. "Well, you need to be able to see those things." I nod, wondering if I ever will. "We'll spend the night here."

Tom's already out of the boat with Samantha Jean, who is "chasing waves." "Go get the waves!" Tom yells. "Come on, Sammy, go chase some waves!" He's taking down the anchors, placing and burying them in the sand. Then he wanders off in search of driftwood for a fire. I've got steaks in lime, corn in salt and lime wrapped in foil, and I start cooking green beans the way my mother cooks them, in butter and soy. Jerry uncorks the merlot.

Jerry gets those steaks off the grill just in time and we eat on my table on the bow in silence, the corn, the steak, those green beans, sipping our merlot. We all agree it's one of the best meals we've ever had. A harvest moon's rising to the northeast—full and orange, the kind that will light fields all night as farmers bring in their corn and we stomp out the fire and head to bed.

I'm settling down to read when Jerry "knocks" on my curtain. "I've been wanting to show you this." He's never invaded my space before and I am a little surprised. But as I pull back my green curtain, he hands me a copy of *People* magazine. He tells me that inside I'll read about his son, Chris, the boy who once swallowed the Liquid-Plumr, and his wife, Kristin. "Is this the rest of the story?" I ask, and Jerry nods. Then he says good night.

Eight years ago, when Chris was thirty-three, his liver failed him. This was in part because of the Liquid-Plumr and years of surgery and medication and finally substance abuse. He was lying in a coma and wasn't expected to live unless an organ donor was found. Jerry and Kathy were trying to come to terms with the situation when they learned that the day before a fourteen-year-old girl from St. Louis named Meghan was on a holiday skiing outing with her school and she crashed into a tree. She was taken to a nearby hospital in Wisconsin, where she was declared brain-dead.

Meghan's parents agreed to take her off life support and have all her organs donated. Chris received the liver. A woman in the next room received the heart and lungs. Another man received her corneas. And so on. A year later Meghan's parents met with all the people willing to meet with them, who had received the organs of their only daughter. At this meeting Chris met Kristin, the woman who had received the heart and lungs. They fell in love, married, and Meghan's parents attended their wedding.

I lie there, listening to the ducks squawking as they settle for the night. How could I worry about my father's clothes? I tell myself. These people donated their daughter in all her parts. I think of Kate, her chocolate brown eyes, her beautiful hair. My daughter is not someone I think of in pieces.

Kate was born during a blizzard in New York. She was a month early, a phenomenon that apparently occurs during snowstorms and full moons. The night before I had taken a baby safety class. What do you do if your baby is on fire? What do you do if your baby is plugged into an electrical outlet? I had gone to the class alone and walked home along Central Park.

Snow was already beginning to fall and I lay down on my back to make a snow angel. I felt tired and my back ached. That night I couldn't sleep. For the past several nights I hadn't been able to sleep. I ran into an elderly neighbor in the lobby of my building and she'd asked how I was doing. "Oh, I'm fine," I told her, "I just can't sleep."

"The baby's coming," she said.

I shook my head. "Not for another month."

She shook her head back to me. "Now," she said.

When I got home, I made myself some soup. I sat up, watching the news, trying to get tired, but sleep wouldn't come. I got into the tub and took a long hot bath and when I got out of the tub, my water broke.

My friend who lived upstairs took me to the hospital. Standing on snowdrifts, we hailed a taxi. It was four in the morning. I was nine months pregnant, carrying a small suitcase. When we got into the cab, the driver said, "I'm not going to the airport."

"I'm not either," I gasped.

When we got to the hospital, I handed him a twenty. "I don't have any change."

"Keep it," I said.

As I entered the hospital's double doors, a man passing a kidney stone tried to beat me to the reception desk. He was holding his side howling in pain as he pushed me out of the way. "We take the pregnant woman first," the intake officer said and the man slumped to a bench. I labored for almost twenty hours. When the doctor told me he was doing a C-section, I told him I didn't care if he did a lobotomy. I wept uncontrollably the first time I heard Kate cry.

Six weeks later we flew down to Florida to spend a week with my parents. Before we arrived, I called my father to ask if he was comfortable with our visit. "Why not?" he replied. "We've got plenty of room." Of course he knew what I meant. My father met Kate for the first time. As I sat in a lounge chair by their pool, trying to sleep, I watched him, walking with her in his arms around and around the pool.

Lying in my berth on the Mississippi River, I'm tired. I am genuinely tired and I don't feel the fast beating in my chest that has been my companion these past months. I flick off the light and pull the covers up to my chin. Only the sound of a passing freight train punctuates the night.

><

I wake in the morning as rested as I've been in months. I dress quickly and tell Tom and Jerry that I'm going to Casey's Convenience Store to see if they have real, brewed coffee and any olive oil, which I consider to be a staple.

"Olive oil?" Tom hoots. "And I'm Popeye." He flexes a muscle for me. "Hey, Jer, you must be Bluto."

"Oh, olive oil. Right." Jerry nods in agreement. "How about motor oil? Can you cook with motor oil? That's more like it."

"Yeah," Tom comes back. "Motor oil. Hey, you don't even need to go to the store. I've got some Valvoline 50 around here."

"Hey, pick up a little chardonnay while you're at it!" Jerry shouts. "French would be nice."

"Okay, boys. I'll catch you later."

Tom raises his big fists into the air. "The Comedy Hour begins," he shouts as I head into town. On my way I stroll by houses with Halloween decorations up in full force—ghosts, witches, jack-o'-lanterns. It's only September 18. I can't imagine what they do around here for Christmas. GO VIKINGS banners are glued to windows. A lawn is planted with wild prairie grass and milkweed.

On a front stoop a red and white tub sits with a sign that reads TUB REFINISHING. A glassed-in porch displays dozens of shoes in all sizes and shapes. Birkenstocks, sneakers, pink platform shoes, flip-flops, high heels, kids' shoes, nurses' shoes, old people's shoes, hiking boots, galoshes.

This is riverfront, Main Street, U.S.A. Picket fences, flagpoles, lawn gnomes, screened-in porches, swings. The kind of houses Tom will later comment remind him of those in the old cowboy movies. Where you shoot a guy and he falls off the roof into a bale of hay. I go into Casey's and Tom's right. I am much more likely to find motor oil than olive oil.

Then I head back to Clark's Landing, the only restaurant in town, where I've agreed to meet the boys for breakfast. I get there first and take a booth near the front. It's Sunday morning and farm families are having breakfast after church. One family has five towheaded children, stabbing at their buttermilk pancakes swimming in syrup. There are men in company caps and Stetsons and a few wearing leather jackets that say on them STURGIS, SOUTH DAKOTA, where the annual Harley festival is held.

I've missed the Friday-night special. Beer-battered or biscuit-battered catfish, served with a nonalcoholic wine cooler. Deep-fried broccoli on the side. My stomach is churning as the boys come in. Tom takes one side of the booth and Jerry sits next to me. "We're both left-handed," he says. "That's a good thing."

Tom orders diet Dew, which comes in a huge white plastic glass, and he manages to down three of these glasses of greenish yellow liquid before his breakfast of two double cheeseburgers and fries is done. I'm having a pair of eggs over easy. Jerry orders the Western omelette, which is smothered in American cheese, cooked with peppers and onions. "I feel like eating light today," he says.

After breakfast we stumble back to the boat. It is a beautiful day and Jerry doesn't seem to be in a rush. Tom starts chasing Samantha Jean up and down the beach and Jerry's tossing water onto the deck. I want to take my first river swim. The water looks clean enough and calm. I tell Jerry and he gives the river an eye. "Good day for it," he says. "Might join you myself." He pauses. "Wear your river shoes."

"I was planning to." I have already been warned of the dangers of clam shells that can slice off your heel.

"And maybe you should wear a life jacket," Jerry adds as a second thought. A life jacket? Oh, he sounds like my dad. River shoes, life jacket. Tie a line around my waist? I am a very strong swimmer and the river is completely still. And I'm not planning to swim across it. Just paddle out a little ways. I cannot imagine why I'd need a life jacket.

I put on my bathing suit and river shoes and start to slip into the water on the upstream side of the boat when Jerry eyes me. "Don't get in on that side. You always want to swim on the shore side of the boat in the direction of the current. Always get in the water downstream from the boat."

I give him a questioning stare.

"People go out swimming in the river and the current carries them under their boats. They get stuck there and drown. Oh gosh, there were these two kids on a raft once . . ."

I put my hands over my ears and pretend to sing a song. "It's okay," I say. "Don't tell me." Good old Jerry. Always a cheerful cautionary tale to go with any misstep you're about to make on the river. So I drag myself out of the water and go to the downstream side of our boat and put my feet into the silt. The bottom sucks at my river shoes.

The river is calm. Its surface is glossy and there is hardly a ripple as I lift my feet out of the silt, which seems to want to suck me back down. I swim out a few dozen yards and feel the first tug of water. Turning, I see that Jerry has gotten into the river as well and is tossing a life ring to Samantha Jean, who proceeds to rip it to pieces. Jerry is trying to get her to stop and I'm watching them play when I realize they are getting smaller and smaller.

It occurs to me that I'm being carried downstream. It is in fact a rather pleasant sensation. A little like being on a waterslide. But as I watch the *River Queen* slip away, and Tom and Jerry diminish in size, and Samantha Jean becomes a speck on the horizon, I grow concerned. I am being taken for a ride.

I try to swim back. At first I do a leisurely breaststroke, but I'm not getting anywhere. I try again, but I still seem to be moving away from the shore. This feels a bit like swimming in one of those continuous pools where you have to use all your strength just to stay in place. And I'm going backward.

I try harder, then switch to a crawl. I use all my might, but I make little progress. If anything it seems that I am being carried backward as if in a riptide. In another moment I'll be halfway to Memphis. I suddenly see why Huck and Jim missed their turnoff up the Ohio. Anyone would. They were riding this conveyor belt too. The river is a team of horses, dragging me with it.

I also see the wisdom of wearing a life jacket and I definitely understand the problem of getting sucked under the boat. But this is all hindsight. I'm fighting like a demon to get back to shore. Tom and Jerry are playing with Samantha Jean and the life ring and I give them a wave. "Hey, guys!" I call. They wave back. I swim, struggling, toward them. "Hello, Jerry? Tom?" I call to my two half-deaf river pilots, hoping they'll get the hint and throw me a line as they frolic at the shore. But they just wave.

Now I put my face in the water and use all the power in my arms. I paddle as if I'm being chased by a giant catfish, the kind rumored to lurk in the muddy depths of this stream. Brave souls "noodle" for them with their bare arms. I swim for my life and finally I reach a place around the bend where, for the first time, I can actually see a wing dam. There it is, a ripple in the water. A thin line of rocks barely revealed. A wing dam. It has eluded me, but I will recognize one from now on. And I know that on the other side the current will be weaker.

I work my way around it, treading water, and soon my river shoes graze the silty bottom. Breathless, I drag myself onto the sand where they notice me. "Hey, Mary," Tom says. "How was your swim?"

"Great." I'm gasping for breath. "That river is strong," I tell them and they concur.

"You didn't need that vest, though, huh?" Jerry asks.

I nod. "Actually, I could've used it," I say.

Jerry nods thoughtfully. "Well, next time you should." Just offshore Samantha Jean frolics on top of the life ring as Tom splashes water into her yelping face.

# AROUND THE BEND

~ 24 ~

EVERYWHERE I look there are stories. Around every bend. Everything you do, every line you throw. There's a tale to tell. Jerry, it seems, has a story for everything, usually one involving mutilation or death. Every waitress, every cabbie, every person at a marina, every boatman you meet will have his or her own. One that will always top yours.

If you saw a storm, they saw a tornado. If you saw a tornado, they were in a tidal wave. If you saw a big catfish, they've always seen a bigger one, no matter how big yours was to start with. If you were in an accident or had a great pet, they were in a worse accident or had a dog who shopped for dinner.

As we go through Lock and Dam 16, Jerry, who is at the helm, says, "Boy I remember the last time we were here. It smelled like brownies. I asked about it, but the lockmaster denied it." He's steering us away from the wall as I take the line in the front and Tom takes his in the back. "I guess he didn't want to give me any."

Holding the line I take a sip of my coffee from my Citgo mug. The boat shifts and scalding liquid sears my tongue. "Ouch!" I cry out. "I burned my tongue." It feels as if somebody sanded it.

Jerry starts to tell me about when he burned his whole mouth. "With this very mug." He holds up his Citgo mug. "Now let her go a little, Mary," Jerry says. "You're holding too tight. Remember what happened to that woman from Trempealeau." And Jerry makes a motion like a knife slitting his throat.

We are leaving the lock and dam, and river scum coats my hands. A sandbar to our starboard side is blanketed in birds. Pelicans, heron, egrets, cormorants, gulls. We're running the engine at fifteen hundred rpm. Jerry says this is a good speed to run it and not burn too much fuel. I stand next to him in the cabin, my face to the wind.

The rhythm of the boat has entered me. The gentle forward movement as we drift at a clip of eight and a half miles per hour. The sound of the engines as they punctuate our journey. As if life is just about forward motion. To go back is a struggle upstream. I'm coming to understand the meaning of "going with the flow."

I check the mile marker, then glance at our maps. We're coming up on Hog Island at Mile 458. There seem to be many markers on this trip. There are the river markers and the day-markers, there are buoys and depth markers. There's the log Jerry keeps. There are the markers on walls to indicate high water and flood crests and on bridges and dams for clearance. Then there are my own personal markers. Eight days on the river and I've stopped taking my pills.

~ 25 ~

"WE'LL KEEP you clean in Muscatine," F. Scott Fitzgerald wrote in 1927 when he worked for the Colliers Advertising Agency. I'm thinking of this as we are heading to Muscatine, a place I only know from Fitzgerald's jingle. He had already published *The Great Gatsby*, but he needed a job. Writers have to do all kinds of things to stay alive, don't they?

I have long identified with migratory patterns of midwestern writers. Cather, Twain, Fitzgerald, Hemingway, Dreiser, to name a few. They went east for opportunity, but they never lost their feeling for the Midwest. Twain's greatest works about thirteen-year-old boys in Hannibal, Missouri, were written from the vantage point of Hartford, Connecticut. Cather wrote her novels of the prairie long after she'd left for good. And Fitzgerald's yearning for the Middle West was always there.

What is it about these flatlands and fields of corn and wheat that holds the imagination? Was it what Proust said in his masterpiece? The only paradise is the one we have lost. For me the Midwest represents a simpler time, one of great clarity and few deceptions. As a friend once said, "It's a good place to be from. . . ."

In 1926 Fred Angell, a resident of Muscatine, steamed a hamburger, instead of frying it, added his own formula of spices, and offered the sandwich to a deliveryman, who declared, "Fred, you know, this sandwich is made right!" Somehow this got translated to "Maid-Rite" and the Maid-Rite sandwich.

Muscatine without Maid-Rite, the saying goes, would be like Muscatine without the Mississippi River. But the river continues to flow, though Maid-Rite, which closed its doors in 1997, is long gone. So are the pearl button factories that once kept this town employed. Once there were eighteen pearl button factories in Muscatine. Now there are three and they only make plastic buttons. The pearl buttons, made from Mississippi mussels, ceased being produced long ago.

Coming into Muscatine, we see old Victorian houses set on the hill above the levee, well out of the flood zone. This is what I'm coming to recognize on the river. The grand houses sit high. We are searching for a landing and hopefully a gas dock and we spot one just below the town. The marina is large and there's a courtesy dock.

"You've got plenty of room," Tom says to Jerry. "You can even back her in if you want."

"Naw, I'll just bring her in forward, I think."

"Looks like you're turning up some sand here."

"Yep," Jerry says, not too happy. "I've only got four feet." But he makes it and we come into a cozy spot on the dock.

Muscatine. The Pearl of the Mississippi. I want to go to the button museum, but it is closed on Sundays. Instead I head for a stroll through downtown. I walk by a plaque. MISSISSIPPI RIVER, RECORD FLOOD CREST, 25.58 FEET, JULY 9, 1993. A mark on the wall shows how high the waters rose.

I walk past Lee's Bakers and The Purple Hedgehog, whose window is filled with—guess what—big purple hedgehogs, fairies, wizards, a Bruce Lee poster, a Bob Marley "Mellow Mood" poster, and some very odd pewter figurines that appear to be dragons. I walk by Hubbles, which seems like a kind of men's store/bar with a wooden Indian in the back, a humidor in front. Nothing appears open in downtown Muscatine—not a coffee shop or a pharmacy, not a corner store—though many shops look abandoned and have FOR RENT signs in the window.

Tucked between Hazel Green and Her Sewing Machine and a carpet store with banners for the Muscatine Muskies in the window is a pawnshop. Inside I see the usual items. A bowie knife, fishing gear, rifles. Bicycles. Elvis photos. Telescope. Television sets. Lava lamps. But then there are the things I don't expect. Someone pawned his kid's basketball, a toy John Deere farm silo, complete with barn. A pair of chopsticks ($2.75). An alarm clock made up of farm animals ($17.29), a lamp with an angel, guarding children ($39).

But the main thing this shop pawns is musical instruments. Dozens of guitars. Shiny blue ones, a black one with flames licking out of its hole. Plain wood acoustical. All hanging by their necks from the ceiling like so many broken dreams, going as far back into the store as I can see. Saxophones ($399). An antique steel reed accordion made in Germany, complete with its box ($159). A slide trombone ($179). A pair of maracas ($3.99). Two boys on scooters zip past me. These are the first people I've seen. They are followed by a pale child on foot. The boys on scooters seem to be Hispanic or perhaps Native American. Or Middle Eastern. One boy has a scar on his cheek. The other wears a Stars & Stripes Band-Aid across his nose. The boy who is walking has bad teeth.

They almost run me over and I have to dash out of their way. On the other side of the street I notice an antiques shop has its door open and I slip inside. It is your usual tchotchke store, filled with ceramic cats, frilly tablecloths, old postcards. I start flipping through the postcards, looking for pictures of the river from earlier times.

A tall man in gray pants comes in with his diminutive blond wife and he's in search of coins. "I want old money," he tells the woman.

I think to myself, "I could use a little old money too."

"I like Civil War coins. Anything you've got." She doesn't have much in the way of old coins, but they start speaking in very loud voices about the price of silver and how it's way up. How nobody can afford silver anymore.

"I've got a Little Daisy butter churn," the wife pipes in. "I bought it at a yard sale. It didn't have its top so I only got the bottom. I thought I'd be able to find a top."

"Bet you haven't," the woman at the desk says as she swats the counter with her flyswatter.

"You're right. I haven't."

"Well, those are real collector's items now. You won't find much in the Little Daisy line."

"I've been having trouble finding those old coins as well," the man booms. "Everywhere I go, I look for them, but silver is getting scarcer and scarcer."

I pick out a few postcards of Muscatine from the 1930s and, as I go pay for them, I ask the owner if she knows where I can get a cup of coffee in town.

She shakes her head. She's sporting a tattered pink sweater and has cropped orangish hair. Probably younger than me, but looks a lot older. She keeps swatting her own back with the flyswatter. "Can't get any coffee in this part of town. You gotta go down to the malls for that."

"Well, I don't have a car. Can I walk there?"

She looks at me like I'm crazy. "You don't have a car? How're you getting around without a car?"

"I'm on a boat, actually."

I may as well have told her that I was traveling by intergalactic spaceship. "You don't have a car?" She's shaking her head.

"No way to get to the malls without a car. There's no busses, no cabs. . . . You have to have a car or you can't get a cup of coffee in this town." She introduces herself as Cindy. "You know, back in the 1970s Muscatine was a booming town. There was a lot going on here. Good restaurants, things to do. Then they built the malls. That just killed the downtown. There's nothing here anymore," Cindy says with a wave of her flyswatter. "You can't buy groceries. You can't get toothpaste. You gotta drive to the malls. It's a conspiracy if you ask me."

"A conspiracy?"

"Yeah, between the chains and the auto industry. I wouldn't put it past them." She swats a fly on the counter, then swats herself again. "And there's no public transportation here. No taxis. If you're working second or third shift in the factory, you can't get home without a car." She's still whipping herself with her own flyswatter as if in an act of self-flagellation. "Look at this downtown. There's no restaurants. No cafés. You can't get a loaf of bread or a cup of coffee here. Nothing. The malls ruined all of that. And the cars. They spent eight million dollars on riverfront restoration. Eight million. And what've we got? A nice place to take a walk. That's all."

Later I will learn something from my husband, who is Canadian. Apparently films that are supposed to take place in the river towns of Middle America (the "fly over" states) are shot in Canada. For example, a film that is supposed to take place in Kansas City is being shot in Winnipeg. This is because Winnipeg looks more like what Americans think river towns should look like—bustling centers of commerce and vitality, not dead centers where nothing happens outside of its strip malls—than Kansas City itself does.

I pay for my postcards and leave. On my way back to the boat, I pass another pawnshop. It too specializes in guitars.

❧

One day, while driving around the Midwest, my father and his brother, Sidney, got an idea. World War II had just ended and my father had gone back to Chicago from Pennsylvania, where he'd been working in the war industry. He had come to run his baby brother's architectural firm. I picture the day. A warm day of Illinois summer. The fields flat, the corn just starting to grow.

They looked at all this vastness and open space and an idea came to them almost simultaneously. What if we put all the stores in one location, they thought, instead of having them scattered all over the place or just on Main Street? What if you drive to these stores? With the war over, the economy was chugging along. So they began building the first shopping centers all over the Midwest. Elgin, Illinois; Green Bay, Wisconsin; Terre Haute, Indiana.

The buildings they built were precursors to the generic Home Depot or Costco boxes we have today. Charmless, depersonalized malls that began the depletion of Main Street and the downtowns. But then, in the 1940s and 1950s, it was all America wanted, and my father and his brother did well for a time. For two summers I worked in his office and I'd gaze at the sketches and models—the plastic trees, the fake families, the cookie-cutter stores. When he wanted to take me on an outing, we would go to a building or a mall under construction. I'd get a hard hat and we'd walk around, usually with an engineer and a set of plans. My father would say things like, "Let's put dressing rooms in the back" or, "Can't we open up those walls?" He seemed happiest walking along the wooden planks of sawdust-strewn floors.

My father had many dreams. One was to be a rich man, which he was for a while. And then he wasn't. He watched his wealth evaporate in bad deals, lavish spending, and taxes on property sold. In some ways he died impoverished. In his final years, when my parents moved to Milwaukee to be near my brother, my father would dissuade his Chicago friends from driving up to see him. He was embarrassed at his fall from grace.

He had other dreams—those he'd put aside. To be a musician, to "angel" Broadway shows. When I visited him in the last year, we'd watch television, which he couldn't hear. Or we'd sit and gaze at the squirrels building their nests. He marveled at how efficient they were. Other times he'd close his eyes and raise his hand and conduct Brahms or Ellington or *South Pacific*. He'd hum along, signaling for the trumpets to come in, for the drums to drop back. I could sit for hours watching him conduct the music he heard in his head.

I encouraged him to work on his memoirs for a while. After all he was a man who'd seen an entire century. And besides he wanted to be remembered for something he did. That mattered to him more than anything. One Christmas I went home and read the pages he'd written. There were dozens of them, single-spaced. They told of business deals he'd done, shopping centers he'd helped design. Real estate he'd developed.

For a man who was to me a musician and a great storyteller, these pages were incredibly dull. Devoid of imagination. I could barely read them. But perhaps most strikingly, there was no mention of my mother, my brother, or me. He even wrote about a shopping center he'd built the year I was born, but never acknowledged my birth.

"Dad," I said when I put the pages down. "I'm not even in here. I want to be born."

"You will be," he told me with a laugh. "You will."

But in the pages of his memoir I never was. We never were mentioned. He talked about bricks and mortar, about deals gone bad and others that came out good. But he never spoke of me. Or my mother. Or John. It was as if we never existed at all.

When he turned 102, he saw an item on the news. It seemed that a ferry called *The Lake Express* was being launched between Milwaukee and Muskegon, Michigan, and my father expressed a desire to go for a ride. I was stunned by this request. He was, after all, very old and frail, and it was a six-hour ride on what could turn out to be a cold and choppy voyage. But he was adamant.

Given that I am married to a newshound, I made a few inquiries. Apparently the public relations people for *The Lake Express* liked the idea that a man who was turning 102 wanted to celebrate his birthday on their ferry. Our family was offered free tickets and we were told the press wanted to interview my dad.

He dressed that day in a navy jacket, a red and white striped tie, gray flannel slacks. He wore his beige cashmere coat and a gray fedora. Nobody looked as good as my father that day. In a folder in his lap he carried a file that read "Memoir." I think he planned to hand this to the press. Instead they asked him one or two questions and snapped his picture.

In response to the question about why he wanted to take the ferry, he replied, "Because my arms will hurt less than if I row." That made the headlines.

For six hours he sat on the deck while my mother, bored and annoyed, grumbled inside. He wore a blanket draped across his legs. When the captain announced that Mr. Morris had just turned 102, Dad gave a wave at the crowd. Strangers came up and congratulated him. He was in his element. He told tales of living through two world wars, of the Great Depression. "Yeah, I remember the invention of the airplane," he quipped with one passenger. "I predicted it would never fly."

But for most of those six hours he just sat, eyes on the water, staring straight ahead.

After he died, people sent me books on the literature of mourning, the nature of grief. A bereavement sampler. None of this did much good except I learned what I already knew. That grief is not a constant, the way love or anger might be. Grief is a sneakier emotion. It comes in waves, when you least expect it, sweeping across you and then it's gone. A sudden storm that comes upon you, then subsides.

જ

In the morning we gas up. Here it costs us $3.96 a gallon. With tax, for one hundred gallons, which is one hundred river miles, I get a fuel bill of four hundred dollars. Later in the year the attorney general of Illinois will charge gas stations with price gouging, but for now this is what I have to pay.

I'm starting to do the math. At this rate, if nothing changes, the fuel costs alone of going to New Orleans from where I am right now would be over five thousand dollars. And that's just one way. If I go with Greg Sadowski, who has suddenly surfaced in Portage Des Sioux, the place where we are headed, he'll have to bring his boat back. No wonder the river is empty. It's not just Katrina or the drought that's keeping barges and pleasure craft off the river. It's the cost of fuel.

The truth is I can't afford it either. As much as I want to get to Memphis and beyond, I'm starting to think that I just can't. I'm going to need a free ride to get myself down the lower Mississippi. It comes to me that it would be perfect to have this boat take me to the end of the upper Mississippi. Then maybe I could hitch a ride south on a friendly vessel that won't charge an arm and a leg. Or fuel costs at least. Jerry has his heart set on ending his journey at Portage Des Sioux, which is at Mile 212, and wintering the *River Queen* there, but I've gotten something else in my head. I want this boat to take me to Cairo. River Mile zero.

With a mug of coffee in hand, I step onto the dock and take Jerry aside. "Can we talk?" I ask him.

"Sure," Jerry says.

"Look, I'm figuring this thing out and I'm thinking it would be better—well, it would be better for me—if you could get me to Cairo. I mean, I know you don't want to go past St. Louis, but I'd really like to do the upper Mississippi with you. If you could just get me to Cairo. It's the place where Huck and Jim missed the Ohio. It's Mile zero. The end of Illinois. Then I can figure out my way from there. . . ."

Jerry's listening, his gaze set on the river, but he doesn't say a word.

"I mean, would you consider . . . ?" I am nervous, shaking as I ask. "Would you think about getting me there?"

For a few moments he says nothing, but looks askance in a way that feels like "no." "Not sure if I can. I've got to figure how many days up and back to Portage Des Sioux. Gotta figure the costs. I need to talk to Tom. And I gotta talk to Kathy."

"Well, would you?"

"Well, I'll think about it." It's not a flat-out no. That's better than what I'd thought. He promises he will, but he doesn't make a call. Later in the morning I take Tom aside.

"So," I tell him, "I've asked Jerry if he'll keep going to Cairo." Tom listens, taking this in. "So what'd he say?"

"He said he'd think about it. Do you think he will?"

"Hard to tell with Jerry," he says. "Never know what he's gonna do." Tom gives me a slap on the arm. "I'll work on him for you."

They are getting ready to push off, but I don't think I can go another day without bathing. I try to broach this subject gently with Jerry. Perhaps there's a way to actually hook up our shower, but apparently this will require some work and time and it also means that we'd be using precious water, which we don't want to run out of. Maybe there's another option. I run this by Jerry. I'm willing to find a gas station that has showers. He shakes his head. "How're you going to get to a gas station?"

I have no idea.

Jerry grumbles for a moment, then talks to Tom. It appears there is some kind of a water pump that they've been saving for just such an occasion. Jerry tells me to go put on my bathing suit and when I come back, they've got this pump operating. It's pumping river water through a hose. The river here at the dock is, well, brown, but if I want a shower, what choice do I have? As Tom pumps and Jerry holds the hose, I stand on the dock, shampooing my hair, rubbing soap under my armpits. Discreetly they look the other way.

~ 26 ~

BOGUS ISLAND, Hail Island, Bell Island, Turkey Island, Otter Island. All these islands south of Muscatine have funny names, I think, as I gaze at the maps and we journey south. My tongue burns and feels numb at the same time from the scalding it took the day before. As I'm heading outside, map in hand, I smash my foot into Jerry's toolbox. "Goddamn it," I say.

Jerry looks up, startled. "Is my toolbox okay?"

"Thanks, Jer." Wounded and chagrined, I take my place at the bow, resting my bruised foot on an extra plastic chair. There are dozens of things to trip on or fall over on this boat. There are mooring lines and anchor lines. There are the places where we pump in and pump out and the caps that are on these, as well as the cap where the anchor line goes. I've stubbed my toe literally half a dozen times on this one alone and the boys laugh heartily whenever I do.

There are three ice chests and plastic chairs, and the long stick and the short stick and firewood, and pretty much anyone's shoes. On three occasions I have smashed my foot into the propped-up hatch above the port engine. When I complain about this, Tom says his engines need to "breathe."

So do I, I want to say, but I resist.

If there is engine trouble, and there often is, I am afraid to come off the flybridge for fear of falling into the bowels of the engines themselves. And of course there is Samantha Jean, who seems to take sadistic pleasure, if a dog is capable of this emotion, in being underfoot. I have a yellow purple bruise on my thigh where I walked into the ice chest and similar bruises on all my toes. Then there are our buoys and fenders and life rings and, of course, the very anchors themselves, which, if they are not stowed, enter my worst dreams.

There's dampness in the air. The edges of my journal and books curl. The cabin is full of flies. My burned tongue feels numb. The banks are lined with trees whose shallow roots are exposed. More pushovers, ready with the slightest shove to tumble down. The river itself is smooth and glossy, the reflection of trees along its bank like a mirror.

It's a slow morning. I have phone reception so I decide to give Kate a ring. I can tell from her voice that she's just gotten up and she's rushing to class. "Hi, honey," I say, "just wondering if you got that package."

"I haven't even gone to the post office yet." Her voice is filled with fatigue and some annoyance. "Look, can I call you later?"

"Sure," I say, "anytime." We hang up and already I'm wishing I hadn't called. I phone home to chat with Larry, but I get the machine. Judging by the time, he's probably out for a run. I try to settle down at the bow while Tom has his breakfast of diet Dew and some sponge candy I picked up in East Davenport. Then he goes back up to his berth on the flybridge and cuddles with his dog. We float free through Lock and Dam 17 and hundreds of white pelicans greet us as the lock opens. "Have fun and be safe," the lockmaster says. When Jerry sees the pelicans, he says, "Cowabunga," and starts snapping pictures.

On the flybridge Tom whispers sweet nothings to Samantha Jean, whom he has tucked into his sleeping bag. "Give Daddy a kiss. Come on, Sammy. Big kiss." Meanwhile Jerry starts talking about having me go from Cairo to Memphis in a towboat. He says that I can just hop a ride. Oh great. I can't wait for that. "I'll make a few calls for you," Jerry says.

We float by a dredging barge that looks as if it landed from outer space. On the shore it's made a huge pile of sand from the river silt it's brought up. All along this part of the river are duck blinds. This must be a major migration route.

We're nearing Lock and Dam 18 and there's a tow and barge ahead. "Looks like she's only six hundred feet," Jerry says. "Maybe she can take us with." But it seems we have to wait.

Jerry explains that when they built the lock and dam system in the 1930s the plan was to build auxiliary locks so that smaller pleasure craft wouldn't have to compete with commercial vessels for lockage. "Then World War II happened, and . . ."— he makes the hand motion he makes when a boat broaches—"that plan went down the tubes."

The sky darkens and the air has a hot, muggy feel. Suddenly a big storm is upon us. Lightning and thunder explode. A deluge pours down. Tom has left his sleeping bag to air out in the dinghy and in minutes it is soaking wet. He races outside and drags all his bedding into our tiny cabin to dry out along with his bomber jacket and the rest of his things, including, of course, Samantha Jean, who is also soaked to the skin. The cabin has an enclosed, musty smell, not to mention that of wet dog. Fork lightning is everywhere and I recall all the cautionary tales from my river planner as Samantha Jean freaks out and races under my bed.

We are locked out by the barge and tow and Jerry puts the marine band radio on Channel 13 so we can hear what the towboat plans to do. I listen to an incomprehensible voice with what sounds like a thick Louisiana accent. "They're all from the bayou," Jerry says. "Cajuns. All them towboat drivers."

It appears we have some time on our hands and not much to do except sit there in the rain, so Jerry lets me maneuver the boat. Gently he shows me how to adjust the shift, which moves the boat forward and in reverse. "Lean into her," he tells me. "You wanta make a right turn, you do the shift like this. Left, you go like this." He shows me how if you pull the shift all the way down she'll go into reverse.

With rain pelting the windshield (and no wipers), I'm not having much luck. On this boat shifting is strictly a right-hand maneuver and I am a lefty. Jerry is also left-handed and I ask him if this isn't difficult for him as well. He thinks about it for a moment. "I suppose it would be," he wrinkles his brow, "if I hadn't been doing it for so long."

"Well, I'm having a hard time. . . ."

I'm struggling with the small adjustments I must make with my right hand as I turn the boat right, then left, but I can't quite get the hang of it. I've long grappled with the perils of being a lefty in a right-handed world—can openers, hotel computer mouses, Metrocards for the New York City subway (which all require right-handed maneuvers). I'm definitely feeling challenged here. "Hey, Jer, what happens if I accidentally throw the shift into reverse rather than neutral?"

"Hmm," Jerry says, "now that's a good question. Let me tell you what happened to my friends, Pete and Jenny. They had a bad marriage to start with, but they were out boating one day and he was going too fast so she wanted to slow them down and he said no so she got angry and went over, trying to pull the throttle back, but she pulled the shift instead and threw the boat into reverse. Melted down the whole transmission." Jerry pauses for effect. "The marriage ended shortly thereafter."

I am careful in the wind and rain as I lean into the shift. A few moments later we get a call from the lockmaster and I breathe a sigh of relief. For whatever reason, the tow and barge has decided to fall back and let us go ahead. "Why're they doing that?" I ask as Jerry takes the wheel to maneuver into the lock. "Well, it could be he has to wait for something. Or it could also be, because of the storm, that he just wants us out of his way. My guess is he wants us gone before he goes ahead." As we move into position on the lock, the barge workers wave. One waves from the rear, but I don't see him so I don't wave back until Tom says, "Mary, he's waving at you," so I wave again.

We pass the tow and barge, slosh a little in its wake as we ease our way into the lock. The lockmaster in a yellow slicker awaits us. "Not a bad day to be a duck," Tom greets the lockmaster as we wait for him to let us through.

"Ducks know enough to stay out of the rain," the lockmaster says. Just then a huge bolt of lightning cracks above us and I scream my head off.

"Bow into the wall," Jerry says.

"Well, you don't have to get pissy," Tom snaps back.

"Hey," Tom says to the lockmaster, pointing to the back of the lock as the gates are closing, "you sprung a leak."

"Yeah, gotta fix that one," the lockmaster says as the water rushes in behind us. I'm standing in the pouring rain. Another crack of lightning right above us, the kind that sounds like a firecracker going off in your brain, and I scream again. Tom laughs his head off. The lockmaster laughs too.

"You can go ahead when I open," he tells us. "No need to wait for the horn on a day like today." The lockmaster leaves us now. "Have fun," he says. "Be safe."

As we leave behind Lock 18 we are listening to the National Weather Service. Chance of rain 60 percent, which I could have told them. Rain may produce hail. Jerry doesn't like this. Hail can damage a boat. Hail is not good for the windshields or the nicely painted fiberglass coat.

"What d'ya think, Tom? Should we head south or tie up behind the wall? Maybe under some trees or something?"

I'm praying for south. I do not want to stay in this fork lightning storm. I really do not want to stay in one place. Tom's staring at the sky. I have no idea what he's looking for or what he sees. "Just looks like a lot of rain. I think we're okay to head south." Though there is no hail, we are on a river of driving rain. Everything in the cabin is wet and lightning crackles all around us. We opt not to stop in Burlington, Iowa, though I'd wanted to. In this storm there's no point.

In the gray mist and drizzle we spot a tow, pulling a boat upriver. It comes upon us like a phantom, and, as she approaches, Tom and Jerry realize that the tow is dragging the *Princess* back to La Crosse. This is the boat Jerry was supposed to move south before he decided upon doing our trip. It is also the boat that Greg Sadowski was piloting when Katrina hit.

On the radio we hear a tow driver refer to her as "an elegant yachtlike boat," but now we see her for what she became after the storm. Her hull has a deep, battered gash. The windows on her starboard side are smashed and boarded up. There is a silence on board as she passes us going north. Jerry shakes his head. "She's a shadow of her former self," he says.

I lie down to take a nap. As I curl up in my nook, I hear a sound under the bed. A desperate, heavy breathing. I look down and see the bleary eyes of Samantha Jean, terrified by the lightning, who has found a safe refuge below me. I ponder this for a moment. Then get up and go to the fridge. I return with a scrap of salami and slip it to her under the bed.

## ~ 27 ~

IN THE 1840s Joseph Smith claimed he was guided by an angel to a place where he found gold plates on which prophets had written divine revelations. Smith founded the Mormon church in upstate New York, then led a small band of followers to Nauvoo, Illinois. Within a few years his following rose to ten thousand and Nauvoo became the second largest town in Illinois, after Chicago.

Considered to be a charlatan by some and a philanderer by others (apparently his belief in polygamy grew out of his own marital woes), Smith made enemies along the way. During a bloody conflict the original temple was destroyed and Joseph Smith was killed. Soon afterward the Mormons set off on their journey to Utah. Two years ago the fully refurbished church, closed to non-Mormons, was reopened.

The new church looms high on a bluff overlooking the Mississippi. Nauvoo was once the center of the Mormon world and is still viewed as a sacred place by the church. Smith had referred to Nauvoo as "the loveliest place and the best people under the heavens," and I wanted to see it. Jerry did too. But, as we approach after the storm, there is no boat landing. The bank of the river on the Illinois side is all farmland. Then Jerry spots a grain elevator and beside it are two barges. Tom and Jerry look at each other and give a shrug. "We'll tie up here," Jerry says.

I am astonished. "But that's private property."

They look at me as if this is a foreign concept. "As they say in Thailand"—Jerry throws up his arms—"c'est la vie."

We are like pirates as we make our way toward the rusty barge, which is riding low in the water. The grain elevator is operating. Yellow kernels fly down a belt, then up into the silos. Others rain down onto the ground. Jerry maneuvers the *River Queen* against the side of the barge. But he doesn't like where he's come in so he reverses and moors our bow to the stern of the barge.

We tie up and Tom opts, as he almost always does, to stay with Samantha Jean and the boat. Jerry will go exploring with me. Tom steadies me with his strong arm as I leap onto the rusty barge, which shifts under my weight. Then I jump to the land.

It is the first time on this journey that I put my feet on Illinois soil. I feel the solid earth, corn kernels beneath my sandals. It is not so different from Iowa, but it's home to me.

The path from the barge to the loading dock is paved with golden corn. Everything around us is corn. Jerry and I tromp through muck and corn around the silo, which churns and grinds and the noise is deafening. Jerry finds his way around the silo and inside to talk to the elevator operator. Kernels rain down as the operator explains he can't be responsible for what happens to us or our boat, and he's going to pretend we aren't here.

This is fine with us. "We won't be more than an hour," Jerry says, checking out the sky and time of day. We cut across the silo property where Jerry points to the safety ladders coming down the sides. "This way you only fall six feet instead of sixty." I nod, glad he explains things in this way to me.

Heading into Nauvoo, we walk by an old quarry from which the original Mormon temple here was built. We pass fields of corn, historic houses with little plaques on them that give a feel of what life was like in the 1840s. We keep trying to get to the temple, but the closer we get, the further it seems to drift away. It is a mirage, an illusion.

There are no shops, no town. At least nothing we can walk to as we keep trudging toward the steeple. Just these historic red brick houses with no one around. There is a ghostlike feel, as if the place had been struck by a neutron bomb. On a tennis court we come upon a group of kids, maybe two dozen teens, playing some kind of game with a sheet and a volleyball. They are all blond and smiling. They seem to be having too much fun. They don't notice us as we pass. The temple remains far away, even as we approach it.

Nauvoo spooks us out. Jerry starts calling the place "Nau-voodoo." "Let's get out of here," he says and I agree. As the light is fading, Jerry goes ahead of me to get the boat ready and make sure the engines are going to start. He definitely wants to leave before dark. I am slower and, as I walk on the path that takes me through the grain elevator, I see that the operator is in the office.

The office is filled with small plastic boxes with labels that read WALK PROGRAM CORN, BUTTER AND HARDY PROGRAM CORN. The grain operator is a short, stocky man with a round face, wearing a hard hat. He seems uncomfortable when I walk into the office.

"Excuse me," I say, "I'm sorry to bother you." He doesn't say anything. "But I'm with that boat. The one that's tied up to your barge." He still doesn't say anything and I have a feeling he's afraid that somehow he's going to get in trouble. "I'm a writer," I tell him, and then perhaps to make him more at ease, "a journalist. Can you tell me something about the grain here? Have you been slow because of New Orleans and the drought?"

"Well, don't quote me, all right? I mean, I wouldn't want you to quote me."

"I'm just curious . . ."

"Well," he tips his hard hat back a bit, "we were running low for a couple weeks, but we're riding hot and heavy now. We're getting ready to load." I ask if he thinks this means the Port of New Orleans is going to be opening soon and again he asks me not to quote him, but, "We're getting ready to load." Our corn, he tells me, goes all over the world. But mostly to Japan.

"Japan?"

"For beer," he says. "The Japanese buy almost all our corn for their beer."

❧

All across the prairie, golden wheat blew in the wind. There were miles of it, flat and waving, seas of winter wheat. When it was ready, the farmers of Illinois, Nebraska, Iowa harvested it, separating the grain from the chaff, then drove their truckloads to the grain elevators where the farmers were paid by the bushel. Winter wheat had already been bought in autumn. September wheat was sold in July.

The farmers were never happy with the price their crops brought. They grumbled and complained among themselves but in the end they had no choice. They took what was offered whether it was a dollar or seventy-five cents to the bushel. They took what was offered because already, months before, some manufacturer had already bought their wheat.

Then Pillsbury or General Mills purchased the grain to make bread and cakes, store-bought items, and what had once flowed like a sea in the prairie was now shipped to the giant mills. As he sat in the order booth, my father tried to make sense out of the journey of the wheat. Or the corn. How it was so young and went so far. How so much happened in its short life. He pictured it in fields and silos, on trains and mills. He was a man who wanted to go places and he was filled with envy.

His hands shot up from the booth as the orders came in. Buy and he waved toward his chest. Sell and he pushed his hand away. A closed fist meant a dollar. Five shakes of the fist, five dollars. Thumbs-up was seven/eighths of a dollar. He showed me once how, when he worked on the Board of Trade, he shot back the same signals, confirming purchases and sales.

During World War II my father lived with a Quaker family. When he talked, they hung on his every word. Once he asked them, "What is it? How is it possible that everything I say is so interesting to you?"

The Quakers laughed and explained they weren't listening to his words. "You talk with your hands," they said, keeping their own demurely folded in their laps.

My father did talk with his hands. It was as if he was conducting a conversation, rather than just speaking it. He talked about business. Futures, commodities. The grain markets. Soy, wheat, barley, corn. He'd point to his chest. "Buy!" I'd shout with glee. Or gesture away with a raised fist. "Sell!"

❧

We sail from Nauvoo beneath a popcorn sky—a bucket of bumpy white and yellow clouds that spill across the horizon. We've taken on swarms of flies and Tom jokes that "this is why they call it the flybridge." Tom says we took them on at the grain elevator where we tied up at Nauvoo. "Lots of flies there," Tom says as he swats them with his bare hands. I've gone topside and am piloting as Tom smashes flies with his broad, bloodied palms on this clear, summer evening. Then he flicks them off the deck into the wind.

The channel is wide and goes into a gentle bend so Jerry thinks the risk of me wreaking havoc is slim. "Keep an eye on her, will you, Tom?" I must admit that I don't like being spoken of in the third person when I am sitting right there, but I try to ignore it.

"So you liked Nauvoo?" Tom asks as he brings his wide hands together and mushes another fly between them. He picks the fly up by its still quivering wings and flicks it overboard.

"Not really," I tell him. "Spooky place."

He nods. He's brought the tin of molasses cookies Jerry's mother made and, between fly smashing, reaches in and eats them by the handful. "Nauvoodoo," Tom says, imitating Jerry. He offers me the tin.

"Naw. Thanks."

"You know what you need," Tom says, munching on a cookie with his bloodied mitt. "You need to kick off your heels and relax." He whacks at the air and catches two. He rubs my head before I can flinch. I'm praying for a marina with showers at Keokuk, where we're headed.

"Hmm . . ." I'm a little stuck on how one kicks off one's heels. I think it's heels you kick up and shoes you kick off. But for the time being I'm just trying to stay in the main channel.

He smashes a few more flies, wipes the blood on his trousers. "Oh, you know. Lighten up, goof off." He jabs at my arm with a bloody paw. "Rock 'n' roll."

"I'm trying," I say. "You mean be an idiot like you?"

"That's right," he says, dipping back into the cookies. "You sure you don't want some?"

"No thanks. I'll pass."

The popcorn sky fades and turns a deep purple. As soon as it gets dark, Jerry takes over below. He is getting nervous. I can feel it. It's palpable on board. He doesn't like the river at night. There are deadheads and wing dams and snags you can't see. It's not like when Mark Twain traveled in these parts, but both Jerry and Tom assure me you can still meet your maker here.

On our radio we chat with a nearby tow, the *Mark Schonen*. He's pushing a six-hundred-foot barge downstream—one of the first barges, riding hard and heavy downstream, we've seen. Even I recognize his Cajun accent by now. We've been passing him and following him in the storm we were in all day. Now it is the blackest of nights and Jerry has a big frown on his face. The tow captain tells us to follow him and he'll get us to a marina in Keokuk.

I don't understand what we're doing, but, as it gets darker, we travel in the *Mark Schonen*'s wake at five miles per hour. I find this pace in the darkness so tedious I could scream. "Why're we going so slowly?" I ask Jerry. I am ready to eat, relax, walk on the planet Earth. And once again I am longing for a shower.

"Because he knows the way," Jerry says, his voice tinged with annoyance. "Because he has radar." His eyes are fixed on the river and he hasn't got time or the inclination to talk to me. We follow at this impossibly slow speed, only slightly faster than if we cut our engines altogether. We hang back in the wake of the tow and barge and in the blackness it feels as if this will take forever.

It is close to nine o'clock when the towboat pilot shines his beacon at a landing. We gaze toward the west bank and there is a dock. As we approach Keokuk, the towboat lights our way. Once he sees that we've spotted the landing, he gives two blasts of his horn, then he disappears into the darkness, but for a long time we can see his wake.

# MAYFLIES

"WHEN I was a boy, there was but one permanent ambition among my comrades in our village on the west bank of the Mississippi River. That was to be a steamboatman," Twain writes in *Life on the Mississippi.* He tells of the two packet boats a day that chugged into Hannibal. One came from St. Louis. The other from Keokuk. And after those boats came and went, "the day was a dead and empty thing."

As we pull into the marina at the Keokuk Yacht Club, I note the significant absence of steamboats or river life or fanfare. It is hard to imagine this Iowa town as a bustling dock as it was in Twain's time. But indeed the huge Victorian homes that line the bluffs, which we will see in the morning, attest to Keokuk's glorious past.

I muse over what has become of these river towns. I recall my conversation with Cindy back in Muscatine and think how the malls and the automobile and the end of the steamboat business and the pearl button factories have decimated them all. As we pull up to the dock, Sally greets us. She's a friendly dark-haired woman with a slightly weathered look as if she's been at this marina too long, and she tells us we've got to change docks if we want to fuel up, which we do. "Fuel dock's back there," Sally says.

"Well, Mary," Jerry says. "You wanta fuel up or you wanta hop off?"

"I'll go check out the facilities," I tell them as they move the boat. Up at the marina there's a nice outdoor shower stall, but it's filled with cobwebs and spiders and I decide to wait for morning when I can see them. The marina restaurant is empty except for a few stragglers who have clearly had one too many, listening to old Kenny Rogers tunes. The smell of cigarette smoke fills the room. The only available food is frozen pizza. One wall is covered with historic pictures. Apparently the Keokuk Lock and Dam 19, which is just below us, holds the title in *The Guinness Book of World Records* for Small Craft Lockthrough (88 small craft). This achievement is immortalized in a photo of dozens of people in their bathing suits and Bermuda shorts, holding lines. What a contrast this is to the empty river we've been on, so devoid of life.

I decide to skip the frozen pizza and return to the boat and scramble some eggs. As I see it, outside of eating a can of Tantalizin' Turkey, which I refuse to do, this is my only viable food option. "You guys want scrambled eggs?" I ask. They are bent over the engine with a flashlight and give me what I can only interpret as disgruntled shrugs. "Gonna get me some of that frozen pizza," Tom says, clearly happy about this.

We are docked beside a pool of standing water and there's a hint of sewage in the air. The dock is illumined with yellow floodlights and the outside of our boat is covered with what looks like a million mosquitoes. I hate mosquitoes. The only one of God's creatures I truly despise and will kill with glee are mosquitoes. Despite whatever purpose they might serve in the food chain, I have spent too many sleepless nights in shoddy hotels and sleeping bags to have any affection or sympathy for them whatsoever.

I slip into the cabin, careful to close the door quickly. I make sure that, despite the heat, all the windows are secured. The only light in the cabin comes from the dock and the bathroom, which I assume one of the boys used while I was up at the marina. These are private fellows and this is their way.

Hungry, I put butter into the omelette pan from Goodwill. When it's sizzling, I pour in my Southwestern egg beaters, drizzle a little cheese on top. I'm stirring them up when I notice the buzzing sound, but I don't pay it much heed. But as I dump the eggs onto a paper plate, the buzzing grows louder. Now I glance up and see thousands of these mosquito-like things, coating the ceiling and windows of the cabin.

As my gaze falls on the gap between the head and the wall, I see them flying out of that lit room. I know it wasn't me who left the light on, but I'm not assigning blame. Not exactly. Hesitantly I open the bathroom door and am greeted with a million of these creatures, lining every inch of the walls. We are completely invaded.

I don't know what they are. They look like mosquitoes and they buzz, but they don't seem to bite. At least they have not bitten me yet, though my skin crawls and I feel as if they are all over me, inside my loose-fitting linen pants, my T-shirt. They have been drawn into the bathroom by the light through an open window. Jerry has yet to install the screens, which are stored in the hold. "It's on the 'to do' list," he likes to say.

Though I do not want to do this, I scream. It is a very loud scream and Jerry yells back, "What is it? What's wrong?"

I race onto the deck where they are still bent over the engines, fiddling with some belts, and the creatures, to which they are oblivious, buzz behind their backs and into the bathroom by the thousands. I shove the bathroom window shut. "I'm sorry," I tell them, "but I'm having a girl moment."

"A girl moment?" They look at me oddly and I can tell they're thinking hormonal.

"There are bugs," I explain. "Everywhere."

Tom and Jerry give each other one of those looks that men exchange when a woman reveals a certain kind of weakness. When a mouse crosses her path or she doesn't know what a red flag in the end zone means. These men are hungry and tired and they have little patience for me. "I'll check it out," Tom says with a sigh, not even bothering to hide his exasperation.

I stand on the deck, hyperventilating and trying to figure out how I'm going to spend the night on the boat, when I hear Tom shout, "Holy shit! This is the worst thing I've ever seen!"

"I told you!" I shout back at him. "I told you it was bad!"

I will learn later that the bugs are mayflies. They live as worms on the river's bottom for up to three years in their larval state. Then for some inexplicable reason they burst onto the adult scene and mate in midair. The females will lay their eggs on the river's surface and promptly die. The males have a few more hours, kicking themselves, I'm sure, under their mayfly breath, "If only I knew."

But sadly mayflies cannot speak. They have no mouths. Though they look like mosquitoes and buzz like them, mayflies do not bite. But they hatch by the millions, especially around brackish standing water, such as where we are moored, and they are attracted to light. This is what I have learned—and all I ever want to know—about mayflies.

Jerry looks at me, at the screenless window of the head, and the light that's been left on. Sheepishly he turns away as the massacre begins. We hear Tom, swearing, swatting, banging, killing whatever he can. He curses and smashes. A few moments later when Tom emerges from the bathroom, sweating and wiping his brow, the floor is a carpet of dead bugs. "This is absolutely disgusting," I say. This time no one argues with me. "I need to vacuum."

"I need some frozen pizza," Tom says.

Though I almost never eat pizza, except on this journey, it seems, I agree that, under the circumstances, it's the best idea. We head up to the restaurant where we all sidle up to the bar. Sally pours us beers, though Tom has, as always, his diet Dew. We order a few frozen pizzas, which Sally sticks in the microwave and in the end are rather tasty. I find myself adjusting to crust.

Jeff who works with Sally pours us our next round of beers. Jeff has several piercings and wears a strand of cowrie shells around his neck and it is obvious to me that he's gay. He's probably the only gay guy in Keokuk, where I'm pretty sure it's not an easy place to be gay.

After we devour three frozen pizzas and a few beers, I ask—no, beg—Jeff if I can use their Internet and check my mail, which I haven't done since I left Brooklyn. He says, "Sure," and, as soon as I log on, I see that I have 137 unanswered messages. As I'm skimming through, deleting the junk, Jeff and I chat.

"So what's it like . . . ," I ask him as I'm waiting for my e-mail to load, "living here in Keokuk?"

"Well," he says with a little snicker, "I'm gay."

I'm a little surprised he said it right off the bat. Clearly he doesn't mind going there. "Yeah, I thought so. . . ."

"Oh yeah?" He laughs. "What gave it away?"

"The cowrie shells," I tell him.

He laughs again. "Yeah, I was married for a while. Now that wasn't going to work out. I tried, but it just wasn't. . . . We're still friends. She lives in town here. But it's okay. Thought my dad was going to disinherit me, though." I was wondering if Jeff meant disown, but, whatever, it didn't sound as if it was easy for him. "But you know, we worked it out. Took a little time."

"What about a social life? What do you do around here?"

He fondles his cowrie beads. "Oh, I don't have much of a social life up here. I drive down to St. Louis for that." Suddenly it occurs to me that we are in range of St. Louis if Jeff can drive there and have a life.

As we're leaving, Sally gives us two flyswatters, a can of bug fumigator, and a beautiful watermelon. Back on board, we put the watermelon in a cooler, then for about half an hour continue our nighttime activity of swatting black flies and mayflies and whatever other flies that have come into our cabin since Nauvoo, and I vacuum.

"We should fumigate," Jerry says, seeing that I'm getting nowhere fast and look like some kind of lunatic, flailing about in the air. I don't want to because I'm not looking forward to sleeping in a fumigated cabin where we can't open the windows, but there seems to be no choice. There are still bugs everywhere. I take the bug bomb that Sally gave us, hold my nose, and spray the cabin.

Then we grab a couple beers and slip onto deck. Tom, of course, is sound asleep on his flybridge. Jerry and I are thinking we'll have a chat, then go to sleep, but from somewhere in the marina comes the sound of incredibly loud rap music. "I don't believe this," I say.

"Let's go check it out," Jerry says.

We take our beers and head toward the sound of this hip-hop music. We follow the pier beside a pool of stagnant water (a happy breeding ground for mayflies, I'm sure) to where the sound is coming from. I anticipate a horde of wasted teenagers holding a wild party, but we come upon two forty-something couples at a picnic table covered with a white tablecloth and candles. They are, however, sloshed out of their minds.

"Hey there," they say, surprised to have company. "Wanta join us?" one of the men asks.

"Is our music keeping you awake?" says the other. It would keep the devil awake, I want to say, but I refrain.

"Oh, no," Jerry replies. "We're just out for a stroll." I look at my watch. We are walking down a short pier past putrid water at midnight, but they're too drunk to wonder. Another nautical term comes to mind. Three sheets to the wind.

"So, you folks like a drink?" We raise our beers and decline. "You traveling?"

We explain our mission. They are old friends on a weekend jaunt up from Quincy, where they're from. "Nice town," the blond wife says.

"Yeah, my dad used to live there. How so?"

"Oh, it's just peaceful. It's a pretty place to live."

"It's safe," her husband says.

"The people are very friendly," the other wife adds. "We moved to Quincy from Springfield and I've found the people very nice."

Her husband laughs. "Well, that was over twenty years ago."

For some reason she blushes when he says this.

"You know the river changes below here," one of the men says. "Gets narrower and faster."

Jerry nods, taking this in. "Hey, do you people know an island somewhere between Quincy and Hannibal where someone could have a farm?" Jerry asks this drunken crew. I look at him oddly, surprised he has remembered. "Didn't your father go to that island?" he asks me.

"Yes, it was an island. There was a farm. Somewhere between Hannibal and Quincy."

"Let's see . . ." Between sips of Jim Beam and Coke, they rattle off names. Goose Island, Hogback, Cottonwood, Deadman. "Now you could have a farm on Poage, couldn't you, dear?" one of the men offers.

His blond, demure wife who can barely sit up without falling backward into the river nods. "You could. Or you could have one on Ward."

"Ward," the other man concludes. "It would definitely be Ward."

I realize listening to them that the truth is I don't know. My father never told me the name. It wasn't in his final note to me. If I don't know it now, I never will know. There is no asking. I am stunned by how final this feels. "Well, thank you," I say. "I'll keep an eye out."

They've turned the music off and want to know more of our adventure. We tell them about the storm. We tell them we've anchored on beaches. They look at us amazed as if Lewis and Clark just stumbled upon them on this pier. "We didn't know you could do that," one of the husbands says. They show us their boats—narrow cruisers named *Young and Reckless* and *Loverboy II*, with sleeping areas below. I'm wondering about *Loverboy I*, but am reluctant to ask.

"Well," Jerry says, after our tour, "we're gonna get some shut-eye."

"Yeah," they slobber, blowing out their candles. "Us too."

"Nice chatting with you," Jerry says.

"Now you have a safe journey and spend a little time in Quincy."

"You do that," another one says. "Check out Quincy. It's a real good town."

"And put us in your book!" one of the husbands shouts.

"I will," I say. As we head back to the boat, I mention to Jerry that they were very drunk.

"Yes, they were," he says, "but they were nice too."

That night I can't sleep. Though I resist at first, I take a sleeping pill, but even as I drift off, mouthless mayflies buzz in my head.

❧

In the morning we're up early, cleaning out the boat. I'm vacuuming more dead bugs. Tom's swabbing the deck. Jerry's busy installing our screens. "Let's water her down and push the bugs out the scuppers," Jerry instructs Tom, who is on his hands and knees with a washcloth and gives Jerry an "aye aye, Sir," salute.

Afterward we head to the showers. Tom takes all of his belongings (he does this every time he showers)—his suitcase and Samantha Jean. She gets a bath whenever he does. I go into the girls' shower, where, with a paper towel, I wipe down the cobwebs and the mayflies that cling to them. The shower stall itself is papered in faux library wallpaper. I have *Bleak House, Mrs. Dalloway,* and *The Sound and the Fury* in mine. When I return to the boat, Jerry is at work, installing all of our screens.

Keokuk Lock and Dam 19 is unusually long—twelve hundred feet—and I can see how it could set a small craft record for lockage. But we are alone in this enormous space and we breeze through. Two white pelicans swimming together greet us on the other side. Afterward we hit a storm and are once more confined to the cabin.

At Mile 359 the rain stops and the river takes on a smooth, glossy flow. We're coming up to Lock and Dam 20 where they show a high water mark of 27.69 feet in the 1993 flood. As we are waiting for lockage, a big fish leaps into the air. Jerry says it's an Asian carp that escaped from a fish farm during the floods.

These carp are merciless creatures and have been making their way north. They have forged upstream through the Mississippi and up its tributaries. Their favorite food seems to be all the fish that inhabit the Great Lakes and their presence in these waters has become a major ecological concern.

We breeze through the lock and dam. Now the houses that line the banks are all on stilts, the results of the 1993 floods. My routines have become, well, routines, simple and defined. Rise, make tasteless brew. Clean cabin. Wash dishes. Wipe dead bugs, of which there seem to be many, off the counters. Fold and refold my clothes. Read, relax. Paint or write. Or just sit at the bow and stare straight ahead. In the afternoon I will pilot if Jerry allows it. The river carries me forward in its relentless course. We are approaching my father's territory and his presence looms. The drunken people from the night before were right: The stream narrows. It's not nearly as wide as it is up north and it seems to quicken its flow.

As we move past the lock and dam and Quincy isn't far, Jerry and I pause on the bow, just gazing at the river. We are silent for a few moments and then I ask Jerry what scuppers are. "Scuppers," I say. "You used the word this morning. You told Tom to push the dead bugs out of the scuppers."

Jerry nods, remembering. "It's those holes in the gunwales," he says. "They're so you can swab the deck. Rinse it off and the water will go out. You know you can put scupper valves on so that a boat doesn't take on a lot of water. I heard about a guy once who had a small commercial vessel, nice little boat he used to take people out fishing. He put scupper covers on, but he put them on backward. They ran into a storm and they took on a lot of water, but it didn't drain. They didn't know where the water was coming from and before they figured it out, they lost an engine, which can happen if you get an engine soaked. And then the boat broached and then—" Jerry makes a whistling sound through his teeth and a hand motion which seems to indicate a boat going down.

"And then?"

"Two people drowned. Just a little mistake, but that's what can happen if you do something wrong. You don't even have time to bend over and kiss the ground."

~ 29 ~

WHEN I was young, my mother had a passion for Abraham Lincoln. She was proud of the fact that the president who freed the slaves came from her home state of Illinois. I don't remember my mother reading that much literature when I was a girl, but she had shelves and shelves of books on Lincoln. Biographies, historical accounts, his speeches and writings. She was actually a bit of a Lincoln scholar, definitely a buff. She used to say if television existed during the Lincoln-Douglas debates, he would never have been elected because he was ugly and had a high, squeaky voice.

Later, for mysterious reasons, her affections for powerful men switched to such role models as O. J. Simpson and William Kennedy Smith, but in my formative years it was Lincoln who attracted her. My parents were actually married on the same date as Lincoln was assassinated—a fact that, despite my mother's interest in the president from Illinois, was perhaps lost on them, but not on me.

When I was ten or so and my brother seven or eight, our mother took us to Springfield, Illinois. We saw the Lincoln museum, the capital building, the log cabin where Abe was said to have lived. I recall that log cabin. How it seemed so tiny for a man who grew to be so big in every sense of the word. My mother was quick to point out that such greatness came from such modest beginnings. We paused before the table where Lincoln as a young student read by candlelight late into the night.

My mother was a progressive in her politics. This was one of the many ways she and my father differed. He was a lifelong conservative (he and I fought bitterly during the Vietnam War years), though he voted for Clinton and Kerry before he died. But my mother espoused liberal causes, even if she did not exactly live by them in her own life.

Once, though, after the Chicago riots of 1968, she accosted a group of Weathermen at a lunch counter. She asked them how many people were members of their organization and they gave her a rather small number. Then she asked how many people rioted during the Democratic convention and they gave her a much larger number. "Oh, just like my synagogue," she told the scruffy crew of boys as she paid for her cup of coffee and sandwich. "Nobody pays dues, but everyone shows up for the holidays." The only time I ever saw her weep over anyone was when John F. Kennedy was killed. And she always forgave Bill Clinton his sins, which she considered "nobody's business but his own."

Though I cannot say that my relationship with my mother has ever been uncomplicated, she always emphasized reading, learning, knowledge of the world. Not that she was a big reader, but I was. As a girl I read everything I could get my hands on. When I was reading a book I truly loved, my mother let me stay home from school. She wrote letters to my teachers saying I was ill and needed to stay in bed. At least the latter part was true. I finished *Little Women, Jane Eyre,* and *Gone With the Wind* in this way. When I returned to school and the nurse asked how I was feeling, I had to remember to lie.

We leave the main channel and sail up a tight canal past Bay Island. Egrets line the banks as we make our way to the Quincy Bay Small Boat Harbor, where we tie up at the courtesy dock. Tom and Jerry opt for a long lunch at the marina restaurant, but I want to see the town.

I stroll through Kessler's Park along the river up to the town square. In the shade of tall trees I stand before the statue of Stephen A. Douglas. It was here that they had their sixth debate. In a tone filled with irony and intelligence, Lincoln drove home his legal arguments against slavery and stated as he would so many times that the Constitution of the United States declares that all men are created equal.

I have to admit that Quincy is, as the drunken people on the boat said the night before, a nice town. It is true that its main street is spelled Maine Street (only later do I realize that Vermont and New Hampshire precede it). The dresses on display in the shop windows are circa 1950 and even then I'm not sure my mother would have worn them, but the town square is lovely and I enjoy the shade. I'm standing beneath the trees, wondering if my father ever stood here. And where he might have lived and worked.

I am not on some secret discovery, some mystery tour. I do not expect to unearth anything I didn't know. I doubt that he had a clandestine past or lived another life, though he played his personal feelings close to the vest. I just would like to walk in his steps one more time and perhaps better understand a person I'm not sure I really knew.

Two elderly women are sitting on a park bench and for some reason I think they might know. "Excuse me," I ask. They look identical as if they must be sisters. "But do either of you know where an old department store might have been?"

"Oh maybe you mean the old Carson Pirie store?"

"I think it was over there on the corner of Fifth."

The other shakes her head. "I'm not sure it was."

"Well, it was definitely on a corner nearby."

Then the younger one says, "You should go over to the library. You know, they have a local history room. Maybe you can find out something there. . . ."

I head along Maine, then down Sixth until I find the library. When I walk into the library, I am struck by the coolness inside. Air conditioning. I've been in the heat and elements for days. My skin is bronzed. I am wearing no makeup. I am filthy, sweating, and I've been more or less in the same clothes, not to mention underwear, for days. Suddenly I find myself in a room full of people in ironed blouses, crisp linen shorts. They have pedicures and shaved legs.

I am feeling like a derelict and must look the part as I ask the librarian if someone can help me with some Quincy, Illinois, history. She tells me that Iris Nelson is the librarian who works in the historic section and points through some double glass doors.

Iris Nelson is shelving some old phone books in the historic section of the library. She's an attractive blond woman, wearing a salmon-colored blouse and beige slacks. I'm in baggy pants, a T-shirt, and flip-flops. I tell her that my dad lived in Quincy and may have worked at Carson Pirie Scott. I want to see if there is any record. Iris begins to take down telephone books and census reports from the early 1920s. But I am fixated on her manicure. As she sits across the table from me, I stare at her nails— perfectly trimmed, painted a shade of salmon pink to match her blouse. Now I do feel like someone who has just gotten off the boat, which, of course, I have.

We can't find my father's name in the resident census or employers' directories, but I tell Iris that I am interested in the history of Quincy and Hannibal. She starts talking about Illinois as a free state and how Missouri came into the Union as a slave state. Iris sits down. "You know," she says, "the trailhead for the Underground Railroad was here in Quincy. There is a great abolitionist tradition in this town."

I recall my high school history days and some of the things my mother taught me. Illinois, which had been part of the Northwest Territory, which included Ohio, Indiana, Michigan, and Wisconsin, became a state in 1818. The Northwest Ordinance of 1787 forbade slavery in the territory or in the states that were eventually formed as a result of it. While Illinois had seen some slavery under the French and British rule, it would soon die out. It would continue in some way in the form of "indentured servitude." But basically by 1839 the Illinois prairie was populated by farmers and artisans who had not practiced slavery in thirty years. Free people throughout Illinois worked for wages and liberal-minded settlers came from all over the continent to live in Illinois.

But Missouri was another story and its history is diametrically opposed to its neighbor across the river. Missouri was part of the Louisiana Purchase, which Thomas Jefferson had bought from France for fifteen million dollars. Under the French and Spanish, slavery had been allowed in the territory and it was deeply entrenched. When Missouri sought to become a state in 1817, it asked to enter as a slave state. However, this would have

upset the balance between free and slave states. After much debate in Congress, the Missouri Compromise was reached. Missouri was admitted as a slave state and the northern portion of
Massachusetts was carved out to become the free state of Maine.

From their beginnings Illinois was a free state and Missouri
a slave state and what separated them was a short mile of river.
No other state this far north was a slave state and Missouri essentially became an island of slavery in an otherwise free territory.
As Iris Nelson is explaining to me about Quincy's role in the
Underground Railroad, I'm thinking about *The Adventures of
Huckleberry Finn* and Jim, the runaway slave. At one point in
the novel Huck considers bringing Jim across the river, but then
makes some excuse. The bounty hunters might catch Huck this
way. But in truth, as Iris explains it to me, many slaves made
their way from Missouri to the start of the Underground Railroad in Quincy in this way. It would have been a sensible thing
for Huck to try.

"So," I ask Iris, "why didn't Huck just bring Jim across the
river? It would just be a mile, right, and he'd reach freedom?"

Iris gives me a knowing smile. "Right. But then Mark Twain
wouldn't have had a story to tell, would he?"

After an hour or so I leave the library. I learned nothing
about my father's presence here, but I did learn some things
about Mark Twain and slavery in Missouri. Now my idea of
going to Cairo on the *River Queen* feels tainted. As I walk back
into town, it's boiling hot and I'm dying for an iced coffee, but
nothing is open. I head back toward the river.

We push on into the hot dry heat of the late afternoon.
There's twenty river miles and one lock and dam between
Quincy and Hannibal and Jerry wants to make it before dark. As
we head south, Jerry is poring over our maps. It's broad daylight
so it can't be that he's worried about shoals or getting lost. "What
is it, Jer?" I ask. "What're you looking for?"

"I'm looking for that island your dad told you about." The island. I'd almost forgotten that it would be between Quincy and
Hannibal. But Jerry remembered. Now I'm looking too. Some-

where in this stretch of twenty miles is the island my father visited with his friends. I want to know its name. I want to know where it is. I wish I could call him and ask.

I shake my head. "It's all right," I tell Jerry. "We can't really know, can we?"

And Jerry nods, agreeing with me. "Nope," he says, a resigned sound to his voice, "I guess we can't."

# HANNIBAL

~ 30 ~

"You know," my father began, "the river is different up here than it is in Hannibal." I'd taken him out to breakfast at Heinemann's in Whitefish Bay in Wisconsin. My father loved breakfast and I was glad to have him alone. My mother was jealous of the attention he always received. It made her angry when we'd sit and talk to him, and she believed, perhaps rightly so, that we were ignoring her. But, as my father liked to say, you couldn't get a word in "edgewise" if she was around.

That morning my father was all dressed up in a brown camel coat, brown fedora, tweed jacket, and silk tie. He was cold even though it was spring. At that time in his life, he was always cold.

We both ordered scrambled eggs, hash browns, crisp, and wheat toast. He was living dangerously and asked for a glass of fresh squeezed juice. "I'm going to be 103 years old," he told the waitress, and she almost fell on the floor.

"I'm going to squeeze that orange juice myself," she said and she went to pay special attention to our order. I was asking him about the river. It didn't take much prodding. He started talking to me about Hannibal. "In Hannibal you can see across it. Up north here there's all these islands. You don't even know where the other side is. You know I lived in Hannibal, don't you?"

"Yes, of course, I know." He told me about living in Hannibal a dozen times. In fact he's told all of his stories dozens of times and it seemed as if he'd reached the end of the line with no more to tell. I braced myself for a rerun.

"Well, I lived in Hannibal. Right next to the house Mark Twain lived in. He'd been dead, oh, ten years when I lived there, and I don't think he'd been back to Hannibal in twenty, but they still remembered him. You know why they called him Mark Twain, right?"

"It's the pilot's cry when they're marking the depths . . ."

"That's right. His real name was Samuel Clemens." Of course I knew all of this. I knew that Samuel Clemens tried out many pseudonyms before he landed on the one that became his signature. "See, if you listen, you learn. Anyway, his house wasn't any bigger than four booths in this restaurant."

"It must be a museum now," I said.

"Well, I don't know how more than one person at a time could go through it. It wasn't bigger than your upstairs bathroom. Anyway I worked in retail. Ladies' garments."

"You mean like dresses, blouses?" I actually didn't know my father worked in ladies' garments.

"Shoes, slips, bras. The whole thing."

"What year was that, Dad?"

"Oh, it was 1921 or 1922. No, it must have been later because that spring, just before I moved to Hannibal, our downstairs neighbor murdered her husband. My parents were very good friends with him. You know, he took her on a cruise, then came home and he's shaving one morning and she blows his head off."

"That's awful," I said, shocked.

"Seems he brought his mistress along on the cruise as well. She was in the next stateroom." My father gave a wave of his hand. "That kind of thing happened all the time."

"It did?" I asked, amazed. I wanted to know more about the downstairs neighbor and his mistress and the wife who blew him away, but our eggs came and my father was on another trajectory. He poked at his hash browns. "I wanted them crisp."

"Shall we send them back?"

He gave a wave of his hand. "Naw, it's all right." But I could tell he was disappointed. He took a few bites of his eggs and the hash browns. "Not so bad. But I like them crisp." Then he took a sip of juice. "Now that's good juice. Here, have some." He pushed the glass my way. "Where was I? Let's see, I was twenty-three years old. So it was later. It was 1925. Anyway, I worked for Klein's Department Store and one day Mr. Klein came in. He came all the way from New York. They were a chain of retail stores. I'm sure you've heard of them. Klein's."

I nodded, though I wasn't sure I'd ever heard of Klein's.

"Anyway, Mr. Klein came in. He was bald as a bat. At that time I had a full head of hair, you know. In 1925 I had hair as thick as yours. So Mr. Klein comes in and the first thing he does is yank on my hair. He says, 'How'd you get a head of hair like that? How come I'm rich and bald and you work for me and haven't got a pot to piss in and you've got a head of hair like that?' Mr. Klein liked to joke around, though I only met him once or twice in the year I lived in Hannibal. Anyway, I had hair then, in 1925, but by the time I was thirty-three, ten years later, all my hair was gone. You know that, right? You've got the portrait."

"The portrait?"

"You know, the picture. We called them portraits then. That's because you went to a studio and sat for them. It wasn't a painting, but we called them portraits. That picture of me. There were only three copies made and one of them is hanging in your house. On your gallery wall."

The waitress came by with her manager to make sure every-thing was all right. "Your eggs are getting cold," she said. "Shall I heat them up for you?"

"Naw, I'm just talking," my father replied in his most polite voice.

"He's 102 years old," she told her boss.

"You must be kidding," the boss said, shaking my father's hand. "What's your secret?"

"Nothing in excess," my father said, admonishing them both.

I was watching their little exchange, trying to envision this portrait of my father. I have a whole wall of pictures. Ancestors and new arrivals. Those gangsterlike shots of my father from the 1920s. My husband's family. Our daughter floating on a raft. Then I see it. In a dark suit, pinstriped shirt, his hands folded across each other, a soft smile on his face. He's holding something in his hand—a pipe, I think. Something he doesn't smoke. I've had this picture for many years. I've probably walked by it ten thousand times, but I've never given it much thought.

"So I never told you about this portrait, did I?"

I shook my head, nibbling on my now cold toast. "It was from 1935 and I was working on the Chicago Board of Trade. On the summer weekends we'd go out to Union Pier and there was this girl from Memphis. But her family summered in Chicago. They had a house on Lake Michigan and we became friendly. She was from the Bloch family. I'm sure you've heard of the Blochs from Memphis."

I nodded, though I never had.

"A very rich girl. Anyway, I dated this Bloch girl a few times one summer, but then the summer was over and she was going back to Memphis."

"Were you still in Hannibal?"

My father waved his hand in the air. "No, you aren't paying attention. I told you. I was in Chicago. At the Board of Trade. Hannibal was a long time ago. This is about the portrait."

I wasn't exactly paying attention. I thought he was telling me a river story, but now his tale had taken a bend I hadn't expected to Union Pier and a girl from Memphis I'd never heard him mention before.

"Anyway, this girl, the Bloch girl, her father committed suicide in 1929. She was a pretty girl. She had red hair like a fire and very green eyes. She reminded me of a party. She was bright and pretty. I liked her and I suppose I felt badly for her because of what had happened in her life. So when she was going back to Memphis I asked her if, when the holidays rolled around, she'd like a gift from me. If there wasn't something I could send her so she would remember me. And she said that she would like a portrait of me. That was all. She just wanted a portrait of me. Now there was this very famous portrait photographer in Chicago, his name was Seymour. He did all kinds of photographs and he was very expensive. So I went over to Seymour's studio one day . . ."

I wasn't completely following the story now about how my father went over to Seymour's studio. I was thinking about the neighbor whose wife blew him away and the rich girl whose father killed himself and who wanted a picture of my father to remember him by.

"What happened to her father?"

"Well," my father said, taking a bite of his eggs, "that's an interesting story. You see, this man, her father, Mr. Bloch, he had a grocery store in Memphis. He was quite successful, but he heard that there was a new kind of grocery store starting up in Minneapolis. A grocery store where employees didn't wait on you. Instead you served yourself. So he told one of his employees that he wanted him to go up to Minneapolis and find out just what kind of new grocery store was being started up in Minneapolis. So the employee went up and said he'd be back in a week or two. Well, a week went by, two, four, six weeks. That employee never came back."

"What happened to him?"

"I don't know. They never found him." My father gave me an impatient look. "This isn't a story about the employee who disappeared." My father made a little explosion sign with his fingers. "It's about the portrait. But since you asked, I'm telling you about Mr. Bloch."

I nod. "Okay."

"So Mr. Bloch sends another employee up to find the one that never came home. His name was Clarence Saunders and he told Mr. Bloch that in Minneapolis the grocery stores were changing and someone had an idea called self-service. He told Mr. Bloch all about how the customers never had to wait for the next clerk but could take the items off the shelves themselves. Butter, rice, beans. They just reached up and took it and put it into a cart. Saved a lot of time. Well, Saunders explained this to

Mr. Bloch and they opened a store together. It was called the Piggly Wiggly and it was the first supermarket. Ever heard of that?" I said I had and my father seemed pleased. "Well," he said, "at least you know something."

"But what about her father?" This story, like so many of my father's, begins on the river, then meanders away much as the river side-winds, leaves its bed, only to come back to itself downstream.

"If you listen, I'll tell you. You keep interrupting me. I'm losing the thread. God, it's freezing in here." He pulled his coat around his thin, frail body. "Anyway, they did very well with the Piggly Wiggly until 1929 and the market crashed. The two men lost everything, and Mr. Bloch, who had a 250,000-dollar life insurance policy, jumped out of a window so his family could have the money. He didn't want his family to have to start over. That's when they changed the law about life insurance policies and suicide. In 1929. And that's how his daughter became rich."

He paused to take another bite. "Good eggs," he said, "but they're ice cold. Anyway, all this girl wanted was a picture of me. I would've sent her a gold bracelet if she'd asked, but that's not what she wanted. She wanted a portrait. So I went over to Mr. Seymour's one day. And there was a doctor there. A famous Chicago doctor. I don't remember his name. But he was having his picture taken. Mr. Seymour was taking it like this and like that." My father turns and dodges, showing me how Mr. Seymour was taking pictures. "Anyway, the doctor recognized me and he says to Mr. Seymour, 'Oh, you have to take that man's picture because he's a famous man. He's on the Board of Trade. You've got to take his picture.'

"Well, while I was waiting for Mr. Seymour to take my picture, I was chatting with his girl and I asked her how much it would cost me to have three pictures taken and she said, 'Oh, three pictures, that would be fifteen dollars.' Well, that sounded okay to me so I told him to go ahead and take my picture. So Mr. Seymour, he smooths down my hair and hands me a pipe. I never smoked a pipe, but I'm holding it in the portrait. He takes my picture for fifteen, twenty minutes, then I leave. About a week later he sends me the proofs and I pick out the one picture."

"The one that's hanging on my wall."

"That's right. So, anyway, I order three copies of the picture and send him the fifteen dollars and a few days later Mr. Seymour calls me up. He's yelling and screaming. 'What's this fifteen dollars? These pictures cost more like a hundred and fifty dollars.' Anyway, Mr. Seymour goes on, blah blah blah, but I tell him talk to your girl. She told me fifteen dollars and fifteen dollars it is. So eventually he agreed and that's how I got the portrait for fifteen instead of a hundred and fifty."

"What happened to the pictures?"

"Well, you have one, that's the one I kept. My mother had one. And I sent one to the girl."

"And what happened to that one?"

"Oh, she probably tore it up. I don't know." He took the last bite of his breakfast. He'd cleaned his plate. "I never heard from her again. I wasn't going to marry her, anyway. I was a confirmed bachelor then. I shoulda stayed that way. Believe me." He tapped my hand. "Of course, I wouldn't have had you." My father shook his head. "I wish I could remember her first name. I think I broke her heart."

~ 31 ~

"AFTER ALL these years I can picture that old time to myself now, just as it was then," Mark Twain writes in one of the most nostalgic passages in American literature, "the white town drowsing in the sunshine of a summer's morning, the streets empty, or pretty nearly so." He was writing of Hannibal, his boyhood home. It had briefly been my father's home as well. Now we are, after ten days on the river, approaching.

Pulling into the small marina, Jerry manages to find the only slip to tie up to in the whole town. As he maneuvers the boat into the narrow passage for the marina, he's shaking his head. "This is literally the only place. If we hadn't found this spot," Jerry says, "we'd be spending the night somewhere else." He seems proud of himself.

I'm heading to a hotel for the night. I decided to do this long ago, but now I really want to. I am ready for land, running water, clean sheets. There is much fanfare as I leave, the boys giving me shouts and a big wave. "Adios, amigo!" they cry. "Hasta la vista!" as I trudge uphill, backpack bouncing on my back, then hang a left.

I come to Main Street—an avenue of souvenir shops, filled with Huck and Tom T-shirts, Mark Twain playing cards, statues of Tom and Huck, a bookstore that apparently only sells books by and about Mark Twain. The last run of the Hannibal trolley drives by and weary tourists wave. At the Becky Thatcher Restaurant a Tom & Huck's Taxi offers me a ride. I decline and instead dial the visitor's center, as a sign instructs, TOLL FREE 1-800-TOM-AND-HUCK, to ask about a hotel, but the tourist office is closed.

Ahead of me I see a big sign—the Hotel Clemens, of course—and I make my way there. In the entrance a giant cardboard cutout of Mark Twain greets me. For a moment I think it's real. Block letters read HEAR MARK TWAIN HIMSELF, LIVE, AT PLANTER'S THEATER.

Wow, they even channel him here.

I'd dreamed of Hannibal all my life. It was the stuff of my father's stories and of the books I read. But as I plodded in the heat of a late summer's afternoon toward my hotel, what greeted me was a theme park. I've come to a place of tacky souvenir shops and cardboard cutouts, of fake "real live" shows and tourist choo choo trains. Disneyland on the Mississippi.

I'm considering turning around and heading back to the boat, but I'm sure the boys already have the satellite dish going. And I am longing for a bed that doesn't roll and a hot meal that doesn't include pizza crust. But the truth is Hannibal is awful. And it is obsessed, literally obsessed, with its prodigal son (who left when he was a young man and only returned sporadically to revisit his boyhood haunts, to reclaim his river, and for photo opportunities).

If I lived here, I'd go mad. Already I feel like someone trapped in the fun house mirrors.

My guess is that at some point Hannibal, not wanting to become a washed-up town like Muscatine, with its pearl button factories closing, or casino-dependent like Dubuque, saw that it had one card to play and it played it well. But how many copies of *Huckleberry Finn* can one town handle? How many ice-cream parlors and postcard shops and souvenirs and T-shirts all with Mark Twain or some version of his famous characters (with the startling exception of the runaway slave, Jim) printed or emblazoned or in neon signs can one small sleepy river hamlet have? The answer is apparently thousands.

My innkeeper is a dour man whose family originated in Fiji and, for reasons he cannot explain to me, has landed here. Circumstances, he says. There is a long, complicated story that involves broken marriages and children scattered in cities throughout the Midwest. I'm getting more and more depressed when he asks to see my driver's license. He gazes at it and says, "Hey, your Yanks sure blew it, didn't they? They had a chance and they blew it."

I'm not quick on the draw here and think we are talking Civil War, but apparently he is a Yankees fan as in baseball and was disappointed in last year's World Series. I feel like sharing so I tell him that in fact I was rooting for the Red Sox and he gives me a look of disbelief that borders on disdain, then turns away, punches in some numbers, and hands me my key.

The hotel, which is several stories high and built around a gigantic atrium, seems deserted. An enormous Jacuzzi bubbles in the center of it. All of the rooms have large picture windows. Privacy is achieved with thick, dark curtains. As I take the glass elevator up to four, I think that this could be a very good setting for a horror film. But inside my room is cozy with big beds, clean, but scratchy, definitely not cotton sheets, and, most important for my purposes, a shower.

I shower like someone who doesn't know where her next shower is coming from, which I don't. Then I get dressed and flip through the guest directory for some dining suggestions. I decide to pass on Huck's Homestead Restaurant, which is right across the street, has lots of fluorescent lighting, and specializes in roast beef.

For my big night out I want more refined fare. When I ask the desk clerk for a recommendation, he says Lula Belle's. Located on Bird Street (the perfect name, it turns out), Lula Belle's is a former house of ill repute turned fine dining establishment, and I stroll there, a woman of leisure for the time being, under the violet sky of a warm summer's night.

In the entryway a pair of bloomers in a Lucite frame greets me. I am led into the main dining room, which is virtually empty, and realize I am the youngest person in the place by about thirty years. The maître d' tries to seat me at a tiny table for two, but I beg for a bigger one. Disgruntled, she seats me at a larger table for four and I thank her. "I can't tell you how much this means to me," I say.

Without a word she hands me a menu and I must admit I haven't seen so much attitude since I left New York. It's rather comforting. But I'm a little afraid of her too and decide not to ask what her favorite things are on the menu. I'll do it on my own. I'm going to pass on the "Awesome Blossom," which is a fried onion, the Missouri equivalent of the Texas Rose. And I know I'm not going to have the Bordello Bombe for dessert. I order a simple New York strip steak, medium rare, fries, and creamed spinach. A glass of cabernet. Comfort food. I am in heaven. For about five minutes, that is.

As I sit, I watch the others eat in a kind of culinary slow-motion silence. No one is speaking. In this dim-lit room, candles flickering, the voice of Dean Martin croons, "See the marketplace in old Algiers. Send me photographs and souvenirs. . . ." "Just remember 'til you're home again/You belong to me," I sing to myself, completing the lines. I must have made a little noise because an elderly woman, sitting at the next table, gives me a glare. The old loneliness creeps up on me. I hate eating alone and want to ask one of the old couples nearby if they'll adopt me.

I get up and wander around. Apparently Lula Belle's also runs a kind of bed and breakfast and one can partake of Belle's River Heritage Collection. Upstairs there's a Safari Room where you can let your inner tiger roam. There's the Renaissance Suite, good for wenches of all kinds, and over on Mark Twain Lake a private house can be had, for family reunions, I assume.

I'm envisioning myself a lady of the evening now in corset and bloomers, leading my wildebeest of a man into our safari room suite. I see a short whip, pith helmet. Lion tamer gear. Next I'm in red vinyl and fishnet hose. But again my vision grows gloomy as I think of all the women who have come to the end of their dreams in these rooms. Everything is less funny than it was. This restaurant oozes sadness from its floorboards. I miss my husband, but my thoughts drift to Tom and Jerry.

I picture them, with their feet up on my worktable, having chili and beans out of a can. The moon overhead, the river lapping at the hull. Samantha Jean licking bowls clean. I see them bedding down for the night. Jerry sipping a beer and Tom his diet Dew. Samantha Jean doing her big leap into Daddy's arms. I contemplate surprising them and returning to the boat.

The waiter signals that my steak is ready. Dutifully I sit down to eat, but my appetite is gone. The steak is, shall we say, not Peter Luger's, but I love the creamed spinach and am happy for real food. I walk back to the Hotel Clemens in darkness and all of Hannibal is shut down.

That night, as is often the case with me, I can't sleep. Or that is, I can sleep, but I wake up at three or four, not sure of what I want to do. I ponder taking something from my drug kit, but decide not to. I want to get an early start in the morning and this would just slow me down.

Since I have a television at my disposal, I check out the menu and find an educational program on the early discoverers. The program begins with a premise that has already been preoccupying me. Why do mining towns and river towns become ghost towns?

It is a show on Lewis and Clark and their journey up the Missouri. What is the frontier? the program asks. And the definition:

The frontier is opportunity in the form of property. Property, the narrator goes on to explain, was a European notion, invented by white men. The native peoples had no sense of property. To them the world belonged to all.

The frontier kept moving. For a time it was in upstate New York, it was the Alleghenies, it was Tennessee. It was the Mississippi. And then when John Charles Frémont introduced the notion of Manifest Destiny—the idea of taking the land and turning it into a profit-making business—it became the whole of the West.

I am engrossed in the program and it goes on for at least an hour, but when it ends I still can't get to sleep. It is the middle of the night and I want ice. I slip out of my room in my T-shirt and yoga pants with my ice bucket. The hotel is eerily quiet. Its atrium opens on the empty lobby, lined with plastic potted palms and plants. A weird gurgling noise comes from the Jacuzzi. I find the machine on my floor and push the button. The sound of ice dropping into the bucket reverberates throughout the atrium like cannon fire.

I expect guests to shoot out of their rooms, prepared to evacuate, but no one stirs. I tiptoe back into my room, make myself a glass of cold water, and try to sleep.

~ 32 ~

SOMEHOW THE Hotel Clemens is less creepy by day than it was by night. People actually seem to inhabit its rooms and they have filed in to, what else?, the Tom Sawyer Dining Room for a breakfast of cold cereal, toast, juices, and very watery, but better than what I've been consuming, coffee. It is true they all have bluish hair and wear pastel pantsuits, but it's human life and I'm glad to be among the living.

I take a table beside two elderly gentlemen, brothers it turns out, who are dressed in plaid shirts, pants with suspenders. They look like well-dressed farmers and they are deeply engrossed in the Hannibal visitor's guide. I hear one say, "Oh, the Gilded Cage. Now what do you think that is?"

The other shakes his head. Then spells out a word. "D-I-O-R-A-M-A. Never heard that word before," the older one says.

They are quiet for a few minutes, then I see they are open to a certain page of the brochure and completely engrossed. Given that I have the same visitor's guide in my pack, I take it out as well. I peruse the entries to see what has captured their eye as I wait for my English muffin to toast.

I breeze by Mark Twain's boyhood home, boyhood home gift shop, Huckleberry Finn House, Becky Thatcher Home, J. M. Clemens Law Office, Mark Twain Museum, Mark Twain Cave Complex, Mark Twain Riverboat, Richard Garey's Mark Twain himself, Twainland Express Sightseeing Tours, Sawyer's Creek Fun Park, Mark Twain Clopper, Tom Sawyer Diorama Museum, Tom and Huck Statue, Tom and Becky Appearances. But none of this has interested these dapper gentlemen.

They are very focused on the last page of the visitor's guide. A page called "Area Agri-Tourism." There is a photograph of a dozen or so cows' behinds, taken in such a way that leaves nothing to the imagination. These cows are being milked on a cow-carousel. "Don't know how they got them up on there," the older man with the white hair says.

"Must use some kind of a step-up ladder," the other replies.

"Well, takes time to get a cow to step up on a stool," the older one says.

Perhaps it's waiting for my muffin or the overwhelming feeling of needing a real moment that doesn't involve fictional characters, but I turn to these gentlemen. "I was wondering about this picture as well . . ." Actually I was wondering why the tourist office would put in such an explicit shot of the private parts of its dairy industry in its tourist paraphernalia, but these guys weren't fazed.

"Yeah, we always milked them in their stalls by hand. And they knew their stalls, let me tell you," the white-haired gentleman said. "Cow always knows her stall."

"This looks pretty complicated to me," the other brother says. "Cow's gotta get up on a platform. Probably doesn't even know where she's going."

"You know, our daddy was a dairy farmer and we've moved a lot of cows in my day. Our daddy gave up the business when I was still a boy, but he made a success of himself in everything he did."

"Is that so . . . ?"

"He opened a store and made a success with that. He started a farm equipment business and he made a success of that too."

The other brother nods. "That's right. Whatever Daddy did, he did it right." Though they are well into their sixties, I see the sadness in their eyes.

On the Muzak, Dolly Parton is singing "Those were the good old days, but I don't care to go back. . . ."

My muffin has popped up and I go to butter it just as the two men get up to leave. "Well, it was nice talking to you," I tell them.

"Sure nice talking to you too," they say.

⌒

In 217 B.C. Hannibal, the Carthaginian general, set out across the Apennines to conquer Rome. Hannibal and his men raped and pillaged for years, laying waste to town after town, during what came to be known as the Second Punic War, but he never managed to subjugate Rome. As I head out after breakfast, I stop at the visitor's center to inquire what connection might exist between the general and the town.

Several women are working at the desk, but no one is sure if or why Hannibal was named after this particular general. They are all shaking their beehived hair. "There is a town named Carthage nearby," one of them says. It appeared that no one had ever asked this question before. One of them gets a big reference book and looks it up. She relays to me that there is no relation to the general, but there is a Hannibal Creek.

As I'm leaving the visitor's center, the Twainland Express chugs past me with tourists sitting in the diminutive cars, chins on their knees. As I stroll through downtown Hannibal, I've lightened my load and only carry a small day pack and my journal.

Passing the local fire station I see I've missed the ham-and-bean dinner at the Methodist church two weeks ago. I descend toward the river where I come to a store that offers INTERNET CAFÉ AND CHRISTIAN GIFTS. But it is closed. I peer inside and see a strange array of Bibles, statues of Mary and Jesus, and computer stations.

Looking up, I realize that I am at the base of Cardiff Hill and begin to climb. It is a hot morning and my pack, though light, weighs me down as I make my way up the many concrete steps of the famed hill where Huck and Tom purportedly played. Twain's father died when he was eleven and the truth is all of his best stories come from his childhood. It is as if he was stuck at this moment and when he had exhausted all his childhood memories, he had little left of great importance to say. At the top of Cardiff Hill, I pause. From here I have a vista of the town and the river, which, as my father described it for me, I can see across.

For Twain the river was the source of all stories—of Tom and Huck and Jim, of lost boys and miserable slaves, of imprisonment and, ultimately, freedom. Twain learned the river and tried to navigate it. He took his pen name from his riverboating experiences, and the river stayed with him long after he'd moved from its banks. He never became a very good steamboatman, but his love of the river permeates his best work.

In his memoir he writes of "the great Mississippi, the majestic, the magnificent Mississippi, rolling its mile-wide tide along, shining in the sun; the dense forest away on the other side, the 'point' above the town, and the 'point' below, bounding the river-glimpse and turning it into a sort of sea, and withal a very still and brilliant and lonely one." And in *The Adventures of Huckleberry Finn*, Huck describes sunrise on the river before him: "Then the river softened up, away off, and warn't black anymore, but gray; you could see little dark spots drifting along—ever so far away . . . then the nice breeze springs up, and comes fanning you from over there, so cool and fresh, and sweet to smell." I wonder if this was the vantage point my father saw. If he climbed this hill himself, perhaps with a girl. For it is a romantic spot. If he stood here and felt the cool river breezes upon his face. But somehow I don't feel his presence. My father seems far away from this town of tourist attractions and T-shirts.

As I work my way down Cardiff Hill, I'm filled with the desire to check my mail. I'm wishing INTERNET CAFÉ AND CHRISTIAN GIFTS was open, but since it's not, I stop in at Becky's Old-Fashioned Ice Cream Parlor, where I pick up a few postcards.

The radio is on and I hear a news report for the first time in weeks. The president has declared parts of Iowa a disaster area and he's offering crop relief. Grain barges aren't moving. The grain is rotting in them. Then Rush Limbaugh comes on. I ask the woman who sells me the postcards if she listens to Rush all day long.

"Nope, just in the morning," she says. "Then I put NPR on for the customers." Well, at least she's honest.

I tell her I want to use the Internet. "Christian Gifts is closed," I tell her.

"Oh, yeah. They aren't open during the week. Why don't you try the public library? They have Internet access there." And she gives me directions, which upon reflection I think were meant for cars.

I wander through the town, passing a store that sells and repairs vacuum cleaners. The window is a display of antique vacuum cleaners. I head out of the tourist part of town, passing a fountain that isn't working and has a statue without a head. I make several wrong turns, climb a hill, and after about half an hour come to where the library was supposed to be, but it turns out to be a funeral parlor.

There's no one in sight on the street so hesitantly I walk in. I enter a room of red velvet curtains, gold carpeting. Two rooms are open and one has a casket. This is not how I want to spend my morning so I head back onto the street where a man is now changing a tire and he tells me the library is up another block. Exhausted, I climb the other block. It is a very hot day now and I am grateful for the air conditioning inside the library.

Two librarians sit in the dark in this cool room of magazines, books, and computer terminals. "I'd like to use the Internet, please," I ask a rather attractive middle-aged librarian with a shock of white hair.

She turns to her bespectacled colleague. "She wants to use the Internet."

"I need to see your picture ID." I realize I'd left my wallet and other items I didn't need for this outing in the hotel.

"Oh, I'm sorry. I'm traveling and it's at the hotel. I'll just be a minute."

"You can't use the Internet without picture ID."

I have my precious journal with me and I think it will serve as collateral as it has in the past so I give it a try. "Look, you can hold on to my credit card and my journal while I log on."

The white-haired librarian who is facing me makes a sympathetic face as if to say "if it was up to me . . ."

"You can't use the Internet without picture ID," her colleague replies.

I am suddenly irate. All that stands between me and communication with the outside world is my New York State driver's license. I am an upstanding citizen. I have never been arrested for a crime. I have never gotten a speeding ticket. No one has ever needed a swab of my throat or my fingerprints. I take in a deep breath. "Is this about Homeland Security? Do you need to track this for the government? Are we all terrorists and you need to keep a record of who uses your library?"

The nice woman keeps smiling and the mean one continues filing whatever she's filing. "It's just the rules."

"I'm a tourist. I'm a traveler. And I'm on a boat. I just want to check my mail."

"You need a photo ID."

Okay. I'm going to lose it. I'm going to leap across the counter and rip her throat out. Instead I storm out of the Hannibal Public Library, past the sculpture without a head, and make my way back toward the more tourist-friendly part of town. I walk for about a mile until I come to a local Java Jive's and suddenly the words "iced latte" float into my brain. I walk in and immediately feel better. Dark brews fill the air.

The woman at the counter seems challenged as she finishes up with the previous customer, handing her her change. Coin by coin. "And what can I get you?" she asks.

"I'll have a half-caf, iced, skim latte," I tell her. She looks at me blankly. "Part decaf, part regular."

"Does that mean you don't want milk?"

"Just make me a regular latte, iced," I tell her.

She starts fiddling with the espresso machine, but she seems distracted and tightly wound. She makes my coffee, but instead of actually giving it to me, she leaves it on the counter and starts cleaning up her work station. "Are you looking for something?" I ask her.

"Yes," she says, "but I can't remember what."

"A straw?" I ask.

She acts as if a bulb has gone off in her head. "Yes, of course. A straw."

"I know what you were doing," I say. "I do that kind of thing all the time. If I can't figure out what I want to do or if I've forgotten something, I'll start straightening up. Multitasking."

"You know," she says, "I'm just always like that. Bet if there was a way to download a woman's brain you'd find like a million things. Take the food out of the freezer, pay the gas bill, walk the dog, go to work, pick the kid up from school, get Christmas cards monogrammed, write thank-you note to your sister, bake cookies for the church bake sale . . ."

"And a man's brain?" I ask, taking my first delicious sip of latte.

"Oh, God, I bet you'd only find about four things in it. Golf, car, women . . . ," she says with some scorn.

"Money."

"Well, that pretty much covers it," she says, handing me my change.

I haven't gone very far when I come to one of those standing cutouts where you can put your face in and take a picture. This one is of Tom and Becky. The theme-park aspect of Hannibal—minus Jim, of course—is getting me down. I am standing, staring at the Tom and Becky photo op, when I run into Jerry, who's just come from breakfast with Tom (no relation to Sawyer) at the Becky Thatcher Restaurant.

Jerry and I greet each other like long-lost friends. It's as if days, weeks have passed since we've seen each other instead of a matter of hours. He tells me that Tom has apparently discovered a 1964 Cadillac in a repair shop and he's got his head in the engine. Jerry's just tooling around.

It's hot out and there's a bench under a tree so we sit while I sip my coffee. "Hey, Jerry," I say, "can I take your picture in the Tom Sawyer cutout?"

Jerry looks over at the cutout. "Nope," he says.

"How about the Becky Thatcher?"

"How about I take yours?" he says.

I stare into my coffee for that one. We both demur.

"Well, I learned a few things about Hannibal," Jerry says. "You can get all the tourist information you want, but if you're traveling on a boat you can't get a loaf of bread or a quart of milk. You need a car to go to the mall to do that."

"Yeah, just like all the other towns we've been to. And you need a picture ID to use the Internet at the library."

We groan. "Don't you just love this country?" he says.

"I sure do."

Then he pulls out a notebook. "So," he says, "I ran some numbers and I figured some things out." He shows me a page of numbers for fuel, for piloting, for a few marinas along the way. For miscellaneous supplies. But not for any boat rental. This is very generous of him. "So," he says, "if this is okay with you, I can take you to Cairo."

"This is great with me," I tell him. I want to leap up and hug him, but I refrain.

If I can get to Cairo, I'm thinking to myself, then I'll have made it to zero in one boat. If I get to zero, I'll change boats and head south. Somehow. I haven't quite figured that one out yet. Maybe I'll hop that tow.

⁂

Leaving Jerry, I wander through Hannibal, looking for Jim. I see the Mark Twain Museum, Tom & Huck's Taxi, the Becky Thatcher Restaurant, Becky's Old-Fashioned Ice Cream Parlor, Cardiff Hill with the statue of Tom and Huck. Tourist office. In this Disneyfied setting, it's all lily white. There's no Jim's Bar, Jim's Gas Station, even. No hint that Jim or any black man in literature was ever around.

I walk into the Becky Thatcher Restaurant where I'm told I can get a good home-cooked meal, though the sign over the counter warns WE RESERVE THE RIGHT TO REFUSE ANYONE. The place is packed, but there's only one black man hunched over his meal at the bar and two black women, sitting in a booth. The women look away when I glance at them.

The restaurant is done in railroad decor. Railroad cars run along the walls. There are railroad pictures, a railroad calendar, a shelf of toy railroad bridges. There's a framed clipping that reads THE MARK TWAIN ZEPHYR REACHES THE END OF THE LINE. And a handwritten sign, maybe ten years old, that reads WANTED: RAILROAD PLATES.

I sit at a table across from three older women and a man. As I'm waiting for Annie, the seventyish-year-old waitress wearing a rhinestone "A" on her chest, I listen to one of the women who does all the talking. "So given the life he's had, you know, I do what I can. You'd be surprised. A little love can go a long ways."

Annie comes by to take the order of the people behind me and I hear a man commenting to her that she looks good. "Just lost thirty pounds," Annie says. "That way I got to get all new clothes."

"You know when he first came to me, well you know how he was . . . ," the woman doing the talking at the table nearby says.

"He'd just stay wherever he wanted. You know, in his chair. He'd had such a rough time of it, I didn't want to rush him or put any pressure on him, you know."

Annie comes by and asks me what I'll have. I feel as if I'm starving and I order the lunch special—baked chicken, hominy, green beans, rice, salad with western dressing, and iced tea. "You gonna want pie? We got lots of homemade pie." I glance over to where the pie is as Annie rings out apple, cherry, blueberry, coconut, banana cream, and key lime. I am tempted, but I see that the flies are resting pretty much all over the pies, which aren't covered.

"I'll pass on the pie."

"I just let him be. Sooner or later he'll want something and come to me. Oh he'll sleep with me, you know, but during the day, never sure when he'll come around. . . ."

I'm thinking foster child. Shell-shocked husband. I am deeply engrossed in their conversation and find myself annoyed when the people behind me start to speak in loud voices and I can't hear what the woman says. I see the solemn nods of her companions.

Annie brings my meal. "You sure you aren't going to want a piece of pie?"

I shake my head and dig in. The chicken is moist and comes off the bones. The hominy has a nice texture and a buttery taste. The green beans were probably cooking for the last few days, but I am starving and it definitely is a home-cooked meal.

"You know," the woman goes on, shaking her head now, with real sadness in her eyes, "some days I don't even see him until I open a can of tuna and then he just jumps right up on the counter." They're paying their check now. "I don't just have a pet," she tells her companions, "I have a friend."

They head out and a new crew is waiting to sit down. Annie comes and waits on them and the man says, "Annie, you look real good."

"Well, I just lost forty pounds. I needed new clothes." Incredible. She's lost ten pounds since I walked in.

⚮

Time is running out and I need to do what I came for. Perhaps I've been avoiding it, I think, as I head to the Mark Twain boyhood home. The entire site is a tourist attraction and I cannot begin to imagine my father living anywhere near this spot. More and more I feel his presence slipping away. It's getting late and Jerry wants to make Two Rivers Marina in Rockport, Illinois, before dark.

I have to skip much of the first part of the tour and the museum and I head right to the house itself. Making my way through the house, I am unsettled by the cardboard cutouts of Mark Twain that pop up everywhere. The only other people in the boyhood home, well, person really, is a man whose wife cannot climb the stairs. I can see her below. She's wearing a pink pantsuit and is quite large.

Her husband, to accommodate her, is shouting down the stairs the various objects he sees. "It's a bedroom with an old brass bed, table, washbasin, baby picture." I rush through the rooms. My father was right. It is a tiny tiny house. But I see no evidence of a house next door where my father claimed he lived.

I decide to try the gift shop. I poke around all the usual Mark Twain memorabilia. Mark Twain books, CDs, videos, maps, statues, Huck and Tom matching mugs, bookends, Becky Thatcher dolls. (Still no Jim.) I want to find a photograph. Proof. Evidence. Why does this matter to me that my father lived next door to Mark Twain's house? Why does it matter if he told the truth or lied? But it matters suddenly more than I can say. What is a family, in the end, except its memories? And the tales it has carried on.

An older woman wearing a thin strand of pearls and a powder blue sweater stands at the cash register. "Excuse me," I ask her, "but my father lived in Hannibal a long time ago. He said he lived next door to this house. But I don't see how he could have. Do you have a picture of this street from, say, 1922?"

"No, I'm sorry . . . I don't believe so." I'm turning to leave when she seems to hesitate. She thinks for a moment, tapping a pencil in her hand. "I do have a picture of the last time Mark Twain visited Hannibal. That was in 1902. He's standing in front of this house. I think it has some of the street. . . ."

She goes to the back of the store and returns with a photograph. In it Mark Twain stands in front of his boyhood home, wearing his classic white suit. A photographer taking his picture is also in the picture. A woman walks by in a white dress and bonnet, carrying a dark umbrella. She wears lace-up boots. A spotted dog sits at the photographer's feet.

This was taken during Twain's last visit to Hannibal. Of course he couldn't have known that at the time. He had simply returned to his boyhood town, which he had written about so lovingly. In the picture his head is turned to the left and a man seems to be speaking to him. Children are gawking. And beside the children is a house that no longer exists. It is a wood frame with back steps that lead to a small balcony. A fence separates it from Twain's house. And I know my father lived there.

My father was a man of stories. And his own set of broken dreams. He was an enigma to me and I knew little of his personal life. But if he got you in his clutches, he'd talk your head off. Once my mother and I went shopping and we left Larry listening to my father. We came back three hours later and Larry was in the same place. My father said, "So, I've got a sore throat and Larry's got an earache." The thing about my father's stories was that they were pretty much one-way events, monologues that as he got older and older he'd get himself trapped inside of and my mother would make a circular gesture with her hands and say, "Here he goes again."

He was himself a very poor listener, but he could go on and on about his friends long gone, about his business interests that had never quite succeeded. He wanted to be as rich as the people he tried to impress. He loved commerce, buildings rising, the smell of paint. Yet he cried during movies and musicals. He couldn't watch anything violent or sad. In truth my father was a

very secretive man, and in the end he didn't really succeed. He
sold buildings and the profits went to taxes. He sold buildings for
peanuts that later went for millions. This was one of the things,
among the many, that made my mother bitter.

I knew little of what was really in his heart. Most of what we
knew of him were his rages. Nobody could do anything right, and
nothing was ever good enough. In the end, life was too entropic.
The center pulled apart. He could not control every waiter, every
family member. His rages could not make everything right. In his
later years he was calmer. He liked to sit in his chair in Milwaukee
and look out at the woods behind the assisted living center where
they lived. In the winter, just before he died, he and I sat, a heavy
snow falling, watching a squirrel secure its nest.

During my last visits he grew confused. He thought the pictures on the wall were real people and he began talking to them.
He talked to his brother. He talked to his grandchildren, who
were living in Hawaii and Brazil.

When I came into the room, he looked up and asked, "Whatever happened to our vaudeville act, Mary? Did you ever take it
on the road?"

I did a little shuffle and soft-shoe. Disappointed, he shook his
head. "Nobody will come and see that," he said.

I am standing in the gift shop of the Mark Twain boyhood
home next door to the house where my father told me he lived as
a young man. I am standing beside this aging woman in a powder blue sweater and pearls and I start to weep. I sob. "I'm so
sorry," I tell her. "I didn't expect this."

She nods, "Oh, I understand. Doesn't matter how old they
were. . . ."

I walk out to compose myself. I stand in front of this house. I
walk up and down the block, which has been turned into a Mark
Twain theme park, and I know that my father walked here. He
stood on this street and looked at the river. He worked in a department store called Klein's. I stand on this little street where
tourists push past me en route to Judge Clemens's office or Becky
Thatcher's house and gaze down toward the river. My father

stood on this spot. He saw the river every day. What he told me was true.

I go back into the gift shop. "Is that picture for sale?" I ask her. "Yes it is. It's eight dollars," the woman says. I nod. "Let me wrap it for you."

She wraps it carefully in tissue, secures it between two pieces of cardboard. As she wraps it, I think how I want to pick up the phone and ask him more. There are a million things I'll never know and I feel a terrible regret. As I head back to the boat, I know that something is over for me in this journey. Tom and Jerry stand impatiently on the dock, waiting. Samantha Jean is doing her guard dog thing on the flybridge. I should hurry, but I do not quicken my pace.

As I approach the boat, I see a small green step the boys have rigged up for me. "The boating equivalent of the red carpet," Tom yuks. Back on board Tom and Jerry are ready to rock 'n' roll. I go to put away my things as Jerry shows me a shelf he has built for me under the sink. "You can keep your books and things there," he says. "Like your work."

I drop my backpack onto the bed. A single chocolate mint rests on my pillow. "Tom," I say, going up to the helm, "did you put a chocolate mint on my pillow?"

He blushes as much as Tom ever will. "You know," he says, "special treatment. Like a hotel."

It's time to push off, but we're in a tricky spot. We have to back way up in order to exit the narrow channel that leads out of the marina. I hear Tom telling Jerry to "spin her hard. Give her all you've got." Jerry is tense, nervous about backing into another boat. "You've got a good hundred feet," Tom tells him, and then as he takes her back, "Okay, that's enough. You're good to go."

As we pull out of the narrow channel, Tom points to a tow anchored on the side. "Hey, we saw her yesterday. She didn't make it. She didn't lock through."

A barge loaded with freight passes us at full throttle and we get bumped in its wake. We're back on the river, chugging along. Hannibal recedes. I'm moving on. I'm leaving all this behind.

✺

At Lock and Dam 22 we have a seven-minute wait. "He sure knows his lock," Jerry says. Tom's come below and he's hanging on to a ladder outside that is covered in cobwebs and bugs. "June bugs," Tom says.

I don't bother to correct him, but under my breath say, "Mayflies."

"You know, two years ago, there were so many over at the Pettibone marina that the harbormaster had to get a snowplow to get rid of them."

"Yuk," I say, pushing off the wall.

Since we've got a little time to kill, Tom tells me he's bought some things for Kim. "You know, cuz she helped so much. And cuz she saved Sammy's life."

"That's nice of you," I tell him.

"I got her a necklace. Wanta see it?"

I tell him I do. He lets go of his line and we both head inside, where he reaches into a cubby above my head and pulls out a brown paper bag. The boat gives a little rock, taking on the exiting barge's wake, and its contents spill onto the couch. I see the necklace, and a gold box, and a pair of silver handcuffs. Tom scoops up the handcuffs with his sheepish smile. "Joke," he says.

"Okay!" Jerry calls. "We're locking through!"

We float free and as soon as we come out Tom and I go above. The river's open. It's a clear evening and I'm piloting now. If all goes well, we should reach Two Rivers by dark. Tom's sitting with Samantha Jean in his lap, keeping me company. "You know what I'll always remember," Tom says with a laugh. "That night when the barge brought us into Keokuk in the dark. That's the kind of people you meet out here."

I nod, moving into the bend.

"You know, this river is a big unknown. She's a bitch and she can take you down if she wants to. Don't quote me on that."

I'm steering and laughing. A flock of pelicans soars above. "But she's big and she's mean and she's full of the unknown."

Ahead we're coming up to a barge, heading north, and I get up from the captain's chair. "You want to take her, Tom?"

"No, you stick with her."

"Really?" I'm nervous. I've never passed another ship before. Thus far my driver's education has consisted of a very wide stretch of empty river. "Are you sure?"

He nods. "You take her."

I'm looking at the barge and its place in the river. I'm seeing which way the tow driver is heading. "I think starboard."

Tom shakes his head. "Port to port."

I don't agree. From the way she's coming, I think I want her to pass me on the starboard side, but Tom's pretty adamant. I'm waiting for the tow to give a signal and I'm at the point where I need to decide when Jerry peeks his head through the little window below. He seems surprised to see me at the wheel, but he doesn't skip a beat. "Take her on the starboard. On one whistle."

"Starboard?" I ask.

"Yeah, their pilot just called."

I give Tom a little wink and he looks away. At Mile 287.1 I get my one whistle and pass the barge on the starboard side. We catch a little wake and I point her nose into the troughs.

"That's good," Tom says. "Now take your river back."

# HURRICANE

## ~ 33 ~

A PLACE with the odd name of Louisiana, Missouri, was once famous for its cigar factories and for the Stark Apple Nurseries, home of the Delicious apple. But we're heading to the Illinois side—the Two Rivers Marina. I ask Jerry if he'll call ahead. He's reluctant to use his cell phone because of the cost (Jerry's a thrifty guy), but now I am officially desperate to do my laundry. It's been a long, hot day and I also wouldn't mind a meal and a shower. "I'll call," I tell him. "Tell me what to say."

"Tell them we're looking for a slip and our L.O.A. is forty-seven feet."

"Our L.O.A.?"

"Length over all."

I use my cell phone and call Two Rivers. A woman answers the phone. "This is houseboat *Friend Ship*," I tell her, "wondering if you have a slip available. Our L.O.A. is forty-seven feet."

"Yes, we can accommodate you. You come on ahead."

I am unbelievably proud of myself for handling this simple communication. I smile so much my face hurts and Jerry just shakes his head. As we sail into this lovely, full-blown marina in a quiet cove, I am in heaven. It actually looks like a real place. It's tucked under the bridge for Interstate 54 and I am content to see trucks and cars and what passes for civilization buzz by.

We moor and plan to head right up to the restaurant. We're all starving but Jerry decides to hang back and make a few notes. As I'm walking up with Tom, I call Kate on the phone, but I get her voice mail. Before I can say anything, Tom grabs the phone away from me. "Whale Kisser," he says, "come in. This is the *River Queen*. Do you read me?" Then he laughs.

As we approach the restaurant, a bevy of teens comes pouring out. "Oh-oh," Tom says, "local hangout." But the restaurant is large and virtually empty. This is, after all, a weekday in the off-season. There are some teenagers playing video games near the bar, perhaps leftovers from the crew we saw leaving, and the bar itself has customers, but the restaurant has only one or two tables filled. A family with a baby is at one.

Tom and I take a seat in the middle of the room and I notice a strange man walking around. He has greasy hair and a blank stare. He plunks himself down next to the family with the baby and lights up a cigarette.

"Can I get you something to drink?" the perky blond waitress asks us.

"I'll have a diet Dew," Tom replies, looking her up and down. I order a glass of chardonnay. My eyes are fixed on the creepy guy. Who'd sit down right next to a baby and light up? But Tom's got his eyes on the leggy waitress. She's just a girl, really, but Tom is fixated.

Our drinks arrive and the waitress starts to tell us the specials when the creepy guy gets up and starts walking around again. Though there are dozens of tables to be had, he goes to the table right next to ours and sits down. Then he lights up.

"I'll have the sirloin tips with asparagus," I tell her, my eyes on this man.

"I'll have the same," Tom says. "But can I have mashed potatoes with mine?"

Tom notices me staring at the man. He turns back to the waitress. "Excuse me, but do you have a nonsmoking section?" I am surprised at how polite and formal he is with her.

"Yes we do, Sir."

"We'd like to go over there."

When we move, the creepy guy moves away as well. Tom gives him an ominous stare. "That was nice of you," I tell Tom.

He shrugs. "Why should you be uncomfortable?" he replies.

Jerry joins us quite a bit later and I'm already falling asleep. I'm grateful when our orders arrive. As our waitress walks off, Tom, who is looking a little the worse for wear, says, "She sure can move from port to starboard. And look at them buoys."

I'm shaking my head as Tom buries his face in his hand. "Oh, God, I'm sinking."

"You definitely are."

Jerry nods, concurring.

I'm tired, and as soon as I'm finished eating, I get up. "I think I'll go to bed," I tell them. Tom rises as well. "Are you leaving Jerry alone?"

"Nope, but I'm walking you back," Tom says.

"You don't need to."

"I'm walking you back."

As we head out the door, I almost crash right into the creepy guy as he heads out the door as well. It is a clear night, filled with stars, and the path back to the marina is paved. We are silent as Tom walks me back. I'm standing on the deck, but he says, "I want you to go inside and lock the boat."

"It's a nice night," I tell him, "I'll go in soon."

But Tom shakes his head. "I'm not leaving until you do."

So I go inside and lock the door. He stands, staring at me until I do. As he's leaving, I hear him tell Samantha Jean, who is topside, "You keep an eye out for things, you hear, Girl? Now give Daddy a kiss on the nose."

Inside the cabin I call Larry first to say good night. Then once more I try to call Kate. On the first ring she picks up. It is so good to hear her voice. She doesn't feel far away at all.

"Who left that message earlier? 'Whale Kisser'?"

"Oh, that was Tom. He saw the picture of you with the beluga."

"Oh." She laughs. "I thought it was some kind of pervert."

I thought how well things had worked out. What a nice little family I'd made. I met Larry at a writer's conference in Richmond, Virginia, when Kate was fifteen months old. He was from Canada and we were both in the same dorm. I had become a bit of a recluse after Jeremy and I broke up, but when Larry and I sat down to lunch together one day, he told me he'd just taken the walking tour of Old Richmond. Taking a walking tour seemed like a wonderful thing to do. The next day we went to a museum. We started seeing each other, eating our meals together, and after a week I knew I had to tell him.

We had gone to Miss Morton's Tea Room, for fried chicken, and over dinner I said, "I just want to let you know that my mother, my nephew, and my baby daughter are arriving on Saturday."

I waited for him to flinch, ask for the bill. To find the way to slip out of the room. Instead he looked me square in the eye. "What time do we need to meet their flight?"

On Saturday he drove me to the airport and, as my mother got off the plane, Kate dashed down the jetway through the terminal. She was heading to the revolving doors. "Larry," I shouted, "get her." He chased her all over that airport.

Two years later Larry adopted Kate in surrogate court. The judge handed her a lollipop and explained to her what it meant to be adopted and did Kate agree. When Kate said yes, the judge asked her to raise her right hand. I can still see that little fist rising into the air.

><

I'm up at the crack of dawn. Stuffing laundry into a pillowcase, I schlep it up to the marina, but the laundry room is locked. I'm amazingly disappointed until I go into the women's bathroom. To my delight there are three sinks, which are just what I need. I use one for whites, one for colors, and one to rinse. I am stunned at the pleasure I take after more than two weeks on board in scrubbing and soaping my personal things, in putting them into the rinse-cycle sink, then hanging them all around the bathroom stalls to drip dry as I take my shower. Despite an odd dream that someone has stolen our axe and plans to use it, I feel vigorous and strong. I let the hot water course over my body, down my back, my thighs. As my clothes drip dry, I soap my body, the top of my skull, scrub my toes.

At about six I run into "Bob," as his shirt reads, who works at the marina. He sees me carting my wet laundry, my sheets and towels, and tells me he'll open the laundry room. "You can wash your linens," he says, opening the door. He says he can't leave it unlocked. "Just look for me when you're done and I'll open it up again." I know Jerry wants to be off on an early start, but surely I can wash my sheets first. I put some of my things in the dryer and the bedding and towels into the machine.

I'm enjoying the simple things again—the sirloin tips and beer from last night's supper, Tom escorting me back to the boat, a moonlit night, two old men fishing in the shade under a bridge, an egret and a blue heron in a territorial struggle. But, as I make my way back to the boat, Jerry, who is sipping his coffee, looks at me askance. He wants to be leaving soon.

Half an hour later I start searching for Bob, who needs to unlock the laundry room, but he is nowhere to be found. There is a man driving a lawn mower, but he can't hear a thing. A fat white cat follows me everywhere I go. "Shoo, shoo," I say to the cat. I keep going back and forth to the marina, but I can't find Bob and Jerry is getting more and more annoyed.

At eight a.m. the marina opens and I find someone to unlock the laundry room. I never do see Bob again. I gather my things, which are only half dry, and head back to the boat, which is once again waiting for me to sail.

I had always believed clothespins were for holding clothes, but I've learned that, on board ship, laundry is in fact the least of their concerns. Clothespins are used as clamps to keep things dry: Honey Nut Cheerios, Wonder Bread, Chips Ahoy, saltines, and opened bags of Dorito chips and potato chips. Whatever moisture will destroy. They are used as markers for maps and books and to keep miscellaneous receipts from blowing away.

In the world of ideal inventions, where function perfectly fits the form (the bicycle, the crowbar, the flyswatter), the clothespin is that most underappreciated of gadgets. As I hold one in my hand on this sunny morning, I examine the way the two pieces of wood and a spring can do so much. But I am actually using them for my damp clothes. As I move through the cabin, collecting them, the boys pretend I'm not there. Not only has my laundry delayed our departure, but I've stolen the clothespins from the chips and saltines to use them for the arcane purpose of drying my clothes.

Now my wet things dangle from the railing. This is clearly a violation, but neither Tom nor Jerry will say it in so many words. Of course, they aren't exactly speaking to me either.

"We're late." Jerry grunts, glaring at my red and blue spandex T-shirts, my shorts, flapping in the wind. My underwear I've hung discreetly in the shower stall, which has never been hooked up anyway. "Late start means late finish," he quips.

Tom glances at the laundry and shakes his head. He doesn't say anything, but I can tell this is not proper ship etiquette. It is as offensive to him as cleaning green beans on the flybridge. This laundry thing is for rural backyards of Nebraska or Italian side streets, but not for a *River Queen* houseboat. Not for our dignified ship. Whatever. I am happy, with clean clothes. As we push off, the man mowing his lawn waves. We pass a cruiser and the couple on board waves. We drift by the two fishermen and they wave. We travel under a railroad bridge and the engineer not only waves but gives us a friendly toot.

Though I still do not exactly understand this odd ritual, I am thrilled by these waves. It is as if the pope or a rock star is waving at me. Though Tom and Jerry are chagrined, I am filled with glee the way babies are, waving hello and "bye-bye" as my sheets and pants and T-shirts, like so many sails, flap in the wind.

~ 34 ~

HURRICANE WEATHER is upon us. Just hours out of Two
Rivers we find ourselves in a hot, sunny day with no place to go.
That muggy, still kind. The doldrums. If we were a sailboat, we'd
be becalmed. The sun beats down on the boat and it's too hot for
any of us to be outside. Tom and Jerry pilot from the inside helm.
They have grown more relaxed with me, I can tell. They have
their shirts off. They leave the toilet seat up.

It's that kind of sultry, sticky weather where you can't do a
thing and there is no respite outside from the sun. I'm sitting in
the cabin with all the windows open. In the heat of the day I am
at the kitchen table (the only table except for the one Jerry lets
me use on the bow to write), with a plastic box in my lap.

I have decided to familiarize myself with the *Chrysler Marine Engine Service Manual.* It occurs to me that, if my pilots
should die simultaneously, say a lightning bolt to the flybridge
while I am below, I would have no idea what to do. I couldn't call
for help. I wouldn't know how to get out of the main channel or
throw an anchor line. And I certainly couldn't get an engine
started if I had to.

I need to inform myself. I peruse the table of contents. Lu-
brication, oil drainage. Controls group: propeller, kick-up inter-
lock, tiller bar control. I check out the outdrive group: removal
from pivot housing. Separation of upper and lower units. Anodes.
There are looping diagrams. Pictures that explain the flow of
fuel, where water meets gas.

As I leaf through a breezy section on the installation and
adjustment of motor parts, I realize I may as well be reading a
neurosurgical handbook with the thought of removing a brain
tumor from myself. Just the pivotal housing diagram is enough
to send shudders through me. Even the 911-M28 marine traveler
toilet manual, with its twenty-four different parts, some of
which I saw my first day on the boat, and its four pages of installation instructions, is beyond me.

Besides, Tom has a special relationship to his motors which I
realize now, defeated in these doldrums, I will never have. He

talks to them the way he talks to his dog. The way a man might whisper about his lover to a friend over a couple of beers. She's lookin' good. She likes my touch. If you give her a little more, you'll get a little more. Come on, Girl. Do it for me.

⚬

It is 11:18 a.m. as we approach Clarksville, Missouri, Lock and Dam 24. Jerry, of course, sees it before I do and he and Tom begin to discuss. Then I see it as well. A huge double barge is going through. It's a short lock, which means they have to take the barge apart and do it in two trips. Jerry is definitely annoyed at me now, but I'm trying to avoid him. I've got "Johnny B. Goode" playing on my computer and I'm trying to look on the bright side. This is a golden opportunity to take down my laundry, which has been baking in the sun.

But about forty-five minutes later it's becoming tedious. It is a very hot day and we are just cooking on the river. "I want to go for a swim," I tell them. They breathe that heavy sigh.

"You can't really swim here. You need to hold on to something," Jerry says. Then he stops and does that stare. A moment later he points to Tom's air mattress, which is secured with bungee cords in the dinghy. "Why don't you float on this and hold on to the anchor line?"

Tom gives me a look. "Hey, that's my air mattress."

Jerry shrugs. "Aw, let's let her float."

I'm pretty much well-done from the heat and decide I'll give it a try. I change into my suit, then go to the bow step, where Jerry holds on to the air mattress and helps me slide on top. It's not the most delicate maneuver I've ever executed, but it does the trick. I take hold of the anchor line and drift out as far as I can.

Cool water laps over me. I dangle on the anchor line, my head lying back. Birds soar overhead, landing in a bank of prairie grass nearby. Dragonflies dart in and out of the reeds. I watch puffy white clouds, shaped like dinosaurs and bears, drift. Splashing water over my legs, here I am, floating free on the Mississippi River. I'm on a raft, just like Huck Finn. At daymarker 273.8, I am happy. I tell this to myself. Put this in your captain's log, Jerry Nelson. I am officially content.

At last we get the signal from the lockmaster that we should prepare for lockage. Jerry gives me a wave and I head to the ship. Coming back up the swim platform, I'm afraid of slipping under the boat. Tom heaves me in a most undignified fashion back on board. "So did you enjoy yourself?"

"Oh, my God," I tell him. "I think that was the most fun I ever had."

"Really? Didn't you have a childhood, Mary?"

I pause, thinking about this. There is a long answer and a short one to this. I opt for the short one. "I had a childhood," I say as I go inside to dry off. "But it was a long time ago."

At last we are given the go-ahead.

Jerry fires up the engine, but Tom makes a face. "Talk sweet to her, Jerry. Don't give her all that throttle at once."

Jerry replies, "Yeah, man," but perhaps nervous about losing our place in line, he fires them up again.

"Easy, easy."

Jerry gives Tom a look. "Actually, I've been in neutral for some time."

We are looking at the tow that should be leaving the lock and dam. "Oh, boy," Tom says, "he's standing tall."

"Is he coming out yet?" I ask, ready to be moving and away from the stagnant heat of the day.

"Shortly," Jerry says.

"Hey, look," Tom quips, "things weren't all bad. I got to work on my valve covers and Mary got her swim and you got to growl at us a little."

"Oh, boy," Jerry says. "Let's bring her in."

I'm looking at the Army Corps of Engineer maps, trying to figure out how we skipped Lock and Dam 23 and jumped to 24. Did I miss something? Was 23 somehow only an upstream dam? "Hey, Jer, this is 24, isn't it? What happened to 23?"

"Good question," Jerry says as he moves into position, ready to enter the lock. "They never built it. They planned for it but decided they didn't need it or something, so, anyway, it doesn't exist. It's a little like that building back in Hannibal—you know, the one Jesse James never robbed cuz they hadn't built it yet."

We laugh over that as the barge five long and three wide, a total of fifteen barges, comes toward us. After a two-hour wait, we float free. It's a boiling hot, dozy day and we've got fifty river miles to cover. The river opens up again and civilization slips away. A water snake slithers by.

After the lock and dam, the day is hot, very hot. Tom, sweat covering his back, is sorting through his things. "Sir," he says to Jerry, "did you secure my air mattress after Mary's swim?"

Jerry looks at Tom, twitches his nose. Tom looks at Jerry. "It's not in the dinghy?"

"No, Sir," Tom says. "It is not."

I expect Jerry to say "Violation," but he doesn't. Probably because it's his fault. We all look upriver. I was so happy on that air mattress and now it's gone. I'm hoping some kids, like those boys back in Muscatine, find it and have a good time. But Tom, I see, is crestfallen. It was, after all, his bed. "Well," Jerry says, "guess we'll have to get another one."

~ 35 ~

SHADE ON the river is a precious thing. You can get it in the morning or late in the day, but in the afternoon, when the sun beats overhead, when the air comes at you like a blast furnace, there is simply nowhere to go. It was what the Indians told Marquette and Joliet to expect. The sun bears down relentlessly. I have come to rely on the breeze off the river to cool us down. But the starboard engine has died. "Gone into a coma," Jerry says. We pause to fix it near a bank where a bunch of kids are fishing.

I'm baking and can tell from the usual assortment of wrenches and oil cans and what-have-you that this is going to take some time. I never thought I'd be on the river longing for a cloudy day; I thought that in mid-September one would move along with a crisp fall breeze. Just another of my misconceptions.

There is news that the new hurricane has been given a name. We are heading into Rita, which is due to strike Galveston in a few days. We've been listening to the National Weather Service on our marine radio and the signs aren't good. Tom fiddles and bangs and after about an hour we're puttering along in this stinking hot day. Tom's listening to his engines out of his good ear. He cocks his head, a robin with his ear to the ground. "She's clanging a little, Sir," he says to Jerry. "Still not sure she's taking all her fuel." He goes back and bangs with a large wrench. Apparently this helps move the fuel along.

Tom has rarely traveled and only been in an airplane once. He flew to Chicago on a job. He said he didn't like flying very much, but he sat next to the engine and as the plane flew, he liked listening to its sound. Tom is listening now. I can tell he wants to do a more extensive repair. At about four o'clock, when it's as hot on the river as it will ever be, we come to Lock and Dam 25. Jerry and Tom see the barges ahead of us and groan. "It's gonna be a long one," Jerry says.

Again I can tell from the tone: This is all my fault. The laundry, the late start. I'm going overboard, that's for sure. We all know that sitting still on this river in this heat is going to be a scorcher, but, given the lateness of the afternoon and the time we will be getting to Portage Des Sioux in Missouri, it is decided that we'll cook dinner now.

Jerry takes my worktable and puts the small grill we bought for $3.99 back in Davenport on it, fills it with charcoal, and sets them aflame. I can't take the heat. The cabin is as sweltering as either of our two decks. I feel oppressed, trapped with nowhere to go. Even the bimini doesn't provide shade because of the angle of the sun. While the grill is heating up, I want to go for another swim. But, given that we've lost Tom's air mattress, I'm not sure what I'll use for flotation. "You can jump in the river," Jerry says, "but you need your life jacket."

While he stokes the coals and Tom fiddles with the starboard engine, trying to revive it once again from its coma, I get into my bathing suit and put on the life jacket I borrowed from my neighbor across the street. It's one of those orange jobs with the plastic snap-on clasps. The kind people wear in movies like *Life Boat* or *Titanic*. I am not a small-breasted woman, and as I snap it on the vest sticks pretty much straight out.

Not wanting to be seen, I jump into the river, but immediately the life vest floats up around my head. I try to push it down, but it rises around my neck, choking me. This seems counterintuitive, but I am having trouble keeping the thing from wrapping itself around my throat. I'm clinging to the boat when Jerry sees me. "My god," he says, "I thought you had a modern life vest. That thing will kill you."

He tosses me a life ring (the "man overboard" ring, Tom calls it), and I heave my life vest back onto the bow step, then work my way around the boat to the swim platform, upon which I fling my body. So much for my swim. Jerry's got some chicken going on the grill, which in this heat I find incomprehensible. When it's cooked, he takes his plate and sits at the table. He doesn't bother getting me or Tom chairs. I know what's on his mind. If I hadn't caused us to have a late start because of my laundry, we wouldn't have wasted half the day at these locks and dams.

Jerry sits at the table with the grill still on it, eating, not talking, and Tom takes his meal and sits on an ice chest. I go into the cabin and eat alone.

At last, almost two hours later, we are given the go-ahead. We are happy to be moving, to catch a breeze again and head out of the heat. As we approach, I see a sign that reads NO LOCK LOCK.

"What's a 'no lock lock'?"

Jerry shakes his head. Then we realize there is an arrow underneath. "No lock" is to the left. "Lock" is to the right. I wonder how many people misread this sign. It is dusk as we sail through, and the heat of the day abates. After waiting more than two hours, we are locked in, floating free, and through in ten minutes.

~ 36 ~

THE WHITE cliffs of Illinois rise, sculpted, to the east. I think of the White Cliffs of Dover. Of home. The sun sets fuschia on the river. Cormorants, lined up like cartoon figures, sit on an up-side-down canoe. Darkness falls and a tension comes over Jerry. He has hooked up a beacon that he can flash on the river as we all scan it for detritus, snags, debris, other boats, whatever can bring our boat down. We've had our harvest moon night and our starry nights and our nights with the riverbanks lit, but this one is pitch-black.

It seems to grow darker as the night goes on, an inky black-ness. On the map I spot Criminal Island and try to imagine what species of man dwelled here, but I cannot see it. There are no lights along the river. Nothing to illumine our way except for our beacon. We are silent on board, all eyes glued to the river and what it might bring.

I think of Captain Bixby's warning to a young Samuel Clemens: "You've got to know the shape of the river perfectly." I wonder at its shape. As I look at it, even in daylight, I have no sense of where it goes. I confuse the main channel for sloughs. When it is wide, as it is right now, it is infinitely mysterious. And in the dark it is unfathomable.

Gazing at the maps with my flashlight, I see the shallows and the islands, sloughs and other rivers that join the Mississippi here. It is the darkest of nights and we are looking for a small lighthouse on the west bank where the main channel merges with a wide slough. We have to make a turn and go up the slough to find the Woodland Marina. Jerry is not happy to be doing this in the dark. I am reading the charts, trying to figure out where we make our turn. We pass a huge dredg-ing barge that has a wide cable coming off of it that at first we do not see.

The depth finder reads 17 feet of good water under us, but Tom quips that you can always tell the water you've got on top. It's the water underneath you don't know about. Jerry agrees, eyes fixed on the river. He's wishing he had radar. He shows me how to use the GPS (global positioning system), which is like a car navigator. "It's not so important to know where you're going," Jerry mutters, "as to know where you're at."

Finally we spot the lighthouse far off the starboard side. It is a very small lighthouse, so at first we aren't sure. "That must be it," Tom says. I am studying the maps.

"Yes, that's it."

Carefully Jerry makes a wide turn up the slough and suddenly there are lights—all the marinas. We pass one after the other until we see the sign for Woodland. Very slowly Jerry makes his turn. Across the marina in the dark two men wave us in. "That's Greg and Glen," Jerry says. We enter a marina of huge houseboats with names like *Whatever* and *Mint-to-Be*. Somewhere on the radio I hear John Lennon singing "Imagine."

We are greeted by a small crowd of people, who have been waiting for us, and two old dogs named Matt and Tux. Matt was found floating down the river during the flood of 1993 on a pile of debris. And Tux, they tell me, just wandered in.

⚓

Captain Greg, as they refer to Greg Sadowski, is the river pilot who was supposed to take me on a fast boat from Memphis to New Orleans. Greg and his twin brother, Glen, have shared a houseboat for the past twenty years. Bachelors, they have made their home at this marina. The brothers also both have their one-hundred-ton captain's licenses, which means they can move huge vessels, though Glen has opted for a land job. Greg is gone much of the time. In a day or so he will be en route to La Crosse to take a paddleboat and move her south.

Everyone is thrilled to see us. Thrilled that we have made it here in one piece. Donna and Bill, Larry and Dixie all give me handshakes and hugs. They live on neighboring houseboats and all invite us to come over for a beer and popcorn. The mosquitoes are biting like crazy, but Donna says she's got a fan going on her porch to keep the bugs away.

We've been sitting on her porch for about five minutes when Donna asks me to come and help her make popcorn. "I'll give you a tour of my boat," she says. Inside, her husband, Dan, is already putting popcorn into the microwave and Donna takes me by the hand. She opens folding doors that display her pantry, pulls out compartments that contain her downward-loading dishwasher, her washer/dryer.

I am struck by her dishes, her well-appointed bar, the cut-glass carafes filled with single malt whiskey, her ceramic tile shower with little fishes swimming all over it, her toilet with a special push button, which she flushes twice to demonstrate its unusual suction.

As I ooh and aah over her cupboards of dishes, her closets with hangers and hooks, her bubbly lava lamps and fish-motif decor, she asks, "What've you got on your boat?"

I think of our meager *River Queen*. My wash dangling from the railing, having to beg Jerry to turn on the water pump so I can do the dishes. My clothes folded in duffels and in cubbies above my head. The green curtain that separates my sleeping area from his. "Oh, the usual stuff," I say.

"Well, I'd love to see it," she says. I can tell that this must be houseboat etiquette. She's shown me hers; now I show her mine.

"It's a little messy right now," I say. I feel like the poor relation, the country mouse visiting the city mouse. "How about another time?"

She gives a shrug and I can tell she's miffed. But what's a girl to do? I want to stay inside the coolness as the smell of fake butter fills the room, but we are expected on deck. It is a sweltering night. Rita is due to make landfall in a day or so and the hot, sultry weather you get before a hurricane presses in around us.

We are sitting in the dark on the deck of Donna and Larry's houseboat. The fan is churning. As we sip our beers and eat popcorn, I ask Captain Greg, who was moving the *Princess* down to New Orleans when Katrina hit, to tell us what happened during the storm.

We all lean in to listen as Greg tells his story.

"We were on the river on a time schedule, really pushing to get to New Orleans, but the forecast kept changing. At first we thought we'd see some wind but didn't anticipate a direct hit. We didn't know that a Category 5 storm was coming our way in twenty hours. We just stayed steady on our course. Then the day before she hit, they said it had intensified and was going to be a direct hit at New Orleans and the Gulf. We were at Mile 112. But as the crow flies, that was only fifty miles to the Gulf."

We are all silent, mesmerized, with only the whir of the fan in the air. "So we had two choices," Greg's voice continues in a flat monotone that betrays no emotion. "We could go back up-river, but at that point the river flows more east/west than north/south. If we'd gone upstream, we would have been going west. At this point the storm was moving west. We'd have a tough time making it to Baton Rouge.

"It might have been safer for the boat to move as far up-stream as we could, but I was more concerned for the safety of my passengers and my crew. There were five of us on board, in-cluding myself. We had a couple traveling with us and they evac-uated. They got a ride north and took it. But me and my crew opted to stay with the ship."

"Could you leave?" I asked, and, "Weren't you scared?"

"Well," Greg goes on, turning his beer can in his hands, "I could leave, but the people who own the boat, they didn't really give us permission, and, well, I didn't think it was the right thing to do. As to being scared, I have a lot of respect for the river. And for the weather. I know what they can do. But I also knew we were pretty far from the Gulf, so I wasn't worried about the surge. But I figured we could get hit hard.

"I was concerned that the *Princess* would sink. So we tied her up with everything we had. We found a couple barges and tied her to that. We spent the afternoon putting out a lot of lines and fenders. We found some old truck tires and we used those as fenders. Tied her up to some twelve-foot steel pilings with extra cable we found on the barge.

"The hurricane winds were swirling by then, so we pointed her port beam into the north/northeast wind. Next to the barge where we tied her was what's called a quarters barge. This barge was anchored to the shore, so we weren't worried we'd drown. It's where barge workers sleep. It's kind of like a hotel below deck. So we brought some mattresses and supplies, water and food, over to the quarters barge. We got some sleep before Katrina hit us. She hits us hard at about five a.m. We stayed below, but every now and then I'd come up and check on things. The water rose about twelve feet." When Greg says this we are all amazed. We look out at the river and try to imagine a sudden rise of twelve feet. "One of the barges tied near us broke free and went downstream. Two barges sank. It went on like this for about five hours. But the worst was for two hours. The barges kept banging together. You can't be scared. It's not going to help, being scared. You just have to keep a clear head and keep checking on things. It was during this banging that a window blew out and the glass cut my elbow open. Right after the hurricane the weather was good. Someone gave me a ride to the emergency room and I could see on the way that all the power lines and all the trees were down."

When Greg is done, he puts down his beer. The fan whirs. The hot, muggy weather tells us that another storm is near.

~ 37 ~

EVEN T. S. Eliot, that most serious of American poets whom everyone seems to forget was from St. Louis, perhaps because of his British accent, writes, "I don't know much about gods, but I think the river is a strong, brown god, sullen, untamed, and intractable." Eliot is also known to have said, "The sea is around us, but the river is in us."

This may have been the case in Eliot's time, but I have a friend who grew up in St. Louis who tells me he never thought about the river. He also says it's the worst town in America. He has told me that his sister, who is rich and lives in the suburbs, has contracts with her servants so that they will never reveal where she lives. This is considered a crime deterrent in the affluent outskirts of the city.

St. Louis native Jonathan Franzen seems to share my friend's view, at least in his novel *The Twenty-Seventh City*. It is the story of a police chief whose ostensible agenda is the revival of St. Louis (once ranked the nation's fourth city and now its twenty-seventh) through the reunification of its depressed inner city and affluent suburbs. I'm going to spend the weekend in St. Louis to see for myself and Tom and Jerry are going to stay at Woodland Marina on the boat. Our plan is to meet up Sunday morning at the airport and we'll be on our way.

At 4:45 in the morning, Glen, Greg's twin, comes knocking on our houseboat. I'd set an alarm, but managed to sleep through it. All of a sudden there's rumbling. Tom topside is shouting for me to get up. I'm scrambling for my clothes and knapsack. But Glen is waiting patiently on deck. He is in a hurry to get to work, but he tells me not to rush.

In his car we go hurtling in silence through St. Charles County. The sky is beginning to turn pale in the east. Staring straight ahead I ask Glen, "So, you and your brother are river pilots, right?"

"That's right," Glen says. "We are both licensed to drive one-hundred-ton vessels."

"Boy, that's amazing. And you're identical twins and you live together in a houseboat."

"Just worked out that way," Glen says.

Clearly Glen is not a man of many words. On the other hand it is only five in the morning as we drive past dim-lit fields and the suburban outskirts of St. Louis and he drops me off. I walk from the street, carrying my own bag, despite the doorman's efforts to grab it, into the glorious lobby of the Hyatt Regency St. Louis, located in the old Union Station. In 1894 St. Louis Union Station opened and it was the largest, most beautiful terminal in the United States. And in my opinion it still is.

I enter the Grand Hall with its gold leaf, Romanesque arches, sixty-five-foot, barrel-vaulted ceiling, and magnificent stained-glass windows. Its "Allegorical Window" shows mythological figures representing New York to the east and San Francisco to the west and in the middle, St. Louis. I find that my room is, surprisingly, ready. I shower right away, which has become my life's great luxury, then head to the dining room. I'm sitting down to breakfast when my cell phone rings. It's on a default ringer and plays a loud, annoying tune. After I chat briefly with my husband, my waitress comes by to ask me about my phone. I think she's going to tell me to put it on silent. Instead she whips out her own. "Just listen to this," she says as she shares her ring tone with me. It's a cat going "meow meow." "I downloaded it off the Purina Web site. You can download just about anything," she says.

After breakfast I'm ready to explore the town. In front of my hotel four huge guys wait for the valet to bring their car around. Their vehicle arrives with a giant barbecue smoker attached to the back. A man wearing a T-shirt that reads EXPERIENCE THE RELIGION OF GOD waits for a cab. I decide to walk to the Jefferson Memorial and on to a gentrified neighborhood along the river known as The Landing. Cars pass with bumper stickers that read MY BLOOD IS BLUE, a reference I'll later learn is to the St. Louis Blues. I pause to pay my respects at Busch Stadium, which is soon to see the wrecker's ball. In the stadium shop a sale of Cardinals memorabilia is on in full force. I pick up a few souvenirs for Jerry and Tom.

Then I pop across the street into the International Bowling Hall of Fame, where I learn that bowling was originally a pagan ritual, performed with human skulls and bones for pins, usually the remains of one's enemies. There were other aspects of this cheery history. Pictures of devils bowling. Judges who executed the innocent were said to spend eternity bowling with their victims' heads.

There's free bowling here, so I get a pair of shoes and bowl four frames. Continuing my walk east, ahead of me the Gateway Arch looms and behind it is the river. I pass a park where a wedding party stands in a giant flowing fountain that acts like a waterfall. The bridesmaids wear cranberry red and matching flip-flops. The groom and groomsmen are bedecked in red St. Louis Cardinals caps and clutch beer cans. A crying flower girl clings to one of their arms. The bride in white flip-flops is perched precariously in the center of the flowing fountain, trying not to fall.

Across the plaza a hundred couples are moving in identical steps. The teacher with a bullhorn tries to explain the complicated move, which the crowd attempts to follow. I'm sure it's a swing dance class, but I can't hear the music. It's odd to see a hundred people moving when there's no beat.

I wish I could find a place for a cup of coffee, but for blocks and blocks there's nothing but government buildings, some of which have been abandoned. There are no little shops, no take-out, nothing but a long path of hard pavement as I walk the long stretch to the arch. I come to the steel Gateway Arch, which was built as a welcome gate to the West. Behind it the river chugs, slow-moving, turgid, and, as T. S. Eliot noted, brown.

Early that evening I head over to the Delmar Loop. In the cab ride, I see how the inner city itself is decimated. There's no life here—no shops, no cafés. And the neighborhoods seem divided between white and black, rich and poor. I recall my friend who comes from St. Louis and wonder if he doesn't have a point.

On the Walk of Fame I locate Miles Davis's star at 6314 Delmar and pay my respects. Then I go to check out Chuck Berry's place, Blueberry Hill, named after the great Fats Domino number (and again my thoughts take me to New Orleans, a place I now know for sure I'm not going to get to on this trip). I'm told I might get a glimpse of Chuck Berry himself, but what I find is a sawdust joint, filled with Elvis dolls, album covers, old jukeboxes, dead animals, and bar food.

After a beer at Blueberry Hill, I pause on the street to listen to a brass band, all black boys, playing a pretty good street rendition of "I Got a Woman." Then I go for dinner at a place called Brandt's. A very large and very good blues singer, dressed entirely in orange, named Kim Massie, is belting out songs in a gospel voice. I take a table near the front and order a salad. Kim Massie's got her eyes closed and she's singing about how she's leaving on that midnight train to Georgia. "I'd rather stay in his world than be without him in mine," she croons and her accompanist hums along with her.

Someone passes her a note and she switches to "Happy Birthday." The woman sitting beside me covers her face and turns to two young women who I determine are her daughters, "I told you not to . . ." Kim Massie starts riffing on "Happy Birthday" and turns it into a kind of old Ella Fitzgerald number and tears fill my eyes.

Tomorrow is my father's 103rd birthday. I've been wanting not to "go there," to push this thought away. I had already planned his party. I'd made out a guest list. I thought he'd make it. I thought he'd just go on and on. And now I'm sitting alone in a restaurant, listening to a blues singer croon "Happy Birthday" to a woman I don't know.

A couple of years before he died, I asked my father to drive around Chicago and show me all the places he remembered and where he'd lived. He was at the wheel, something that scared me as he was almost a hundred years old. A few weeks later he would turn on to four lanes of oncoming traffic on the Outer Drive and stop driving forever. But on that day he took me to all his old haunts. We rode to see an old limestone building on the West Side, where they'd lived in a cold-water flat. We drove down to 47th Street and the old Bronzeville district of the South Side, where the music was. Then we went to another neighborhood and pulled up in front of a house.

My father got out of the car and stared at the tidy brick building with a front porch. An elderly black woman with graying hair sat on the front stoop. Around her, small children, grandchildren I assumed, were playing. As we stood in front of her house, she eyed us suspiciously. I don't blame her. We were the only white people on this block of well-appointed row houses. Her gaze turned to anger. "May I help you?" she asked, her voice thick with irony and a tinge of fear.

"I'm sorry," my father said, "I didn't mean to stare. It's just that I used to live here and I'm showing my daughter around."

Now she was very suspicious. She didn't believe a word of it. "Well, we've been here since '49."

"Oh, no, I lived here long before that," he said. "We were here in 1907."

"1907?" she shrieked, a stunned look in her eyes. "What are you?" she asked. "A ghost?"

My father laughed. "No," he said, "I'm just a very old man."

On his eightieth birthday my father called me and wept into the phone. "I had a dream last night," he said. "I dreamed about the night before we moved to Nashville and I went to stay with my aunt and uncle. She was very fat and he was very skinny and I slept between them with a big comforter over my head. All night I thought I couldn't breathe. I couldn't have been more than five years old when we were moved to Nashville. I'm eighty years old," he told me, "and I remember that night as if it were yesterday. My whole life lives inside of me."

✂

It is late as I hop a cab to take me over to the Soulard district, a restored neighborhood of back porches and red brick houses and alleyways. It has a distinctly New Orleans feel. A pair of extraordinary transvestites in blond wigs and four-inch heels pass me. I follow them and stumble into, then out of, a gay bar.

I am roaming when a man staggers up to me out of the shadows. He starts talking for no reason. He is a small, slight man. Not particularly old. He's talking about a place I've never heard of called Bay St. Louis and I think it's somewhere in this town. "No," he says, "Bay St. Louis. It's in Mississippi. Right on the water. Prettiest town you ever saw. I was a chef there for ten years. But now it's all gone."

He tells me he left before Katrina hit and went to Florida, and now Bay St. Louis where he lived and had all his friends is no more. "I got my cat and my dog with me. That's what matters. I got out. My cat and my dog, they're with me here. I come up here and my brother helped me get two jobs. I was doing all right, but now with this new storm coming . . ." His voice trails off.

"You mean Rita."

"You know, it's like a flashback. It's like it's happening all over again. I had these friends down in Bay St. Louis. This old guy who fishes. He's never lived anywhere else. That's the kind of people who are my friends. But he's gone. Or I don't know what happened to him. It's just happening all over again. But I got my cat and my dog. And my brother got me two jobs."

"Have you talked to anyone about this?" I ask him. "Maybe you need some help?"

"Maybe," he says as he staggers back into the shadows as quickly as he'd come.

In the morning I head to the airport to meet Tom and Jerry, who are going to pick me up and take me back up north to the boat. I am hungry but there is only fast food. I can't get a drink that doesn't have sugar. I get a coffee and a breakfast muffin. Over the loudspeaker comes a call to prayer in the chapel near the Food Court.

As we drive in the car back in Portage Des Sioux, Tom is glee-ful. "Hey, Mary," Tom says, "we did a big shop for you yesterday."

"Oh, yeah, what'd you get?"

"Let's see: We got four cases of diet Dew, diet Coke, beer, some frozen pizzas, sliced meats, candy bars, chips, a hunk of cheese, and a four-bean salad." He pauses, obviously proud of himself. "All the healthy stuff is for you." I'm actually not sure what the healthy stuff is, but I'm assuming it's the cheese and the bean salad.

~ 38 ~

WE ARE caught in a great gauzy storm, the remnants of Hurri-cane Rita. A drenching soup. We have to batten down the hatches. Take everything off the deck that we don't want to get soaked. Back at the marina Greg gave us an electric fan to keep the bugs off and I say to Tom, "Maybe we should put the fan away." Disgruntled, Tom drags it off, I assume to stow it below. As we depart in a driving rain, Tom moves all his bedding and the new air mattress he picked up while I was in St. Louis and dumps them in the middle of the cabin on the floor.

It's tight quarters already, but I try not to complain. Here, this is just another storm. After all, thousands have had to evacuate in the South. But everything is wet. We are trapped inside the cabin. And there appears to be some cause for concern. "I'm not finding the buoys, Sir," Tom says.

"Just keep her straight," Jerry replies as they scan the water. I'm searching for buoys as well. The two of them are chattering away about engines and about some boat ride they took three years ago on Lake Superior and who knows what else. The river is surprisingly choppy and for the first time I feel woozy. Everything around us is gray—the river, the sky, the air—all a misty impenetrable gray. Samantha Jean, wet and neglected, shivers under several bomber jackets at the helm. Sitting beside her, I hesitantly stroke her fur.

At Grafton we pass the mouth of the Illinois River. I know we are gliding beneath the rocks on the eastern shore, but in the fog I can see nothing. In *LaSalle and the Discovery of the Great West* Francis Parkman wrote that these rocks were once "cut into fantastic forms by the elements" and were marked as "The Ruined Castles" on some of the early French maps. Somewhere along these cliffs, Marquette and Joliet spotted the sight that reminded them that "the Devil was still lord paramount of this wilderness."

Looming above, Parkman tells us, was an image painted in red, black, and green on the flat face of a high rock. Marquette saw "a pair of monsters, each as large as a calf, with horns like a deer, red eyes, a beard like a tiger, and a frightful expression of countenance. The face is something like that of a man, the body covered with scales and the tail so long that it passes entirely around the body, over the head and between the legs, ending like that of a fish." This demon, etched by the native people, served as a warning to those who dared to venture on.

At Mile 212, just past the confluence, instead of the face of the devil, a huge white statue appears from behind the curtain of rain and fog. It seems as if she is rising out of the depths itself. Our Lady of the River stands fifty feet over the banks on a seventeen-foot pedestal. Built in 1951 in gratitude after a great flood, the

Madonna blesses and protects travelers. She seems eerily real against the opaque sky, dominating the river and showing the culmination of Marquette's vision. Now it is the Christian God instead of the pagan that rules here.

We keep searching for buoys but the visibility is low. Tom is at the wheel, shaking his head. He eyes our captain for guidance. "I'm looking," Jerry says.

"I'm looking at a pile of rocks, Sir," Tom replies. At river marker 193.5 at Chain of Rocks Canal, we have almost no visibility. "I'm not going to get lost, am I, Sir?"

Jerry, using his binoculars, says back to him, "It looks like it's a straight line. Just steer her ahead." He pauses to pat Samantha Jean on the head. "Samantha is the biggest dog of her size I've ever seen," he says by way of senseless non sequitur, then gazes back at the river. He stares down at the Army Corps of Engineers maps, trying to get our location, and realizes I've already flipped the page. "Violation," he says, "but not punishable."

Tom checks the instrument panels. "We're going nine point eight, Sir, but it feels as if we're going a lot slower."

Jerry nods. "We are. We're about one point five miles per hour slower. We don't have the power of the river behind us here in Chain of Rocks. This is a man-made cutoff. I was trying to make Hoppie's last January with Captain Greg. We had a 150-foot ship made by SkipperLiner in La Crosse. We had to break ice to go. *The Majestic.* . . . Rode her from La Crosse to Florida and up to Montauk. Almost did the Great Loop, but not quite." The Great Loop is a trip through the Great Lakes, down the Mississippi, up the Atlantic Coast, back to the St. Lawrence, returning to the place where you began. Many people we met on the river would be making this journey.

I'm staring out at the grayness and the rain. Then I start to tell them about the man who talked to me last night in the Soulard district. How he'd been in Katrina and now in Rita. "I told him he should get some help."

"He should get a boat," Tom says. "If you've been in two hurricanes like that, you need a boat. What did God say to Noah?

How long can you tread water?" Tom chortles to himself, then pauses. "Oh-oh, something's coming my way. Barge ahead."

I look out at the gray water, the obscure horizon. "How can you see that?"

"I can just feel it coming. Sometimes you can see something better by not looking at it."

I am pondering this when a voice comes over the radio. Another incomprehensible Cajun accent, a barge pilot. "Looks like he wants to take us on the starboard side," Jerry says.

Now the barge, just barely visible, comes into the horizon. Tom reaches down for Samantha Jean, who lies buried beneath several coats. "How'ya doing, Brown Eyes? Rain's letting up," he tells her, which it isn't. "Looks like I could run an engine check." The wind has shifted and Tom apologizes for the smell of his engines. "But some high octane is good for the head."

I disagree. My head is full of fumes. But there isn't anything we can do. One huge barge comes alongside and passes us like a giant beast, gray, waves rising against our hull from its wake.

We are coming up to Lock and Dam 27. "This is pleasure craft *Friend Ship*, requesting lockage," Jerry calls in, but the lockmaster does not reply. "Guess he's having lunch," Jerry says as he idles the engines. There's a barge coming up behind us with a tow. "Maybe he's going to put that barge through first."

But the lockmaster calls. "*Friend Ship*," he says, "give us a few minutes."

Now the red light starts flashing yellow. "Okay," Jerry says. "Get ready." We can't see the lock gates opening, but we see the green light. I've got Tina Turner playing "Proud Mary" on my computer and our mood is more elevated than it's been. In the driving rain and mist Jerry moves into the lock and we tie up on the port side to a short, thick post that Tom calls a bollard.

As we move into position, we see the tow and a huge barge coming in behind us. Jerry gets on his radio, "Lock 27, this is *Friend Ship*. Is that tow coming with us?"

The lockmaster says back in a scolding tone, "Yes, it is. You were supposed to call." The lockmaster is obviously irritated and I look at Jerry, who is irritated as well.

"But we did call," I say.

Jerry shuts off his radio. "Nothing to be done."

Tom turns to Samantha Jean. "Get up on your jacket, Sam. You're worse than your mother."

Jerry makes a snap decision that we need to move our boat over to the western side of the lock so that the barge and tow can have as much room behind us as possible. "I'm going to the other side," he says. Tom and I are on deck in the pouring rain as we cross the lock to the first bollard.

"There's a plant growing out of this one, Sir," Tom says.

"I don't want that one. We're going up ahead. Tie to the mid-cleat. I want to give him all the room he needs."

We tie up, then in the downpour wait for what seems to be a long time. Tom keeps the cabin door open with his pole sticking out against the wall and once again the cabin is filling with flies. I'm not in the mood for more. I'm also nervous that we will all have to spend the night together in the cabin, along with the flies. "Tom," I ask in my sweetest voice, "can you close the door around the pole?"

He gives me a look, then walks out into the driving rain and pulls the door shut with a bang. I look at Jerry. "I didn't mean for him to go outside. I just wanted him to close the door."

"Well, you created a minor firestorm," Jerry says. Then he adds his own annoyance. "Don't mess with a man doing his job." I look outside and see Tom standing in the rain, and I go outside.

"Tom," I say, rain sliding down the back of my neck, "I'm sorry. . . . I didn't mean for you to leave the cabin." I'm standing in my New York City Marathon rain slicker and flip-flops, holding our lines. "I just didn't want the flies . . ."

Tom stares at his stick and at the cement lock wall. "It's okay," he says, not looking me in the eye.

"I'm making sandwiches. Ham, roast beef?"

"Whatever," he says. Then as an afterthought, "No mustard on mine." This is our truce, as good as it gets with Tom.

As I head in to make lunch, I hear Jerry. "We've got company," he says. We all look back as the barge and tow move into the lock and after a few moments Tom and Jerry exchange glances. "He needs more room," Jerry says. "We've got to move forward." He revs the engines as Tom unties us from the bollard. Jerry moves the River Queen up to the very front of the lock gates, which are huge, looming in the driving gray rain. Even I can see that our nose is too far forward and that if these gates open now and we are in this position, we will be crushed.

"Okay," Jerry shouts at us, "we've got to push her back! Get her front tied up to that bollard! Push hard! Now!" Tom and I are pushing off the wall, trying to get our nose away from the lock gates, which at any moment will open and, as far as I can tell, pulverize us with their massive power. I cannot help but feel somewhat as if I am sitting in the front row at an IMAX theater, except this is actually happening.

Jerry is maneuvering the boat into reverse when suddenly we hear the silence. We all hear it. It is an unmistakable sound. The starboard engine has died. "Tom!" Jerry yells.

"Can't do anything about her right now, Sir. You gotta go with one." Tom and I are shoving the River Queen as hard as we can, tugging on the lines, trying to move an eighteen-thousand-pound boat backward before the enormous lock gates open and smash our bow. I feel the power in my own hands as we move our boat, down by an engine, backward in the driving rain. Just as we get her pushed back and tied, the huge lock gates begin to open right at our nose.

A wave, created by the gates, strikes our bow, but the gates open smoothly and we clear them by a few feet. We all breathe a sigh of relief, shaking our heads. "Now that was a close one," Tom says.

"Too close for comfort," Jerry replies.

Ahead of us is more gray, driving rain. As we move out of the lock, we are in the same gray soup as we were before. But we are lockless now. It's open river from here to Cairo. The lockless monster, I call ourselves. We can barely see anything ahead. The sides of the riverbank are obliterated in the mist and fog.

Suddenly we reach the confluence with the Missouri River. In the storm we almost miss it. Like a quiet herd of elephants, it comes upon us, gray, placid, barely noticeable. But I recall the fury of its flood, which I'd witnessed in Kansas City in 1993. Marquette had seen it as well. As told by Parkman, here they met with a real danger: "a torrent of yellow mud rushed furiously athwart the calm blue current of the Mississippi; boiling and surging and sweeping in its course logs, branches, and uprooted trees. . . . They reached the mouth of the Missouri, where that savage river descending from its mad career through a vast unknown of barbarians, poured its turbid floods into the bosom of its gentler sister. Their light canoes whirled on the miry vortex like dry leaves on an angry brook. 'I never,' Marquette writes, 'saw anything more terrific.'"

# CONFLUENCE

~ 39 ~

IN 1803 Thomas Jefferson sent Meriwether Lewis and his friend William Clark upstream on a mission from St. Louis. Their goal was to reach the sea, but they fully expected to find woolly mammoths and mastodons along the way. What they were hoping for was a water route to the Pacific. They found an overland passage instead. Clearly the Lewis and Clark expedition was the highlight of Lewis's life. He committed suicide three years later. But Clark went on to father ten children and live a full and fruitful life.

Now we come to the point in our journey where they began theirs. I have only seen this place once before, from the air. In 1993 when I flew over this confluence, the Mississippi and Missouri had converged into a single body of water. Now with what is left of Rita, I can hardly see a thing. "I can't see any buoys, Sir," Tom says.

"Just keep in the main channel," Jerry replies.

We are coming down from Portage Des Sioux to the north and are only just now drifting by St. Louis, which we can barely discern. The Gateway Arch resembles two hands rising out of a grave, disappearing into the clouds, a half circle, no longer complete. The city is obliterated as we slip past, but the river seems wider than it did from the land and the water level appears to have risen slightly with the storm.

The day drags on and we must make Hoppie's. It is our only landing ahead. In the rain and fog the day feels long, but now darkness falls. Passing a river dredge, we are once more navigating at night, trying to find our way. The dredge is illumined like a Christmas tree—all red and green and yellow. Suddenly we are in shallow water and Tom sounds an alarm. "Sir," he says, "we are in four feet. The water is very thin."

Quickly Jerry maneuvers into a deeper part of the channel and there is a heavy sigh. I have made us some kind of dinner on boat—a pasta dish with Italian sausage and parsley. They gobble it down as we look for our landing for the night. The storm is breaking up. I see it in the sky. Little patches of blue gray appear where it had been just dense, socked-in clouds. The river turns glassy. A fog rises as we call ahead to Hoppie's and they say they'll have a place waiting.

We come out of the mist into the blackness of night. It is as if the storm just comes to a stop. We have reached its edge and ahead of us is a starry night. Jerry shines the beacon light and it bounces off the banks of the river. We scan the water with our binoculars, searching for debris, logs, snags, anything that might catch our rudder, grind into our gears.

We are silent as we search the water, eyes on the beacon, looking for Hoppie's. A ghostlike haze skims the surface. We pass a brilliantly lit paddleboat that churns slowly upstream, then see the string of lights for Hoppie's. White with a shade of pink on the river, lighting our way.

Before he died, I had this dream about my father. I dreamed we were on a river at night in a speedboat, going to a party. Ahead of us Japanese lanterns illumined the way. My father pulled up to the dock. I thought he was going to tie up, but instead he stayed at the wheel.

"Aren't you coming?" I asked as he started to leave. He shook his head.

"I'm not going with you," he told me as he headed upstream. "You'll be coming back alone."

~ 40 ~

GREEN TURTLE Bay. I have no idea where this is, but I like
the sound of the name. I envision turtles, the color of moss and
evergreens. A quiet cove. I wake to hear Tom and another man
talking about it. They are speaking in loud voices and don't seem
to care that I am sleeping. I hear the man say, "It's a good place to
leave a boat in Tennessee."

Tennessee. Annoyed at being awakened in this way, but taking in their conversation, I perk up. Jerry has made a decision I
don't know about. He will not return to Portage Des Sioux or
leave his boat at the Woodland Marina where his friends moor
theirs. He has decided to go farther south. Up the Ohio and down
the Tennessee. Below the freeze line. It never occurred to me that
Jerry wouldn't just go back up the Mississippi to Portage Des
Sioux. That he'd want to keep going. As much as I want to get to
Memphis and beyond, the fact is, I'm pretty much broke. When I
budgeted this trip, it was fuel at $1.50 to $2.00 a gallon, not $4.00.
But something else beyond finances is sinking into my brain. As
difficult as this is for me to admit, I want to stay with these guys.
I don't want to change boats, hop a tow. I want to stay with the
*River Queen* for as long as she'll carry me.

As John Banvard understood, and perhaps this was the source
of his obsession, the river is its own story that many will want to
find the way to tell. But it's coming to me now that the upper
river is my story and I want to tell it in my own way. I am starting
to know this river in my head. I can see it with my eyes closed. I
don't know that I have to do all two thousand miles of it when
this part of the journey has already brought me home.

I make my Folgers with three "tea" bags and find Jerry on
the landing. He's chatting with someone he's just met on the
dock, a guy with a big cruiser named *Bronx Cheer*. As he sees me
coming, I give him a wave. "Are you talkable to, Jerry?"

"Roger," he replies.

"I understand you're thinking about going up the Ohio and
taking the *River Queen* down the Tennessee. Is that right?"

"It's a thought," he says in his inimitable way.

"Well, are you going to keep going?"

"Yeah, that's right. I figured if we're moving south, I may as well keep moving her."

I nod, taking this in. "Well, I was wondering, do I have to leave the boat at Cairo? I'd like to keep going. . . ." I find these conversations with Jerry inscrutable and incredibly complicated. But now I know what it is I want. "I'd like to go as far as you guys are going."

Jerry shows no emotion one way or the other. "Well, we're going to end up somewhere in Tennessee."

"Then I'd like to go with you." As it is with all decisions Jerry makes, nothing is said. It is just understood that this is what will happen. I'll go where they go. Jerry and I stand, sipping our coffee, eyes on the river. Just then Tom's cell phone rings and I hear him talking. When he is done, he opens the aft door and shouts to us, "That was big sis! She says this weather's gonna be clear ahead."

"Great," Jerry says and I agree.

"But there's tornadoes in Tennessee." And then he gives us his big whooping laugh.

We need fuel before we can leave—an experience I'm starting to dread like a trip to the dentist—and I was hoping for a shower, but the one at Hoppie's isn't working. Jerry is annoyed because *Bronx Cheer*, which has just gassed up, is holding a space at the gas dock while his friend gasses up. This is slowing us down and for Jerry this behavior is rude.

But I guess my disappointment is palpable because Jerry asks, "What's wrong?"

"I was hoping for a shower."

"Well, we could hook up that river pump again." But I don't want to. There are lots of boats moored here, some big fancy ones, and I just can't see myself bathing on the dock. "Well," Jerry grumbles, "I suppose you could do the shower."

The shower. Our elusive shower. The thing I have yet to try. I'm all over it. "Yes," I say. But first there's a hose that has to be hooked up and a warning that there's no hot water. "I don't care. Cold water is fine."

While they do the hose, I remove the axe, vacuum, and baseball bat being stowed there. I am actually going to shower, naked, on our boat. I wait a few moments and when they say they are ready, I slip in. I turn on the water.

Nothing happens for a moment, but then it does. A trickle of freezing water sputters over me, chilling me to the bone. I stand under it for two minutes, shivering, not bothering with the soap or shampoo. I can hear the water pump, banging away, and picture Jerry standing there, timing me with his watch.

Fern and Hoppie are an aging married couple, two old salts, and they have braced their landing on the hull of a Civil War gunboat, Fern tells us. "We don't know which side they were fighting for, but they went down here." Fern leads me to the river's edge, where I'm trying to warm up in the sun. In the water I see the remnants of the Civil War vessel. The front, she tells me, is a sharp rammer, used to bring other boats down. "We just don't know if it was for the North or the South," she says.

A few other people join us. Two of the women have very large dogs—a Bernese Mountain Dog and an Irish Wolfhound puppy. It turns out they are doing the Great Loop. They've given themselves a year to complete this. I am amazed, not only that they are doing this trip, but that they intend to do it with two huge dogs.

We've got a little time before we have to "rock 'n' roll" and we sit down with Fern, who wears an anchor necklace. She adjusts her barrels of potted plants, then settles into a lawn chair. She lights up a cigarette and starts talking about women on the river. "I give lessons, you know. . . . Women need to know how to operate a vessel," she says. "How to get help. They need to know how to anchor, dock, start, and operate. . . ." I'm nodding my head. I can now maneuver on the river. I can start the boat and

I could anchor if I had to. But Jerry doesn't let anyone but himself dock or go through the locks and dams.

"Women need to know how to take care of themselves," Fern tells me. "I take 'em out on the river and show them. I've taught women to be first mates and captains. I don't like to see a woman out there, not knowing what she's doing. Men," she says, "they don't have the patience for teaching."

~ 41 ~

IT IS a glorious day as we set off for Cape Girardeau. The end of Rita has left the weather cool and clear. Just warm enough, a sweet, precious day. We have maybe six hours and about a hundred river miles ahead of us. The boys are hungry as we depart, so I heat up some of the Italian sausage with some pasta leftovers and make a salad for myself. I slip Samantha Jean a little sausage and she licks my hand. Now I'm ready to listen to Fern's advice.

It is time for me to learn the basic seaman's knot. I am tired of standing back as they tie up lines. I want to do it too. It is midday and I take a piece of rope. "Show me how you tie that knot," I say to Tom and Jerry as we all relax on the flybridge.

"You mean a bowline?" Jerry asks. "It's easy." He twists the rope into four or five directions, using the hand that is missing half its fingers.

"Can you do that more slowly?" I ask.

"Here," Tom says, taking the rope from Jerry. He holds it between his hands. "The rabbit goes down in the hole, out of the hole, around the tree, and back in the hole again."

I watch as he twists the rope. Rabbit goes down the hole, out, around the tree. Down, out, around, and in. Down, out, around, and in. I'm watching, but it looks more like out, around, down, and in to me. They tell me to take the piece of rope and practice tying it to the chair or to my own leg. My own leg is actually easier and I hold it up in the air. Down, out, around, and in. No matter what I do it still resembles a kid's shoelace knot.

Tom takes the rope again into his big thick hands and makes it move like a trapeze act. He ties up to things he claims would

hold a hundred-foot barge. He ties his knot to the captain's chair
and lifts it into the sky. I take my piece of rope back down to the
bow to practice. Rabbit goes down or out. What exactly does it do
around that tree?

I envision a small furry bunny, a fluffy brown thing. Once
when I was little a mother rabbit gave birth to four bunnies in
our yard, but our dog killed them all. A few years later I got a
white rabbit with red eyes as an Easter gift. I would hold that
rabbit by the ears and toss it around the yard. It wasn't the only
animal I ever tormented. I killed my mother guppy when she ate
her young. I tied up a neighbor's dog and beat it with a stick,
wanting it to obey.

Now I know, of course, that such action is a sign of socio-
pathic behavior in children. Was I a sociopath? If I could control
the world around me—the world of rabbits, fish, dogs—the way
my father wanted to control us, keep us in line, if I could get
them to do it, then maybe everything would be all right. I
wanted these creatures to obey me as I tried to obey him.

"If there's a wrong way to do something, you'll find it," I
hear him say as I try to do my knot. This is the voice I prefer not
to hear. It is not where I want to go. Why is my mind taking me
to this place? But love is never simple, is it? Never really so cut
and dried.

Down, out, around, in.

At Mile 110 I take the wheel. Underneath I feel the current
and it is very strong. I am having trouble keeping a straight
course. I struggle with it.

Jerry tells me the current is strong here because the bottom is
uneven. There are forces beneath the surface you can't really see.
"It would be difficult for anyone to pilot here," he says.

I return to my place on the bow. Dozens of monarch butter-
flies flutter past.

We pass the Chester State Prison. A sign reads LANDING—
PRIVATE. I'm sure it is. I'm using my binoculars all the time now
to read daymarkers, indicators on bridges, at the locks and dams,
to locate our whereabouts. After the prison, I return to my knot.

*Cowboy Carl*, a tow with barge, comes by us too fast on the starboard side and soaks us in his wake.

They've given me enough rope to hang myself, shall we say. I go back up to the flybridge, where Jerry who is left-handed and a bit more patient tries to show me again. Still, my knots look more like something you'd put on a Christmas gift than use to tie up an eighteen-thousand-pound boat.

But left to right has never been my strength. Tying knots never came easily to me. I flunked the shoelace tying lesson in Ms. Partlow's second grade. If someone taught me how to hit a baseball right-handed, I played, and still play, as a righty. I throw and kick, such as it is, as a lefty; I play golf as a righty, but can barely swipe my Metrocard in New York City, which is always a right-handed motion. And so on.

I recall shoe tying as a trauma of a left-handed youth. I only succeeded when my seatmate and best friend, Tommy Hinds, patiently instructed me. But I never learned very well. For the whole school year Tommy stooped down at my feet and tied my shoes. I can still see him. His blond head bent over my sneakers.

He was the first boy to show me real kindness and we were true friends. Perhaps he was my first boyfriend. We remained that way until third grade when he broke his leg during a simple fall from his bed and he died from bone cancer the following year.

We want to reach Cape Girardeau by dark, but there's only a gas dock there, not really a place to tie up for the night. We decide to bivouac on the Illinois side of the river. At Mile 61.7 I spot a lovely strip of beach. "Can we go there?" We locate it on our navigational maps. It is a sandbar called Dusky's Bar beside a channel called the Picayune Chute. "This is good," Jerry tells me as we gaze at the maps. "It's accessible only by boat. There's no access road. No one can come near us. You don't want to tempt fate, you know. . . ."

Please, I whisper, please, don't tell me a story about someone being murdered on a beach. It is a missed opportunity perhaps, but Jerry lets it pass. But there are other issues, he says, as we make our way toward it. We are a distance from the fueling dock and we need fuel. We have an eight a.m. appointment with the gas man, who will make a special trip if you call ahead for gas. "It means we'll have to leave by six a.m.," Jerry says.

But he is more concerned about anchoring just off the main channel. He is worried about the wake of barges and tows. "I don't want to get pushed up onto a beach," he says. "Or trapped by a loose barge."

Trapped by a loose barge. I am calculating what the chances are of this happening. "I know a guy back at the marina in La Crosse. Twice he said he got stuck on the beach by a loose barge." Somehow I feel willing to take the odds against being pinned against the sandbar by a runaway barge. In the end I convince Jerry that it's a perfect little strip of beach—isolated and pristine. And though he's loath to agree with me or even tell me that he has agreed, he points the *River Queen*'s nose toward shore and heads her straight toward the inlet, next to the Picayune Chute.

Checking the draft, he nods, and this seems to mean we're all right. I feel the bow as she begins to rub up against the sand and in another moment we are tucked onto the shore. Tom jumps off with an anchorline and pulls her ahead as hard as he can. Then he sets the anchor lines, burying each one in the sand.

As soon as we are anchored, Tom pulls Samantha Jean onto our beach for a run in the waves and I announce I'm going to take a bath before it gets dark. "Knock yourself out," Jerry tells me.

This time I do it right. I put on my river shoes and borrow Jerry's fashionable L. L. Bean snug zip-up life vest. No more of that antique orange thing for me, though here the tug of the current isn't so strong. I take my towel, shampoo, and soap. I am sweaty. My body smells. I walk out into the river and scrub my face and hands. The back of my neck. My armpits. I scrub and wash. I dive into the murky water, then wash again.

"Hey," Tom shouts as he heads off, axe in hand to chop wood, "Mary's taking a mud bath!" This is a new level of Mississippi baptism, but one I am prepared to make. I turn my back to him, pretending to give him a snub. But now I've been christened in the waters of the river too. I float on my back, watching the sun crest the tops of trees on the western bank.

In the final few moments of daylight I walk the beach as Tom gathers wood for a fire. Jerry has the grill going. It is a cool, calm night. A breeze blows. I'm sitting on a log. There are no mosquitoes and just a hint of fall. I watch the sky turn a shade of crimson, then purple, as the sun quite literally sets in the west.

Tom returns, lugging half a tree above his head like the hunter and gatherer he is. He builds a huge campfire, but then gets pouty because we don't want to sit right in front of it. We have grilled chicken breasts with orange slices, rice pilaf, carrots, and broccoli. He eats his dinner alone in front of the fire. "Let him be," Jerry says. "He's just being Tom."

Without a word Tom goes right to bed after dinner as he always does and Jerry and I sit by the fire, which is dying down. The "genie" is off and there isn't a sound, except crickets and the lapping of the waves. "This is what I love," Jerry tells me. "I could just live like this all the time. On a beach on the river. Not many people know what this is like."

The night is full of stars and I tip my head back to see them. Jerry's brought out some beers and he gives me a bottle of his best imported, an honor, I believe. I don't really drink beer, but this one tastes good and cold. "It's so quiet," I tell him.

"This is one of the last free places," Jerry says. "I just love being out here."

We sit, each with a stick, poking at the fire. "You're probably right about that."

"Where else can you just stop and spend the night? That's all gone. Freedom is pretty much over in this country." As the fire crackles, we talk about America, about Bush, and God, and our families. We finish our beers. Soon I am tired and I turn in. The sound of the cicadas and crickets fills the night. The only other

sound is an outboard motor, which races incongruously up the
river. The moonlight shines into the cabin, casting a dappled
light on my wall. The North Star rises right over Missouri. I see
Orion from my window. I realize I am cold. I'm surprised by the
chill in the night air. I crawl into my sleeping bag. I snuggle
inside, and before I know it I am asleep.

I awake to the cabin filled with brightness. It is the middle of
the night but a light shines in like a beacon. Are we being ab-
ducted by aliens? Or is it the police, coming to arrest us? Looking
out, I see a passing barge, the kind that Jerry feared. But it moves
slowly, causing no wake.

~ 42 ~

I'M UP before six, working on my knot. Jerry has instructed me
to do it backward. As he eases us off our sandbar at six a.m., I lie in
bed, rope in my hands, struggling to get it right. Take it apart in
its reverse order, he has told me. Then you will see how it is made.

I am taking it apart as we head toward the gas dock in Cape
Girardeau. It is a pristine morning and from my nook I see the
river bend. I am sad to leave our beach on the shore. Gazing out,
the water churns. Behind us Dusky's Bar recedes. I go back to my
rope. I see how it comes into its hole. How it winds around the
tree. It is seven a.m. and I haven't had my coffee, but I'm working
away. Once I've analyzed the knot, I try it for myself. I try it three
or four different ways.

Finally I think I've got it. I slip into a pair of flannel pants
and a sweatshirt. Jerry has boiled water and I drop my three bags
of Folgers into my Citgo cup. Then I go up to the helm where he
is at the wheel. I hold it up to him and he takes a look. He holds
my knot in his hands as if it's a dead animal. "You're missing a
loop," he tells me. Clutching the piece of rope, I go back to my
nook, determined to get it right.

I am practiced in this kind of thing. I recall a rainy, spring
morning and I am three or four years old. My mother says to me
that I can play in the den, but I can't disturb my father because

he is doing our taxes. But of course if I go into the den, I am
going to disturb him. I have nothing else to do. The den has sliding doors and I like to slide them back and forth. I can do this
hundreds of times in an hour. Another thing I like to do is sit on
the couch that looks out onto the garden and blow my breath
onto the glass, then scribble on it.

I do not know how to write. I do not know how to read. But
my father, for lack of anything better to do with me, writes my
name across the top of a yellow pad. MARY. "There," he says,
"that's your name. Now you write it."

He knows I can't, but it is a distraction good for half an hour
or so. I take a pencil and the yellow pad. I am surprised by the
point of this pencil. My father always kept his pencils very sharp.
I do not know if I have ever held a pencil before, but I grip it in
my left fist. I hold it the way you'd hold a knife if you were planning on stabbing someone in the chest.

I start to copy what my father has written at the top of the
page. I do not know why, but I recall this moment with perfect
precision. The grayness of the day. My father's somber, serious
face. The yellow pad and MARY written across the top. I work for
what seems like a very long time and, when I am satisfied, I stop.
I take the pad to the card table where my father works. My nose
just reaches the table. I can smell my father's cologne, his fresh-
shaved face. And the slight odor of talc I have always associated
with him. Now I see my father's finger coming down as he points
to the page. "The R is backward," he says.

I have certainly read worse critiques of my work over the
years, but this was the first. It did not make me want to stop. To
the contrary, it made me want to persevere. I went back to the
scratchy carpet, the pencil hard in my tiny fist, and I struggled
until I got it right.

✺

Haruki Murakami writes, "Your heart is like a great river after a
long spell of rain, spilling over its banks. All signposts that once
stood on the ground are gone, inundated and carried away by

that rush of water. And still the rain beats down on the surface of the river. Every time you see a flood like that on the news you tell yourself: That's it. That's my heart."

I have underlined this quote. Committed it to memory. How a rush of water can become a heart. It is not why I planned this journey in the first place, but it has become a large part of the reason to me. I am trying to understand why I have decided at this time to undertake this. But my heart is a river, gushing forth too.

There is perhaps only one story I really have to tell. It is the one I could not tell until now. It is the story of home and the one I have wanted to write for years. I wanted to write about my father as I knew him and not as others saw him. But his long life prevented me from doing so. This journey began in a different place but it has taken me where I never thought it would. What began as an adventure and a lark has become a passage into memory, childhood, and the past. I began writing some of this material long ago, when my father was alive. But I knew that no one would read it until he was dead.

I waited for him. As a little girl, I waited every day for my father to come home. I waited with his slippers, newspaper, and robe. A courtesan. His lady-in-waiting. He would come in, beaming, and for a while it was good. But then a minor incident would happen. Some small thing would go wrong. "If there's a wrong way to do something, you'll find it."

I recall carrying a tray of dishes from our playroom back to the kitchen. I am holding the tray and my father says, "You're carrying too many dishes. You're going to drop them."

The tray I had a good grip on moments before starts to slip from my hands. The dishes crash to the floor. "I told you," he says, "you were going to drop that tray."

I ran up to my room, sobbing. I stood in a tightfisted pout, a stubborn pose it would take years of love and therapy to untie. My mother came up and told me to apologize. "Just say you're sorry," she begged.

I went downstairs where my father was hammering some paneling in the basement. "I'm sorry, Daddy," I said, though I'm not sure for what.

He turned, knelt, and held me as I cried. That was what he wanted. He wanted me to be sorry. And I was. I would do everything right. If I did it all right, then no one would be mad at me again.

If there is a secret vein I still have to mine it is this. I grew up trying to figure out how to get it right. I lived in terror of the left-on lightbulb, the horror of the incorrectly buttered piece of bread. ("Always break your bread before you butter it"— a tongue twister for me). The way to eat soup. With cold soup the spoon went one way, with hot soup the other. "Let me let you in on a secret," he'd begin, and then we knew what was coming. He was articulate and precise. A dry drunk, a friend once referred to that rage.

The dragon eyes would turn red. The fire that almost came out of the nose. In fairy tales I knew what the dragon looked like. He looked like my father.

Once he lost his temper with Kate. She was about eight years old and she and her friend Amanda had gone to visit my parents in Florida for a winter break. They were at dinner and one of the girls burped. They both started laughing and couldn't stop. For some reason, my father thought they were making fun of him.

When he asked what they were laughing at, they only laughed more. He asked, "Are you making fun of me?"

They shook their heads, trying not to convulse. Then he flared. "I've been around for ninety-five years and I know when someone's lying to me!" He screamed at them and ordered them to leave the table. It is a scene I know only too well. In a sense it is a reality check for me.

My mother decided to separate the two girls until they calmed down. She put Amanda in a bathroom and locked Kate in my parents' walk-in closet, where she spent the better part of an hour, trying on my father's wigs.

"By GEOGRAPHICAL standards the lower Mississippi is a young, even infant stream, and runs through what is known as the Mississippi Embayment, a declivity covering approximately 35,000 square miles that begins 30 miles north of Cairo to Cape Girardeau," John M. Barry writes in *Rising Tides*. It is here at Cape Girardeau that the true head of the Mississippi Delta, which will extend to the Gulf of Mexico, begins. Already I feel the landscape flattening where the banks are rich in alluvial soil.

As we approach the gas dock at Cape Girardeau, a cruiser speeds toward us. It is a big white boat and it's coming full throttle. There is a woman on the deck, shouting and waving something in her hands. I think there's something wrong with her boat or someone on board. "Excuse me!" she yells. "Excuse me!"

"Hey," Tom says, "she's racing us for the dock."

Jerry glances at the cruiser out of the corner of his eye. "Well, we are here first," Jerry replies. He is concerned that we were low on fuel and relieved that we've gotten here at all. But the cruiser keeps coming. I have no idea what she wants. It seems as if there is some kind of emergency. A heart attack. Her boat's on fire. But Tom and Jerry chose to ignore her.

The woman is screaming and shaking something in her hand and I now see it's a set of keys. For some reason I think they are our keys or that she has a message for us. Then I realize that they just want to tie up on the dock ahead of us.

She shouts again as they come closer, this time with attitude in her voice. "Excuse me!" I recognize her as the woman with the Bernese Mountain Dog from Hoppie's Landing. She and her husband are doing the Great Loop. On the bow I see the other woman, who has the Irish Wolfhound.

"Hey, hello!" she's shouting, shaking these keys.

Jerry sees her and, disgusted, turns away.

"We've got the key to the gas dock," she cries. She shouts that the gasman gave it to them the night before so they could take their dogs for a walk in the morning. "So if you'd just move your boat, we can walk our dogs."

Jerry shouts back. "You are welcome to tie up to us and we'll carry your dogs onto the dock."

But she is adamant and insists that we move. "We have the key," she says. "The gasman gave it to us."

Still Jerry won't budge. He looks at me and says, "We're already tied up here. They can tie up to us."

"We can't tie up to you. How're we going to get our dogs off the boat?"

"We'd be glad to help you there," Jerry offers.

I'm not really sure of the proper boat etiquette at this moment. But suddenly the woman screams at us: "You should change your name because you aren't *Friend Ship*. You're bull-shit."

"Ouch," Tom says, pretending to ward off a blow.

"Whew, that hurt," Jerry grabs his heart and goes into the cabin. As she's cussing us out, my binoculars focus on the name of their boat and I groan. Of course, it's *Bronx Cheer*. Just my luck that the only rude people we've met thus far on the trip have to come from New York.

There is silence for a few moments as their boat makes a wide circle. When we hear the voice come over the radio, Jerry quips, "I knew he'd call."

"Hello, *Friend Ship*, this is *Bronx Cheer*. Come in, please."

Jerry gives me one of his shrugs. "*Bronx Cheer*, this is *Friend Ship*. I read you."

"I'm not sure if my first mate explained very well what we want to do."

Jerry flicks the guy off. "His first mate," he says to me. "Glad I don't have to live with that first mate." Then he puts him back on again.

"We have the key to the fuel dock. We don't want fuel. We just want to tie up and give our dogs a walk."

"I understand that," Jerry replies. "That is why I invited you to tie up to me." There are some grumbling sounds on the radio and the captain says he'll get back to us.

"Why don't we just move?" I ask Jerry.

"Because," he says, "we were here before they were. I don't want to have to maneuver the boat twice. I don't want to take any risks. What if their boat doesn't start and we can't get to the dock? We might be here all day. We're here. We'll stay here. Safety first. And besides, they were rude. And they were also inconsiderate at the gas dock at Hoppie's. Remember that boat that wouldn't move out of the way?" Jerry nods in their direction. "That was them." He gets back on his radio. "If you'd like to tie up to our boat, we'll help your dogs get onto the dock."

"The dogs are very heavy."

"We can handle that," Jerry says, and I see Tom flexing his muscles in Charles Atlas poses on the bow.

There is another pause, a sigh. "Thank you, Captain. We'd appreciate your help." As they come alongside us, I take the bow and drop the bumpers down. Jerry holds the boat at midship. Tom takes his newly purchased air mattress down from the flybridge and puts it on the floor. "What's that for?" I ask.

"So the dogs don't hurt themselves." He puts blankets over it as well. As soon as they're tied up, the women hand Tom the huge Bernese Mountain Dog, which Tom deftly lifts and places on all fours on the deck as if they are ballet dancers, completing a delicate jump. He does the same with the Wolfhound. Then he assists the four adults to move onto our boat and onto the dock. Not a word is spoken. No apology is heard.

As they head up through the gas dock gate to the walkway along the levee, Tom turns to me and says, "Friendship is all about attitude. And I don't have to take any of her wake." Then he laughs his head off.

⋈

Laura Ingalls Wilder, Tennessee Williams, T. S. Eliot, Langston Hughes, Jess Stacy, Scott Joplin, Burt Bacharach, J. C. Penney, Dale Carnegie. Inside the southern flood wall of Cape Girardeau I stroll the Missouri Wall of Fame. Among other things Cape Girardeau prides itself in being home to Rush Limbaugh.

I opt, however, to skip the Rush Limbaugh self-guided tour, which includes the hospital where he was born, the middle school he attended, and the barbershop where he once shined shoes.

Instead I amble through the rather happening little town, past a Furniture Elimination Outlet, Nick's Family Sports Pub, Mudsuckers Liquid Lounge (alas FOR RENT). I pause at the Yacht Club to see if I can get a couple of scrambled eggs, but the waitresses, puffing away, tell me they don't open until noon.

I keep walking past the First Baptist Church, which is closed and for lease, then pop into a café. A jazzy version of "Get Your Kicks on Route 66" plays, and I order a cappuccino and scrambled-egg croissant. The only misstep is the maraschino cherry in the canned fruit compote. Otherwise I am in heaven. After breakfast I see a red-tailed hawk gnawing on a pigeon in a park.

In the visitor's center I run into Jerry, who is chatting it up with the ladies there. "Hey, Jerry," I say, "they let you out again?"

He chuckles as he's signing the guestbook. "Oh, look," one of the women says, "he's a lefty."

"I'm a lefty too," I chime in, but they only have eyes for Jerry.

"All the best people are lefties," one of the women says. "You know, my brother was a left-handed surgeon and he had trouble finding instruments." I silently commiserate.

Jerry wants to get breakfast somewhere. He also says he needs to find navigational maps for the Ohio. "We have no maps of that river," he tells me.

And I tell him about the little jazz café. "You can skip the fruit compote," I say. "It tastes like . . ."

"The bottom of an owl's foot."

"Exactly."

Jerry cocks his head. "Is that Norwegian?"

"No," I say, "actually I think it's Yiddish."

"Thought so." Then he heads off to find my café.

~ 44 ~

WE ARE going to Paris, Jerry says. I picture sidewalk cafés, the Louvre. "Not *that* Paris," Jerry adds as I imagine our *River Queen* lifting herself out of the river and carrying us across the seas. Apparently there is a place called Paris, Tennessee, and we are now headed to a marina called Paris Landing, where Jerry thinks he can moor his houseboat for the winter. "Okay, Paris, Tennessee, it is." I take a sip of my coffee, which is hot, and slurp so as not to burn my tongue, which is still sore from the last time I burned it.

"Don't slurp," Jerry says.

"Okay." I head into the bathroom and on the way out close the door. "And don't slam the door," he says. Then I leave it ajar and he tells me not to leave it open. For whatever reason he is in a bad mood and starting to remind me of my father so I decide to go topside where Tom is piloting.

"I'm giving our captain wide berth," I tell him and Tom nods, understanding.

"Yeah, sometimes you gotta do that." That's all he says. He'll never say a disloyal word about Jerry. But a few miles out of Cape Girardeau he says, "Why don't you take over for me now?"

I take the wheel just below Buffalo Island as we come into Dog Tooth Bend. Here the river arches and we're going to go several miles east, then north before we're heading south again. A beautiful, long S curve. It's twenty river miles to zero and I'm at the helm. The river is wide and there isn't a thing along its flat, scrub banks. Not a house or a grain elevator. The river is empty as well. The sun streams down with afternoon light. We could be anywhere in the world.

Tom checks his cell phone and he's got a message from his aunt Sue. "She told me I forgot to cut Grandma's grass. I guess she forgot I'm out of town."

"Grandma?"

"Yeah, my mother's mom. She's been around a long time, but Aunt Sue kinda raised me. You know the older she gets, the more she looks like my mom." He takes a deep sigh. "I just stick to her like glue." We're in the delta now—flat, green land without a house or building in sight stretches as far as the eye can see. From this land and its flooding comes some of the richest farmland in the world.

Dog Tooth Bend becomes Greenleaf Bend. Another big, gentle curve. We're moving fast, it seems to me, and I'm right. Jerry comes topside to announce that we're averaging twelve miles per hour now. That's because we have no locks and dams to slow us down and also because the river, as it narrows, is growing swifter. "I want to go slower," I tell him.

"We're getting good mileage," Jerry says. "Less than a gallon a mile at speed. That's good because we're going on two engines."

But I don't want this trip to end. I'm just starting to see the river. To see its ripples and whirls. To read its surface the way I'd read any good book and learn to look at what lies beneath. There are no more secrets from me. I know so much more than when I began. This river has become a friend.

I gaze down at the water and suddenly it is boiling with swells and eddies and backward swirls. So much for no more secrets. "What's this?" I ask as we continue up Greenleaf Bend.

"It's an uneven bottom," Jerry says. "Because of the delta. It collects silt."

I nod, taking this in.

The sun burns into the horizon as I hold the wheel. Even through the eddies where I feel the tug, no one tries to take it away from me. We ride silently on the flybridge, knowing our journey on the Mississippi is coming to an end. I ease us around one more S curve bend.

"So what do you think of the way our girl is piloting?" Tom says with a laugh, poking me in the arm.

And Jerry pays me what I assume must be his highest compliment. "What girl?" he says.

We are approaching zero. I invite Tom or Jerry to take the wheel, but they both refuse. "You take her to zero," Tom says.

"This one's for you." As a surprise Jerry pulls out a bottle of apple fruit wine, apparently the only wine to be had at Fred's Gas Station in Cape Girardeau and a few Dixie cups, which he fills. We pour ourselves glasses. I probably shouldn't drink and drive, but, as we pass beneath Cairo Highway Bridge, we click our paper cups together, take a gulp of sweet apple wine, and congratulate ourselves on getting here in one piece.

As we do, I see a flash, like lightning, coming from behind us. "What was that?" I ask Tom as he makes a small adjustment to the wheel.

"Oh, that was just your next idea."

We come on to the Ohio. Ahead on a hill in Kentucky a giant white cross looms. The South is below us and I reach a deeper understanding of the term "sold down the river." It was what slaves dreaded—to be sold deeper into the South.

Barges, lined up by the dozens, are moving tons of fuel, grain, manure, and plumbing supplies up and down the Ohio. Smokestacks to the south puff away and the sky is rimmed by a gray brown horizon of smog. I can see where the waters meet. A marriage, Jerry calls it. Below is the lower Mississippi, a river that for now eludes me. Behind is where we have been and ahead the Ohio, a big unknown. I'm glad I made the decision to stay with this boat. I know, as I leave the upper Mississippi behind, that I lay claim to its wide vistas and gentle bends, its white pelicans and locks and dams. I am a northerner to the core. For now there'll be no side-winding waterways for me.

Still, as we enter the lake-wide confluence and I hand the wheel to Jerry, Tom and I get a despondent look in our eyes. What had been a quiet, peaceful cruise is suddenly a bustling highway of commerce and trade. We don't like it. None of us does. A few miles up the Ohio we start to talk. We don't want to spend the night here. There are no marinas in sight. At least nothing for sure. We see a beach on the eastern end of the confluence and Jerry decides to make for it, then he balks. Because of the delta and the layers of silt the water is too shallow. And he doesn't like all the barges coming up and down. This time I see his point. We could get trapped here.

"Let's go for a ride," Jerry says. He is turning the *River Queen*, scanning the banks of the Ohio, then making for the Cairo Highway Bridge. We pass beneath it once again and then it is clear. We are heading back up the Mississippi to find a beach where we'll bivouac for the night. None of us wants to drop anchor anywhere near where we came onto the Ohio. The sun is setting on the Missouri side as we head upstream. We go four or five miles around the bend, and then we see it.

A wide strip of pristine sand. There's a gravel elevator nearby, but it is silent with only a single barge off to the side. As deserted as we could hope for and, as we beach, we see that this sandbar is perfect for our last night on the Mississippi. We drop anchor and scramble onto the beach. Samantha Jean does her usual runs up and down and I walk across a surface made from silt and clay—a thick, crusty mud. Where it has dried, it is cracked.

Samantha Jean is racing up and down and Tom shouts, "Go get 'em, Sammy, big waves! Go get 'em, Girl!" I'm actually wishing he'd be quiet, but he keeps yelling and his voice echoes across the river. "Come on, Sammy, big waves, big waves!"

Then he calls to me, "Hey, Mary, can you get me the axe?"

"Gee, I thought you'd never ask."

I go back inside and retrieve our axe and carry it up to Tom. As I walk along the beach, I feel like an ant on a Firestone tire. The clay grooves cut into my bare feet, but I don't care. The axe is heavy in my hand.

As I carry it to him, he keeps yelling at Samantha Jean. "Come on, Girl, here's a big one! Let's jump!" Jerry stands on the bow, laughing, sipping his beer. The male energy is starting to wear thin. I could do with some peace and quiet and a little less guffawing. On the other hand we've been on the boat for almost three weeks and no one is dead. It doesn't even occur to me to smash this axe into someone's skull. That in and of itself is a kind of miracle to me.

Instead I hand the axe to Tom and he heads off toward the end of the sandbar. He goes into a muddy, wooded realm and hacks away at some brush and comes back, as he always does, dragging huge logs. He builds the biggest fire he can make and we sit around it. Jerry throws some steaks we've been saving on the grill and keeps them there for about an hour, until I beg him to take mine off. They cook theirs twice as long and we eat without a word around the fire. As soon as dinner's done, Tom heads off to bed, but Jerry and I sit, sipping our beers until the embers cool. We sit in silence, heads tilted back, just gazing at the stars. Finally, reluctantly, we stumble off to bed, knowing that our nights on this river are done.

I wake early, take my coffee and journal for a long walk along the deserted beach. As I'm heading out, Jerry says, "Guess we had company." I see where he is pointing. The tracks of two deer, heading past our boat, are carved into the sand.

# UPSTREAM

~ 45 ~

IN 1967 a black man was found hanging in a jail cell in Cairo, Illinois, and for Cairo, this was the beginning of the end. Protests erupted. The whites fled and many never returned. Since then the town has struggled. I have read reports about Cairo. The mayor was quoted as saying that what his town needs is a McDonald's and a mall. But nothing prepared me for the ghost town I saw.

As we pass the Civil War site of Fort Defiance, just up the Ohio, I decide I must stop at Cairo. But there is no courtesy dock so we have to bring the dinghy down. It is the only time we use it, and Jerry is very proud of the way it descends smoothly from the aft transom into the water. Tom and I hop on the dinghy and he drives me up to the levee and leaves me there. I tell him I'll give a shout when I'm ready for him to come and get me. He gives me a wary look. "You gonna be all right here?"

"I'm going to be fine."

I walk through the gate in the flood wall onto HISTORIC 8TH STREET. A wrought iron sign arches across the street, and I come to an avenue of boarded-up shops, plate glass shattered on the ground. A corner building on the main street is completely in ruins and in the distance I see another sign that reads HISTORIC DOWNTOWN CAIRO. In the middle of the road is a pedestal for a statue that was never installed. The beauty shop is closed. The flower shop too.

A black man sits on a folding chair in front of a boarded-up building. I say "Good morning" and he doesn't respond. He doesn't look away. He doesn't do anything. Behind him is a storefront where the windows have been soaped to read "Leadership? Cairo? Why?" I pause at the Gem Theater Restoration Project. Which has been halted.

Cairo, Illinois, which sits at the confluence of the Ohio and the Mississippi, used to be one of the most significant towns in the Midwest. During the Civil War it was of great strategic importance. On either side of the rivers were states sympathetic to the Confederate cause. They provided supplies to the Southern troops. Cairo was home to many regiments of the Illinois infantry and served as the staging area for Union army expeditions into Missouri, Kentucky, Tennessee, and Mississippi.

Now it is a town in ruins. The Mighty River Church is shuttered. In front of it prisoners in orange uniforms are picking up trash. All of them are black. Cairo was a place where many blacks settled after the Civil War. One of the prisoners looks up at me with red, rheumy eyes, and says, "Good morning, Miss," and I say "good morning" back. Then he returns to picking up trash. In front of an insurance agency I eavesdrop on two men. The one says to the other, "Doing that in a place like this is suicide."

"What is wrong with Cairo?" I ask a woman at a local newsstand. "Bad government," she says. I suppose that's true, but the fact is Cairo hasn't found its Mark Twain; it hasn't embraced its Superman. There are no casinos, no waterfront development. The town feels as if it is falling down.

I hear, however, that the Custom House and Old Courthouse have been turned into a museum and I make my way there. The Custom House is indeed filled with tons of artifacts— arrowheads, old wagons, pictures of Cairo's founding fathers, its Civil War heroes, cradles where children once slept. I'm not there long, browsing, when Fred Shelton, who runs the place, starts telling me his story. I don't even have to ask for it. Fred, a tall gray-haired man, just starts to talk.

"I moved to Cairo in 1943 with my mom and stepdad. His name was Vernon 'Turkey' Curtis and he was a famous baseball player from Chattanooga. He was about 90 percent Illinois Indian and he had a hot temper. He married a woman named Ruth Elizabeth. They had two children. Then he went off to war and when he returned, they divorced. Then he married my mother. Her name was also Ruth Elizabeth. Odd coincidence, no?"

"Oh, that's a coincidence, all right." I'm trying not to gaze at my watch, but I know Jerry's going to want to push off and that Tom will be waiting for me soon with the dinghy, but Fred gives no hint of pausing.

"My mother worked at a fancy restaurant in town and the ballplayers stayed in the hotel. My stepfather played for the Senators and other teams. Anyway, one thing led to another and they got married. We moved up to Cairo when I was nine. . . ."

"Nine, wow . . ."

"Yep." Fred doesn't skip a beat. "That was a while ago. When I was a kid, Cairo was the most important town in southern Illinois. People came here from Paducah, from Carbondale, on Friday nights. The stores stayed open until nine p.m. and you couldn't even get a parking spot. People came from Paducah just to people watch. They used to have all kinds of stores—J. C. Penney, Sears, Woolworths. You name it." I glance around the museum and through the open windows. It is hard to imagine Cairo as the cutting edge of fine fashion. But apparently it was.

"We used to have professional baseball here in Cairo. The Cardinals trained here. The lady who drew the Cardinal logo, she was from Cairo. I was the mail carrier. From 1964 I used to make two trips a day through the business section. I had to load up two or three times. When I retired in 1999 I could carry the mail in one hand. There used to be 30,000 people, then 15,000. Now it's 3,000. It just went down. When the black people started protesting, the whites left town. I carried the mail all through that time as well. I sat with my wife and kids in the car and watched them firebomb the police station in 1968. I was a boy in Chattanooga and there was a white counter and a black counter. Here you'd get on the bus and the blacks could sit wherever. But after that man was found hung . . . I guess there's just hatred everywhere."

Now it is getting late, but I am reluctant to go. I have a feeling I'm the only person who's stopped by here in days.

But Fred is cheerful and resilient. "Nice talking to you. You see anybody else out there, you just send 'em around."

As I'm leaving Cairo I pick up a local events brochure. The next evening there's a Yard Decorating Contest. "Judging Starts at 6 p.m. Remember the theme, have your decorating completed, and your lights on." I want to know the theme. I'm dying to know the theme, but nowhere is it written. And then on Saturday it's the Little Miss Pageant. "Contestants between the ages of 4 and 6 compete for this honor. Come and see cuteness at its finest." The judging starts at 7. Past my bedtime.

I give Tom a call on his cell and he asks me if I can find some ice on my way back to the dinghy. I do find some in a grocery store and lug two giant sacks on my shoulders, more than I can carry, really, back down Historic 8th Street, through the flood wall opening. I come back to the dinghy and find Tom, waiting for me. "Hey," he says. "You giving me the cold shoulder?"

He helps me on board. "Hey, we're not in such a rush," he says. Then he takes me for an unauthorized ride in the dinghy around the Ohio River for a few minutes, while Jerry, shirtless and perplexed, stares as we whiz by.

~ 46 ~

SOMEHOW WE missed the wicket dam, which is down for high water. A warning in Quimby's tells us, "Recreational Boats Advised That Navigation Is Hazardous During These Times and Should Be Avoided." "Well, great," Jerry says. "We just went over it."

Jerry has been avoiding sharing something with me, but now he does. "We don't have any more maps. Just the Quimby's," he says.

By maps he means navigational maps. We don't have any detailed drawings of the Ohio or the Tennessee. What we have from the Army Corps of Engineers stops at Cairo. We were never planning on going this far. "Will we be okay?"

Jerry shrugs. "If nothing bad happens, we'll be fine."

"Right . . ."

Approaching Lock and Dam 53 we have to lock through no matter what. A tow who doesn't speak Cajun passes and tells us he'll take us on starboard on two whistles. He's loaded with manure and we aren't exactly upwind. We pass Harrah's casino as we're looking for a dock, but don't see a place to tie up. Heading farther downstream, I'm tired and the day feels long. Suddenly I see that we are slowing down. I look up and there is, well, a fort. A real fort, or so it seems. It looks so much like a real fort that I anticipate the U.S. cavalry coming to our aid. And to my great joy I see that we are mooring here.

"Can I stretch my legs?" I ask.

"Well, considering that we have six double barges ahead of us, I don't see why not."

I look and see them all lined up. Half a dozen of them and they're riding low and heavy. Technically, if we're willing to wait a while, they'll put us through, but who knows how long that wait might be? "Does that mean we're here for the night?"

Jerry nods. "Unless traffic suddenly eases up, guess so."

I head up to visit the fort on shaky legs. It has been a long day from our beachhead on the Mississippi to here. I make my way up a road through a grove of hills to the visitor's center, which is closed, but I pick up a brochure, slightly sodden and mildewed, that sits in a little Lucite box. I read the following: "The replica of the 1802 American fort was finished in October of 2003. The new replica replaces the 1794 American fort built 30 years ago. The 1794 fort had been a reproduction of the first American fort built at Fort Massac. The 1802 fort was selected to replace the 1794 fort."

Okay, when is the exam? I'm sure there's a niche industry for writers willing to compose local tourist pamphlets, but I'm not applying for the job. Crossing a wooden bridge and a dry moat, I enter the fenced-in compound. It is almost dusk on a fall evening and yet the fort is wide open. It is what one would expect—rustic, made of logs—but actually quite lovely.

It is growing darker and amber lights go on. I am alone with this replica of the past until suddenly a bus arrives. I'm hoping for reenactors. I see from the brochure that there are all kinds of "Living History" programs here. "French and Indian War reenactors are welcome." You can actually take a basic training class for "French soldiers and militia during the 1760s" that includes military drills, mock battles, and camp life.

But for now it's just kids. They race into the fort and surround me. They're whooping it up and I am overrun. I assume it is a history lesson as I slip away. Sometimes in the half light of dusk, I still see Kate as a child. It's hard to grasp that that little girl who raced through fields is no more.

It's late when I get back to the boat and I can see a houseboat coming up alongside ours. Jerry is talking to their captain. Apparently this houseboat, named *It's Magic*, sees the same problem with the lock ahead we saw. I hear their captain ask Jerry, "Can we tie up to you for the night?"

This is proper houseboat etiquette, unlike that of the unfortunate *Bronx Cheer* encounter. "Sure," Jerry says. "Do you have a bottle of wine?" He's joking, but they say they do. "Good, because my second officer here could use some."

I am delighted by this exchange, thrilled to be referred to as second officer, though actually this makes me the last officer, and almost equally delighted even as they hand me a nice warm bottle of pink zinfandel. My fave. They introduce themselves. Ron and Lizzie are from Indiana and they are doing the Great Loop. Their boat is an elegantly appointed houseboat but with a cruiser engine. It has a fancy white vinyl couch and they invite us to come on board for a drink. Tom doesn't want to go. He's shy of rich people with big boats. But Jerry agrees.

We climb onto their boat and rest ourselves in wicker lounge chairs as Ron pours the pink zinfandel. "So," he says, "I see you

folks are on a houseboat too. Well we've been coming down from
Lake Michigan. We started in Muskegon."

"We started up in La Crosse," Jerry says.

"We're going to take a whole year. I took a leave from my law
firm. Well, it really is *my* law firm. That is, I started it, so I guess
I can walk away from it for a while, can't I, Honey?"

Lizzie looks at him adoringly and smiles. "Of course you can."

"I can do whatever I want. Worked hard enough to get to this
point, so I'm going to enjoy it, right?" He gazes at us through his
somewhat beady eyes.

We sip some of the sweet, syrupy zinfandel, but after a few
minutes Jerry leaves, saying he's got work to do on the boat. I
look at my watch. It's almost nine o'clock and I'm sure he doesn't
have any work to do. I'm also sure he doesn't like this guy very
much but I'm intrigued and glad to be sitting in a wicker chair
on an elaborate white vinyl deck with Burt Bacharach on the
stereo.

After Jerry's gone, Ron turns to me. "Do you believe in
meant to be's?"

"Sure," I tell him. And I do.

"Well, I just have a feeling about you, Mary. I think we were
supposed to meet." As he says this, it begins to rain. Ron looks up
at the heavens. "Do you ever feel that way?"

"Well, I think we can know things. I think some things are
supposed to happen. . . ."

"I know exactly what you mean."

"You know," I tell him, "once my daughter was getting on a
ride at Coney Island. She stood in line for forty-five minutes for
that ride and all of a sudden I went berserk. I started shouting at
her that she can't go on that ride. I make my husband go and get
her and everyone is angry at me. Then a few weeks later I open
the newspaper and see that two children were killed on that very
ride."

Ron nods thoughtfully. "Are you a Christian, Mary?" he
asks me.

I decide to answer honestly. "No, I am not."

I expect he might ask me what I am, or display a shred of interest in my response, but he does not. "Neither am I," he says, staring deep into my eyes. We are coconspirators now. "I'm a heathen. I've lived many times before. I'm a sorcerer. I traffic in white magic." Why me? I want to ask. Why do I wind up with guys like this? But he goes on. "In a previous life I was a Viking. I have raped and pillaged. I have done horrible things I am not proud of and I have gone through several life cycles of repentance."

His sweet wife, Lizzie, gazes at him with adoring eyes. Clearly she has heard this before and is unfazed.

I suppose this beats alien abduction, but I am at a loss for words. I only know I'm on their boat in the dark and Tom and Jerry are nowhere to be seen. They've probably gone off into the woods to pee. And I'll never see them again. "How do you know you are a sorcerer?" I ask, trying to be polite.

He gazes at his wife. "Shall I tell her?"

Lizzie smiles demurely. "I think you can."

"Well, you see, one day, a few years ago, I was driving and there was this guy, riding my tail. He annoyed me and I threw my hand back, just in an impatient gesture, you understand. . . ." I assume this is the sorcerer's equivalent of flicking someone the bird. "And all of a sudden I heard this big boom and I looked back and saw that his engine had caught fire and exploded."

"Wow," I say, my eyes popping out of my head.

"I've done this one or two other times. You know, when someone really deserved it, but since then I've had to be very careful. I have to learn how to manage my anger. I can't just go do that anymore, can I, Lizzie?"

Lizzie shakes her head. "You certainly cannot."

"I've known about my powers for a while. I try to use them sparingly. I try to help people. Tell them if they are in danger, if they are safe."

The zinfandel is starting to make me swoon. Outside I can hear a driving rain. I am wondering how I can make my exit gracefully. "So am I in danger? Am I safe?" I am trying not to make these questions seem rhetorical.

Ron reaches across and puts my hands in his chubby fists. His hands are exceptionally warm and at any moment I expect to be vaporized. He closes his eyes and begins to hyperventilate. Then he stares at me with piercing eyes. "You are safe for now," he tells me in a deep preacher's voice. "But you are very very lucky. This time you were lucky. I cannot say what will happen next."

And all I can think is that I am very lucky that I didn't wind up on his boat. I am very lucky that Tom and Jerry aren't nut jobs or psychos and I am willing them to come rescue me. I'm starting to think about what to do next when I see Jerry poking his head over the side. "Hi there, Mary. Just wondering what you're up to."

"Oh, I was thinking of coming back."

"Well, we've got some dinner ready."

I look at him puzzled. I know this is a lie. Jerry would never have dinner ready. I want to leap up and hug him, but I remain calm. "Oh," I say to the sorcerer and his wife, "my captain calls. Guess I'd better go."

He clasps my hand in his and I anticipate self-immolation. Instead he helps me off the ladder of his boat onto mine. When I land on our deck, I gaze at Jerry. "I thought you might need rescuing," he says.

"He's a sorcerer," I tell Tom and Jerry when we finally sit down for a bite. "In his previous life he was a Viking."

Tom and Jerry look at me askance. "Sure, Mary, of course he is."

"Give me a little potato vodka," Tom says, "and I'm a sorcerer too."

~ 47 ~

FASTER THAN a speeding bullet, more powerful than a locomotive. Able to leap tall buildings in a single bound. Look up in the sky. It's a bird; it's a plane; it's Superman. How is it that I distinctly recall such adages of my youth? The Jiminy Cricket song.

"You are a human animal. . . ." Or Roy Rogers on Trigger, crooning "Happy Trails." These things stick like glue in my head. Like childhood itself. So when I saw that Metropolis, Illinois, is on our way up the Ohio, I told Jerry we had to stop.

Metropolis, Illinois, is the only town in America named Metropolis. In the early 1970s when other river towns, such as Cairo just downstream, were dying, Metropolis was looking for a public relations plug. For years since Superman's inception as a comic book character in 1938, the Metropolis post office had been receiving mail addressed to Superman, Metropolis, USA. So, with huge fanfare, the town leaders decided that the way to secure their future was to adopt Superman and declare their town his.

In the middle of Metropolis a twelve-foot statue of Superman looms and there is a Superman museum and I want to see it, though neither of the boys do. I push on alone. It's a chilly morning, perhaps not much more than fifty. Last night's storm brought a cold front down from the north. A promise of fall, or even winter in the air. As I walk, I anticipate phone booths where you could make a quick change into your red cape and jersey, but Metropolis is a fairly ordinary hamlet. There is a good-size grocery store within walking distance of the boat, right outside the fort, and I intend to avail myself of supplies later on.

I stroll the four or five blocks into town, pausing for a visit at the *Metropolis Planet.* Because it is a weekly, the town newspaper cannot call itself the *Daily Planet,* but along with the adoption of Superman, the local newspaper changed its name. I pick up a few copies of the *Metropolis Planet,* along with a souvenir copy, for which I paid five dollars, telling about how it came to be that Metropolis, Illinois, became home to a superhero.

Outside of the Superman museum there's actually a phone booth and a sign for the *Daily Planet.* Let's face it; the guys who have played Superman haven't had much luck. Some have postulated that there is a curse on those who take on the Superman role, and two of them have been named, coincidentally, Reeves and Reeve. Christopher Reeve suffered a tragic horseback riding accident that left him paralyzed, but George Reeves is another story.

In the 1950s his star was rising. He took the part of Superman and was typecast from then on. When the television series ended in 1959, Reeves fell on hard times. He was found with a single bullet wound to the head on June 16, 1959, three days before he was to be married. The coroner's office declared it a suicide. But there were no fingerprints on the gun. No powder burns to the head. The shell gun casing was found under the body and the gun was at his feet. Downstairs his fiancée and guests were waiting for him to come to dinner. Los Angeles murder buffs have never come to a consensus on what really happened to George Reeves. But both Noel Neill, who played Lois Lane, and Jack Larsen, who played Jimmy Olsen, believed it was foul play.

The Superman museum, however, doesn't dwell on such things. There are no suggestions of mob hits, jealous lovers, or cover-ups, all of which the buffs have posited. This is a place of memorabilia. Everything that has ever happened to Superman or had his face on it, they've got. Buttons, comic books, dolls, paintings, statuettes, costumes, stills from Superman movies, including both George and Christopher flying through space, and other would-be Supermen performing various amazing feats. In the end, given that I'm not much of a superhero girl myself, I grow bored of looking at the buttons and seeing the sad faces of the young couple who work there. I buy a few postcards for the children in my life who still believe they can fly, and leave.

As I head back past the giant statue of Superman that looms over the town, I stop at the grocery store and buy, among other things, olive oil. A pointless purchase, really, as we only have a day or so left. As I walk by Fort Massac, prisoners in black-and-white prison stripes and matching hats chop trees and pile the wood. After a few minutes their guard gives them a command and the men line up and march, single file, into a waiting van.

~ 48 ~

THREE MILES north of Paducah, Kentucky, we lock through. This time because we are going upstream, we rise ten feet. I hold the line and Jerry shows me once again how to loop it through. On the radio the lockmaster calls us, "Northbound *Friend Ship,* come in on your port side. You'll need all your bumpers and fenders out and two twenty-five-foot lines."

"Roger," Jerry says. We've never had to use our own lines before, or put all our fenders and bumpers down, but Jerry explains that each lock and each lockmaster has its own rules and regulations. "Tom, get us two lines."

Tom starts to secure the bowline and Jerry snaps at him. "Not the bowline. We've got loose lines. I don't want to risk our bowline."

Tom shrugs and looks up at me. "Same difference," he mumbles, but Jerry hears him.

"Not the same," he says. "Safety first. We need the bowlines."

Tom and I go about gathering two twenty-five-foot lines, which we loop around two bollards as we lock through. We're running low on fuel and Jerry is getting nervous about this. We assume there's a fuel dock in Paducah, but as we come to Paducah, and pass it, we don't see a fuel dock.

About half a mile past Paducah, we see what looks like a fueling platform. "What about there?" I ask Jerry.

"Worth a shot."

As we approach the platform, we see it is covered in cables and old tires and made of wooden slats. A guy in greasy overalls works there alone. "Hello!" Jerry calls, but the guy ignores us. "Excuse me!" Jerry says, and the worker turns away.

We pull up alongside despite the very obvious cold shoulder. "I'm sorry to bother you. I see how much you're working here," Jerry says, "but we're low on fuel. Can you help us out?"

"Nope," is our one-word reply. This is starting to feel like an outtake from *Deliverance* and Tom and Jerry are uncomfortable as well.

"Know where we can?"

"Twenty-two miles south at Kentucky Dam."

We look at one another. "We aren't going to make that," Jerry says.

"Can't we just get gas from a gas station?" I ask them, and they nod. It seems that we can. "So . . . why don't we?"

Tom and Jerry agree that we'll go back to Paducah, where there's a courtesy dock. We'll tie up there and see if we can't figure out how to take our gas drums to the nearest gas station. None of us is very optimistic, but it's worth a shot.

Paducah, Kentucky, is a pretty hip town. Known for its harness racing at the Players Bluegrass Downs, it also has lots of cute shops, restaurants, old cobblestone streets, and a river history museum. This is the place where John Banvard began his artistic career modestly enough on the banks of the Ohio.

Tom plans to try and rustle up some gasoline. He never wants to explore or see where we are. He wants to be near the boat, his dog, and his engines, and he seems content with this. It is a chilly morning as we leave him and Jerry and I head off to visit the river museum. Afterward we stop in the Bayou Cajun Restaurant for some takeout. While we're waiting, we decide to have a beer. Though it's only a little after noon, the bar is open and there's a couple of regulars (you just know they are regulars) in jean jackets. One has no teeth. We take a pint of what's on draft and I must admit, though it is the middle of the day, the cold beer tastes good.

There are various stuffed animals—a monkey crawling up a rope, a stuffed frog—and I compliment the bartender on her taste in stuffed animals. "Oh, these ain't just stuffed animals," the man with no teeth says, "show her Big Mouth Bill Bass."

She takes down this fish, mounted on a piece of wood, winds something, and the bass starts to sing, "Take me to the river, drop me in the water," its thick red lips flapping. When she sees I am laughing hysterically, she pulls a frog down and he sits in front of me, singing "It's a Wonderful World" in an excellent Louis Armstrong rendition.

As we get back to the boat, Tom is happily pouring gasoline into the engines. "I got gas," he says, clearly pleased with himself. "I got gas." He tells us he was walking to find a gas station and a woman stopped him. She asked if he had a boat and was he looking for gasoline. He replied he was.

"It's a disgrace we don't have a gas dock in Paducah," this woman said.

"She made two trips with me," Tom tells us. "She even waited while I filled up, then took me back for more." He pauses, shaking his head as he's gassing up. "That's the kind of people you want to meet on the river," Tom says.

~ 49 ~

A FEW more miles up the Ohio and the river forks. We make our turn onto the Tennessee and I feel this trip is coming to an end for me. Perhaps it already ended when we left our little campsite on the Mississippi and turned onto the Ohio. I felt a spirit leave me then. This Tennessee River is wide and beautiful, but I have left something behind. For a time I had found home. Now I am once again on my way.

Tom agrees with me. As we sit on the flybridge, he says he wasn't "a fan" of the Ohio. He wants his river back. I'm nodding as Samantha Jean gets out of her bomber jacket and stands, whining, at my feet. I decide to give it a try. "Okay, Sammy girl, big jump," and she propels herself from the floor into my arms.

The dog nestles in my lap as Tom pilots straight ahead. I think he's a bit stunned and perhaps a little jealous that his ornery dog has found her way onto my lap. As the sun starts to go down, a chill is in the air. It's been our coldest day yet, anyway, but now with the sun dropping it's just cold. Jerry won't let me navigate here because we are traveling without maps in uncharted terrain, and I find myself growing colder and bored, even with Samantha Jean on my lap.

Even the landscape is altered. Here it is all flat. The reddish brown beaches of the delta. It is dusk as we near the Kentucky Dam. I am topside, catching the fading light, and I see right away that we've got two barges ahead of us, going downriver. That's at least a two-hour wait. Quimby's warned us of this. They said that this is the busiest lock on the river and long delays are possible.

This doesn't seem to bother the boys, but I am anxious to be on our way. Jerry and Tom are gabbing back and forth and I can hear their guffaws, which I've grown weary of now. I am tired of the confines of this space. It's cold and there's nowhere to go. I sit on my yoga mat, wrapped in my moon and stars flannel blanket on the flybridge. Silver fish are jumping as the sun is setting on the Tennessee. On the shore a blue heron stalks them. After the sun goes down, it's too cold to stay on top and I go below. I find Tom, sitting silently on the bow, staring at the lock. "It's our last lock," he says.

I nod. It's true, it is. "I guess I don't want this trip to end," he says. He's got Samantha Jean wrapped up in his jacket like a baby in a Snugli. Even in the dark I can see his eyes well up. "Do you want to talk about it?" I ask him.

"Naw," he says. "Not now." He gets up and leaves. A few minutes later I hear him topside, making his bed, and before I know it, he's laughing with Jerry over something someone I've never met before said.

At 7:30 it's pitch-black and there's a tow named the *Tennessee Hunter* with a six-hundred-foot barge, filled with sand and gravel. We are moving into position ahead of it, but still waiting for another barge to clear. Tom wants to drop anchor, but Jerry says we'll idle here. "Really?" Tom says.

"Yeah, I think so."

The big black barge moves into place behind us. "We'll get through after this tow. Tom, check the aft light over the transom. Make sure she's on. Looks like the *Tennessee Hunter*'s just gonna hang back."

The lockmaster comes on to our radio. "*Friend Ship*, hold back to port in case he has to reverse." I'm watching Jerry hang back as we start to swing into the levee.

"Let's try an anchor," he says to Tom. "Which way's the wind coming from?"

"Across the port bow," Tom says.

"Okay, let's throw an anchor over her port bow," and Tom throws it. In the darkness we hear it splash.

"I'm gonna leave her running because we're awfully close to shore."

Tom seems nervous and I can tell he doesn't like the look of this. "We're getting some current here, Sir. It's from the lock. She's really kicking up bubbles and pushing us back. Shove your ass that way," Tom says, pointing in the opposite direction we are drifting.

"I'm going to try and move us from the shore." Jerry looks concerned as we are drifting closer and closer to the shore.

"Want me to pull the anchor?"

"If you can. Yeah, they must be draining the lock and the valves are pushing us into the shore."

Jerry revs the engines and Tom tugs on the anchor line. "Okay, now we're off the shore."

"Just kick back." Then more sharply to Tom, "Just kick back! Let me do this." After he's made his maneuver he looks sheepishly at Tom. "Sorry. I just wanted concentration. . . ."

"Rock 'n' roll," Tom says. "Hey, that *Tennessee Hunter*, he's hanging way back. . . ."

It appears that *Tennessee Hunter* is going to perform the river courtesy of letting us go ahead of him. He could easily come in with us or exert his right-of-way as a commercial vessel, but he chooses to hang back and after a two-and-a-half-hour wait we proceed into Kentucky Lake. We enter a huge, dark pool of water, illumined with amber lights, where we will rise fifty-seven feet. The gates of the lock are an eerie golden color as suddenly the water begins to pour into the lock.

We find ourselves on a roiling sea. The water, the color of pea soup, literally swirls beneath us, boiling up. It is the kind of water where you know if you fell in, you'd be sucked down, and we all quickly put on our life jackets and Tom hurls Samantha Jean into the cabin. We churn in this cauldron from hell, a pit from which it seems we will be pulled down. We rise higher and higher in this bubbling broth until suddenly the churning stops. Everything is calm as if nothing was ever wrong. The yellow gates open and the siren blares. We sail into the blackened night.

We are looking for the Kentucky Dam Marina. But we have come onto a huge lake in the darkest of nights. Across the lake we see lights, but they are far away. Closer to where we are there is an inlet and more lights. "Well," Jerry says, "which way should we go?"

Across the lake looks very far in this darkness so we opt for the closer inlet. It is close to midnight as our *River Queen* floats into a marina, filled with hundreds of sailboats. Tom and Jerry shake their heads. It's the wrong place, but we're all too tired and cold to go anywhere else now. We find a slip at the dock and tie up. Tom hands me the bowline. "You do it," he says. "I'll take the stern."

I'm exhausted and shivering, holding the line in my hand. I wrap it a few times around the cleat, then try to remember "the rabbit." Down, out, around, in. I do it once and it doesn't seem right. Angling myself for better light, I try again. Tom comes by as I finish and yanks the line. "That'll hold," he says, adjusting the fenders. It is a cold clear night with just a crescent moon. The sails around us clang into their masts like hundreds of wind chimes.

~ 50 ~

AT SIX in the morning there's frost on the glass. The cabin is freezing cold, except right in front of the space heater Jerry's dug up from the hold, which smells of gas. I huddle down inside my sleeping bag. But Jerry's stirring about, putting on water for our tea bag coffee, so I get up. Outside I hear the clanging as wind blows through sails. I gaze out and see the dozens and dozens of boats, their sails flapping in the wind. It is clear we are at the wrong marina. We need fuel and a pump out. I haven't had a shower, a real shower, in six days. I don't mean hot water either. I just mean relatively clean water that comes from above and falls over my head.

No matter what, we need to find the Kentucky Dam Marina, which is probably across the lake. I'm so cold I put on all my heavy clothes, which isn't a lot. There's a lighthouse on a spit of land and I walk there. I take my binoculars to see if I can see the marina. The sunshine feels warm, but I can almost see my breath.

On the dock, lines are coiled in an orderly fashion like garden snakes. The sailboats have such earnest names, like *Relentless, Persistence, Tranquillity*. There's nothing fun or playful here. No *Ms. Chief, Mint-to-Be*, or *Naughty Buoys* at this marina. I go out through the gate and head along the short trail to the lighthouse. With my binoculars I spot what looks like a marina far across the blue stretch of lake. The wind is blowing and I'm shivering as I head back and find that someone has shut the gate and I'm locked out.

I start to shout for Jerry, but it's not even seven in the morning and I'm sure people are asleep on their boats. I call him on his phone, but he doesn't answer. I wait a few moments for someone to come. At last Jerry answers and comes and gets me. When I return to the boat, Tom is sitting on the bow, eating a pepperoni pizza. He has another one cooking in the oven. He's on his third can of diet Dew. "Breakfast," he says. "Missed dinner last night."

There's something about the smell of pepperoni pizza at seven a.m. that doesn't sit well with me. Still, I help myself to a slice.

"I have an idea," I say. "While you guys gas up and pump out at Kentucky Dam, I'll take a shower."

"I have an idea," Tom says. "Why don't we all wait and take showers at Paris Landing?"

"Because I want a shower now."

"Well, I say we all take showers at the same time."

We huff and I walk away. Tom does too and for the next half hour we don't speak. We are preparing to leave, untying our lines. As we are about to push off, Tom turns to me. "I guess I was kinda testy."

"No, I was being selfish," I tell him.

"I just don't want this trip to end," he tells me.

"I don't either." Then we finish up with our chores.

✺

An hour later we are riding across Kentucky Lake to the marina where we will pump out and gas up. We will also all take showers. The sun starts to warm up the day and we aren't in a rush. I meet a man who tells me he's sailing around the world.

"Sailing?" I ask him.

"Yes, in a sailboat." He's a short, stocky, gray-haired man with a mustache, and he doesn't exactly look like a sailor.

"How long are you going to spend?"

"Four years."

I am stunned. "Four years." He starts to tell me his route. Down the Mississippi to Florida, Florida across the Atlantic to the Mediterranean, the Mediterranean to Africa. Around the tip of Africa. I am completely amazed and now my little journey feels paltry in comparison. "Can I see your boat?"

"Sure," he says.

As we're walking over, I ask if he's going alone. "Oh, no, my wife and our daughter are coming with."

I find it incredible that a daughter would want to spend four years sailing with her parents. "It's nice that your daughter wants to come with."

"Oh, she doesn't have much choice."

"She doesn't?"

"No, she's fifteen."

Now I am really stunned. I can't imagine taking my daughter out of high school. And when I see their boat—a rather small, black sailboat with no real deck topside—I truly can't believe it. The wife and daughter come out of the hull to greet me. The wife is a large, blond woman and their daughter has a weak handshake and dark eyes.

"We're homeschooling her. She's doing the ACE program," her father explains when they've gone back below.

"ACE?"

"Accelerated Christian Education."

"Really . . ." I'm trying to imagine what this would be like—to be homeschooled with your Christian education, or any education for that matter, by your parents in the hull of a boat as you sail across the Atlantic. I would never get my daughter on board. As I head back to our boat, I feel sorry for that girl. I still feel her limp hand in mine and sometimes at night I think of her, drifting at sea.

I think of our empty house. Our daughter gone. I recall a night when she was a little girl. I was tucking her in. Like my father I always read to Kate and sang her a song. As I was turning off the light, she said, "I love you more than anything, Mommy."

"And why is that?" I asked her.

Without hesitating, she replied, "Because you let me be what I want to be."

I closed her door behind me and breathed a deep sigh. This is what I wanted for her. When I get home from this journey, the house will not be filled with her blaring music and mess, her night owl hours and raucous laughter. But I know she'll be back—in whatever form that might be.

>O

In the late afternoon we set out across Kentucky Lake. It is a beautiful, warm, sunny day now and the lake is big and wide. Though we still have no maps, Jerry doesn't mind letting me pilot. At the Blood River I take the helm. With my binoculars I navigate the red and green buoys. As we are going upstream on the Tennessee, it's red buoys right. Tom and I are stunned by the beauty. "We had to come through the gates of hell to get to this paradise," he says.

We're at Mile 61.4 and our journey ends just a few miles ahead. I want to slow it down, but Tom, who stands beside me, gazing out across the river, says, "We've got issues."

"We do . . . ?"

He lists them for me. "We've got an oil leak, a crack in the manifold. The carburetor's gotta come out. I'm not sure how long

the fuel pump's gonna hold." Tom leans back, puts his feet up.
"You know what I'm going to do when I get home? I'm going to
sit back and put my feet up and rewind."

I smile at Tom. "That's a great idea. I think I need to
rewind too."

"Yeah," Tom says, smiling as he gazes upriver. "We all do."
As I steer between buoys, he starts to muse. "I guess you've seen
it all on this trip, haven't you, Mary? You've seen hooters and
shakers. You've been in tornadoes and hurricanes and lightning
storms and bugs. You've bivouacked on beaches and swam in the
river's mud. You've met sorcerers and sea captains, river rats and
gypsies. You've seen its tired towns and you've been in God's
Country. What more could you ask for?"

I shake my head. "I don't know, Tom. I really don't know."
We ride in silence for a few moments. Then he says, "You okay if
I go below?"

He has never asked to go below before when I'm at the helm.
I look at the wide Kentucky Lake. There's nothing ahead; nothing behind. Just open river. I tell him I'm fine. "Sure, go ahead."
And with that Tom leaves me. When he gets below, Jerry must
realize I'm at the wheel, but he doesn't take her below. I'm alone
at the helm for the first time. No one's with me, no one telling
me what to do. Only Samantha Jean is topside, asleep in her black
bomber jacket, dreaming in the sun. What was it Captain Jack
Sparrow in *Pirates of the Caribbean* says about a boat? That it's
not just a rudder and keel and a hull. "What a ship is, what a ship
really is, is freedom."

"The moon belongs to everyone," my father used to croon,
his head tilted back, "the best things in life are free." His hands
glide up and down the keys. "And love can come to anyone." I
hear his voice, slightly cracking, a little off-key. He plays a stride
with his left hand, keeping the melody with his right. His foot on
the pedal as he holds the beat.

I need to find a way to put his bones to rest. My brother still
talks of scattering them at the Sportsman's Country Club golf

course in suburban Illinois. I'm torn between downtown Chicago and Prospect Park in Brooklyn where I live. But my father doesn't know anyone in Brooklyn besides me, I tell myself. He always wanted to be free. I understand this. On some level he wanted none of the encumbrances. I want my own kind of freedom as well.

Then it comes to me. Perhaps he'd like his ashes to mingle with the river. The one we left a few days back. Perhaps somewhere between Hannibal or Quincy. The place where Huck could've taken Jim, were it not for the sake of a story. I'll find that island. Or one that looks like a place where cattle grazed. In the spring when the water is high and rushing, I'll bring him home.

Kentucky Lake casts its spell. It is so wide and open and blue. I ease the throttle back and slow her down a little, not enough so even Tom can tell. I'm not in a rush to get anywhere and nobody even bothers to ask me what I'm doing. With binoculars around my neck, I navigate the buoys. A heron rises, skimming the water off my port side.

As I steer alone down the middle of Kentucky Lake, I'm reminded of a conversation I had with Tom a few days before. It was another sunny day like this, close to dusk. A sun-drenched evening and I was piloting through a series of bends. I was asking him about his life and what it was like, living as he did in his houseboat in all seasons. Wasn't he cold in winter? Didn't the bugs bother him in summer? He just shook his head the way he always did. "I've made my home on this river," Tom told me. "I've given it my life."

"It must be hard," I replied.

He shook his head again, with that twinkle in his eye. "It's a hard life," he said. "And it's a happy life. It's an easy life. It's a sad life. Hey!" He bumped me on the arm in that evening light in what now seems like a long time ago. "Maybe that's your ending, Mary? Maybe your story should stop right here."

Maybe it should. Maybe it does. I hear the clang of footsteps on the ladder as Tom and Jerry come topside. We are coming to a bridge and on the other side is Paris Landing, where our journey will end. I'm assuming Jerry wants to take the wheel, but instead they both stand, side by side, staring into the blue of Kentucky Lake. As I'm making a diagonal to the bridge, Jerry says, "Take her straight for the middle."

I shake my head. "I've got a red buoy at ten o'clock, Sir." I point across the lake, almost to the other shore.

Tom and Jerry are silent for a moment. Hesitantly Tom agrees. "She's right, Sir."

Jerry nods, never looking my way. "Then proceed as you are."

# ACKNOWLEDGMENTS

First I must thank Tom Hafner and Jerry Nelson, the best river pilots and most decent guys a girl could stumble upon on a July afternoon in the North Country. I cannot think of a luckier set of circumstances. They made my journey, and this story, happen as it did. I want to thank my brother, John Morris, and his wife, Gloria, for their generous help. And my nephew, Matthew Morris, his wife, Gail, and her family, who showed me around La Crosse and gave me the keys to their house. I am not sure I would have found Tom and Jerry without their efforts or their hospitality.

I want to thank my wonderful agent, Ellen Levine, as always, for her incredible dedication and support. And everyone at Trident Media Group, including Lara Allen and Alanna Ramirez for the enthusiasm and professional expertise they brought to this book. My editor, George Hodgman, has been with me all the way in this project and it is safe to say that this book would not be what it is without George's determination and unflinching eye. I am also indebted to Sarah Lawrence College for a Bogert fund release time grant and the very important assistance it provided.

I want to thank my friends Marc Kaufman for his careful reading of this manuscript, Krin Gabbard who has taught me much of what I know about jazz and shared with me his extensive collection, Anne Adams Lang, who was always on the other end of the phone, Julian Shapiro for the lyrics to songs and favorite paintings, Mary and Philip Elmer-DeWitt for lending me books and magazines I have yet to return, my neighbors Joel and Diana Robinson for the last-minute loan of a duffel and life vest, Jane Supino for being there, even when I tested her, and the Comfortzone on Fifth Avenue in Brooklyn that provided a place where I could sit and work all day. I want to thank Carol Wise whose generosity and almost thirty years of friendship gave me a week's peace and time to think in Mexico.

A number of books provided important sources and I will just list some of them here. *The Army Corps of Engineers Upper Mississippi River Navigational Charts, Quimby's 2005 Cruising Guide*, and the fine *River Event Planner: Boating and Travel Guide* all provided excellent maps, marina and nautical information, and travel materials. Books I came to cherish included *Rising Tides* by J. M. Barry, *Old Glory* by Jonathan Raban, *La Salle and the Discovery of the Great West* by Francis Parkman, *Upper Mississippi River History* by Captain Ron Larson, *Jazz on the River* by William Howland Kenney, and of course the writings of Mark Twain.

Several people along the river shared with me their knowledge and offered their assistance, including Assistant Lockmaster Bill Stute from Genoa Lock and Dam 8, Iris Nelson from the Quincy Public Library, and Henry Sweets from the Mark Twain Museum in Hannibal, and I am grateful to the many people on the river who shared with me their stories and experiences of life on the Mississippi.

And, finally, to the "Whale Kisser," my daughter, Kate, who asked to read the manuscript and gave me some of the smartest, most thoughtful comments I've ever gotten from anyone, ever, let alone a nineteen-year-old. I do believe she has aerial vision. And I am sure I will never find in this life (or any other) words to thank Larry—partner, guide, and, always, friend.

# ABOUT THE AUTHOR

MARY MORRIS is the author of three other travel memoirs, each one representing a different stage in her life: *Nothing to Declare: Memoirs of a Woman Traveling Alone; Wall to Wall: From Beijing to Berlin by Rail;* and *Angels and Aliens.* She is also the author of six novels, including *The Night Sky; House Arrest; Acts of God;* and *Revenge,* and three collections of short stories, including *The Lifeguard: Stories.* When she is not traveling and writing, Morris is on the faculty of Sarah Lawrence College, where she teaches creative writing. The recipient of the Rome Prize in Literature, Morris lives in Brooklyn.